AHU-4654
18.95
917
.446
GA
AUG 1 2 2002

P9-DFP-378
05442798

Relocating to

Boston

and Surrounding Areas

Everything You Need to Know Before You Move

and After You Get There!

ADAM GAFFIN

PRIMA PUBLISHING

With love to Nancy and Greta,
the two best things about Boston.

Copyright © 2002 by Random House, Inc.

All rights reserved. No part of this book may be reproduced or transmitted in any form or by any means, electronic or mechanical, including photocopying, recording, or by any information storage or retrieval system, without written permission from Random House, Inc., except for the inclusion of brief quotations in a review.

Published by Prima Publishing, Roseville, California. Member of the Crown Publishing Group, a division of Random House, Inc.

The RELOCATING series is a trademark of Random House, Inc. PRIMA PUBLISHING and colophon are trademarks of Random House, Inc., registered with the United States Patent and Trademark Office.

All products mentioned are trademarks of their respective companies.

Every effort has been made to make this book complete and accurate as of the date of publication. In a time of rapid change, however, it is difficult to ensure that all information is entirely up-to-date. Although the publisher and author cannot be liable for any inaccuracies or omissions in this book, they are always grateful for corrections and suggestions for improvement.

Library of Congress Cataloging-in-Publication Data
Gaffin, Adam.
    Relocating to Boston and Surrounding Areas : everything you need to know before you move and after you get there / Adam Gaffin
        p.   cm.
    Includes bibliographical references and index.
    ISBN 0-7615-3563-2
    1. Boston Region (Mass.)—Guidebooks. 2. Boston Region (Mass.)—Handbooks, manuals, etc. 3. Moving, Household—Massachusetts—Boston Region—Handbooks, manuals, etc. I. Title. II. Series.
F73.18.R45   2001
917.44'610444—dc21   2001040915

01 02 03 04 HH 10 9 8 7 6 5 4 3 2 1
Printed in the United States of America

First Edition

Visit us online at www.primapublishing.com

CONTENTS

ACKNOWLEDGMENTS

Thanks to John Gallant, Neal Weinberg, Sandy Gittlen, Melissa Shaw, and Nancy Reynolds for their advice on specific neighborhoods.

INTRODUCTION

One of my favorite spots in Boston is the Copps Hill Cemetery in the North End. As you enter from Hull Street, you pass the narrowest house in Boston—just 10 feet wide and built mainly to annoy the people living behind it. Climbing the hill, you see colonial-era tombstones still pockmarked by musket fire from target-practicing Redcoats during their brief occupation of Boston. At the top, you rest while you look out over the blue water of Boston Harbor. It's a peaceful place to ponder the way the city has grown over the centuries.

Then you descend to the ramparts over Commercial Street. And you try to picture 2½ million gallons of molasses exploding down the street one unseasonably warm January day in 1919, destroying buildings, bending the supports of the elevated railroad, and drowning 21 people and 12 horses in a thick, brown gooey mess.

So much history in one small spot. Boston is like that—layer upon layer of things to discover. You could live here all your life and not run out of new things to learn about the city. Like Copps Hill, Boston is many things at once:

- It's historic Boston, where the colonial and Revolutionary sites attract millions of visitors from around the world.
- It's cutting-edge Boston, where for hundreds of years, people have made new discoveries, from ether to the telephone to the computer.
- It's quirky Boston, where commuters from the south daily pass under the world's largest profile of Ho Chi Minh and a major bridge is marked off in units of length based on the height of a 1958 MIT fraternity pledge.
- It's ethnic Boston. On a per-capita basis, Boston is the most Irish-American city in America. But it also has large communities of blacks, Hispanics, Italians, Jews, and Lithuanians. Recent years have seen an influx of Vietnamese, Haitians, Brazilians, and Russians. A bit further out, you'll find areas with large numbers of Armenians, Portuguese, French-Canadian, and even Finnish.

But most of all, it is home. If you've never been here, your view of Boston might be colored by media portrayals (no, we don't all share unisex bathrooms and spend every evening dancing with our co-workers) or tourist guides (yes, the Swan Boats are really quaint). But beyond *Ally McBeal* and Quincy Market lie scores of neighborhoods and towns, each with its own unique character and charm.

Sure, Boston is the largest city in New England and known around the world for its cultural attractions, medical facilities, and high-tech companies. But Boston is also Wednesday-evening concerts at Adams Park in Roslindale and kite flying in Franklin Park. It's the annual Puerto Rican festival and the Gay Pride Parade, the country's largest St. Patrick's Day Parade in South Boston and the annual Dorchester Day Parade.

And beyond Boston lie the scores of cities and towns of greater Boston, many still run by that historic exercise in direct democracy, the town meeting (see chapter 1 for more info on town meetings). From the sea views of Hull to the town-common gazebo of Natick, from the preppy/Yankee Wellesley center to the ethnic downtown of Framingham, greater Boston offers a wealth of community and housing options.

Is Boston perfect? Hardly. Yes, there is crime and pollution here. But the community policing pioneered here has reduced crime in recent years. And an expensive cleanup project means the most polluted harbor in America is now once again home to seals and a port of call for visiting dolphins.

One unique Boston ailment is its inferiority complex. Not content with its past and forever fretting about its future (not to mention a certain large city to our south), some Bostonians seem to do little more than fret over whether Boston is failing to become a "world-class" city. No, nobody knows exactly just what makes a world-class city, but politicians use the fear to push expensive projects like convention centers and sports stadiums.

Fortunately, there's a sure cure for world-class-itis. Get a towel, stretch it out on the Esplanade and laze about watching the sailboats on the Charles. Or take one of those Swan Boat rides. Or a water taxi out to one of the Harbor Islands. Or spend an afternoon with the masters in the Museum of Fine Arts. Soon, you won't have a worry in the world.

History

The basic outlines of Boston history are familiar to every American schoolchild: Pilgrims, Thanksgiving, Puritans, Boston Tea Party, whites of their eyes, one if by sea, the shot heard 'round the world. . . .

But there's a lot more to Boston history than that. Just take a look at some of the firsts of Boston history:

> First public park in the U.S. (Boston Common, 1634)
> Oldest American public school (Boston Latin, 1635)
> Oldest American college (Harvard, 1636)
> First American post office (1639)
> First American lighthouse (Boston Light, 1716)
> Oldest constitution still in use (1780)
> Oldest continuously operated restaurant
>   (Union Oyster House, 1826)
> First sewing machine (1845)
> First use of ether (1846)
> First telephone conversation
>   ("Mr. Watson, come here . . ." 1876)
> First U.S. YMCA (1851)
> First public library in the U.S. (1854)
> First subway in North America (1897)
> First computer (1928)

Among the Boston area's more famous natives and residents:

> Authors: Henry Adams, Louisa May Alcott, Horatio Alger, e.e. cummings (buried in a Boston cemetery under a tombstone that reads EDWARD ESTLIN CUMMINGS), Ralph Waldo Emerson, the poet Robert Lowell, Sylvia Plath, Edgar Allan Poe (who, truth be told, couldn't wait to get out of town), Anne Sexton, Paul Theroux, and Henry David Thoreau.
> Inventors: Alexander Graham Bell, Samuel Morse, and Eli Whitney.
> Performing artists: Aerosmith, Ben Affleck, Jane Alexander, Ray Bolger, Mama Cass, Chick Corea, Jane Curtin, Matt Damon, Olympia Dukakis, Arlene Francis, Tammy

Grimes, Ann Jillian, Madeleine Kahn, Jack Lemmon, Leonard Nimoy, Conan O'Brien, Estelle Parsons, Donna Summer, James Taylor, Sam Waterston, and Mark Wahlberg.

Political figures: John Adams, John Quincy Adams, Sam Adams, George H. W. Bush (born in Milton, just south of Boston), James Michael Curley (*The Last Hurrah*), Benjamin Franklin, John Hancock, John F. Kennedy, Tip O'Neill, and Paul Revere.

Boston English

Yes, Bostonians have their own unique form of English. But it's a lot more than just dropped Rs. There is a Boston-only vocabulary ("Friendly's makes a wicked good frappe" is how a Bostonian would say "Friendly's makes a very nice milkshake") and even a local grammatical construct, the positive negative (Say "I love frappes!" to a Bostonian and she'll agree by saying "Oh, so don't I!").

Sports

Boston has a reputation for tough but knowledgeable fans in every major-league sport. Red Sox fans, though, know the anguish of heartbreak. Only the Chicago Cubs have gone longer in not winning a World Series.

Resources

(617) NERVOUS

Call this number when you need to know the time and temperature.

BOSTON A TO Z

By Thomas H. O'Connor
Harvard University Press
A quick introduction to all things Bostonian.

BOSTON.COM

www.boston.com

The *Boston Globe*'s portal site: News, classifieds, arts and restaurant listings and reviews and forums.

BOSTON ONLINE

www.boston-online.com

OK, I'm partial to this site, because I run it. Features the Wicked Good Guides to Boston English (which will show you how to understand Bostonians) and Public Restrooms (they're well hidden in Boston), along with a forum to talk about Boston with the locals.

CITYSCAPES OF BOSTON: AN AMERICAN CITY THROUGH TIME

By Robert Campbell and Peter Vanderwarker
Houghton Mifflin
See how Boston has developed as a city. With extensive photos and maps.

MAKE WAY FOR DUCKLINGS

By Robert McCloskey
Viking Press
The classic children's book. Each Mother's Day, scores of little kids dressed as ducklings retrace the brood's path through Beacon Hill.

THE PROPER BOSTONIANS

By Cleveland Amory
No longer in print, but still fairly easy to find, this is a wonderful introduction to the now gone world of the Boston Brahmins who once ruled the city.

SMARTRAVELER

www.smartraveler.com/scripts/bosmap
.asp?city=bos&cityname=Boston
Current traffic reports and highway Webcams.

WXUSA

www.wxusa.com/MA/Boston
Latest local weather and forecast.

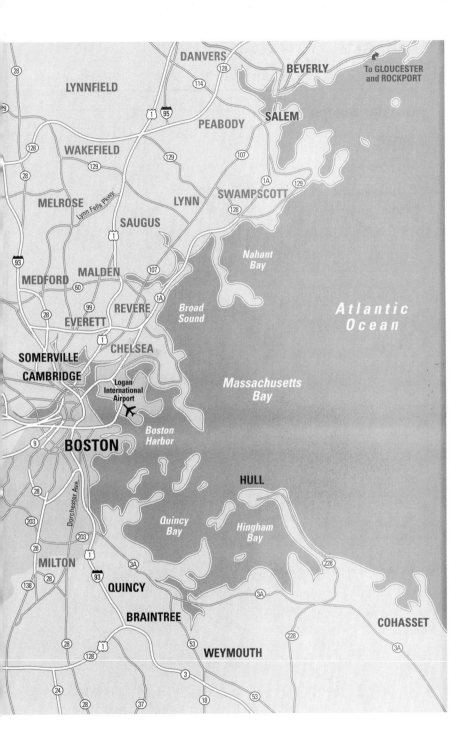

Greater Boston

Population
Total: *3,406, 829*

Population by Gender
Female: *51.9%*
Male: *48.1%*

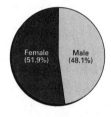

Population by Age

Under 19:	*25.1%*
20–24:	*6.7%*
25–44:	*32.8%*
45–64:	*22.2%*
65+:	*13.1%*
Median age:	*36.2*

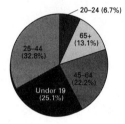

Population by Ethnicity

White:	*80%*
Black:	*6.6%*
Hispanic:	*6%*
Asian/Pacific Islander:	*5%*
Native American:	*0.1%*
Other single race:	*0.6%*
Multi-racial:	*1.7%*

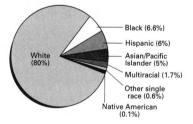

City of Boston

Population
Total :   589,141

Population by Age

Under 18:	19.8 %
18–24:	16.2 %
25–44:	35.8 %
45–64:	17.8 %
65 and over:	10.4 %
Median age:	31.1

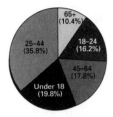

Population by Ethnicity

White:	291,561	*(49.5%)*
Black:	140,305	*(23.8%)*
Hispanic:	85,089	*(14.4%)*
Asian/Pacific Islander:	44,280	*(7.%)*
Native American:	1,517	*(0.03%)*
Other single race:	8,215	*(1.4%)*
Multi-racial:	18,174	*(3.1%)*

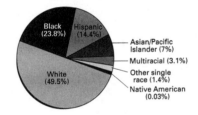

Cost of Living
High
Boston: 132.5
National: 100

Housing
Boston: 171.2
National: 100
Source: 2000 ACCRA Cost of Living Index

TEMPERATURES

January

Max.:	35.7 degrees F
Min.:	21.6 degrees F
Monthly:	28.6 degrees F

February

Max.:	37.5 degrees F
Min.:	23 degrees F
Monthly:	30.3 degrees F

March

Max.:	45.8 degrees F
Min.:	31.3 degrees F
Monthly:	38.6 degrees F

April

Max.:	55.9 degrees F
Min.:	40.2 degrees F
Monthly:	48.1 degrees F

May

Max.:	66.6 degrees F
Min.:	49.8 degrees F
Monthly:	58.2 degrees F

June

Max.:	76.3 degrees F
Min.:	59.1 degrees F
Monthly:	67.7 degrees F

July

Max.:	81.8 degrees F
Min.:	65.1 degrees F
Monthly:	73.5 degrees F

August

Max.:	79.8 degrees F
Min.:	64 degrees F
Monthly:	71.9 degrees F

September

Max.:	72.8 degrees F
Min.:	56.8 degrees F
Monthly:	64.8 degrees F

October

Max.:	62.7 degrees F
Min.:	46.9 degrees F
Monthly:	54.8 degrees F

November

Max.:	52.2 degrees F
Min.:	38.3 degrees F
Monthly:	45.3 degrees F

December

Max.:	40.4 degrees F
Min.:	26.7 degrees F
Monthly:	33.6 degrees F

Yearly

Max.:	59 degrees F
Min.:	43.6 degrees F
Average:	51.3 degrees F

MBTA COMMUTER RAIL SYSTEM

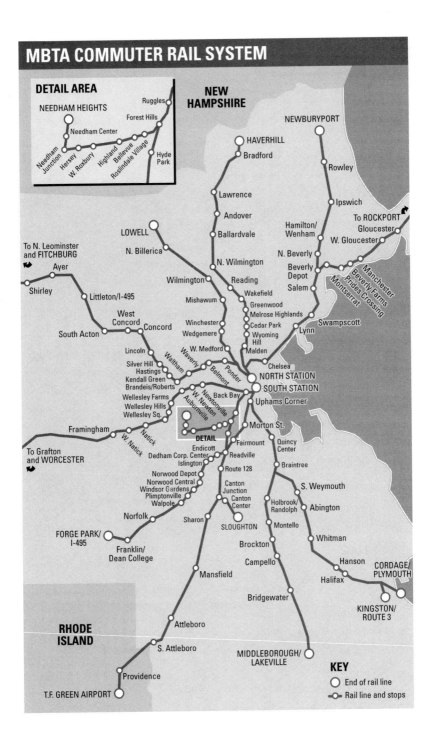

DETAIL AREA

NEEDHAM HEIGHTS
Ruggles
Forest Hills
Needham Center
Needham Junction
Hersey
W. Roxbury
Highland
Bellevue
Roslindale Village
Hyde Park

NEW HAMPSHIRE

NEWBURYPORT
HAVERHILL
Bradford
Rowley
Lawrence
Ipswich
To ROCKPORT
Andover
Hamilton/Wenham
Gloucester
LOWELL
Ballardvale
W. Gloucester
To N. Leominster and FITCHBURG
N. Billerica
N. Wilmington
N. Beverly
Ayer
Wilmington
Reading
Beverly Depot
Manchester
Shirley
Littleton/I-495
Mishawum
Wakefield
Salem
Beverly Farms
Prides Crossing
Montserrat
West Concord
Greenwood
Concord
Winchester
Melrose Highlands
Swampscott
South Acton
Wedgemere
Cedar Park
Lynn
Lincoln
Wyoming Hill
Silver Hill
W. Medford
Malden
Hastings
Waverly
Ponder
Chelsea
Kendall Green
Belmont
NORTH STATION
Brandeis/Roberts
SOUTH STATION
Wellesley Farms
Newtonville
Back Bay
Wellesley Hills
W. Newton
Uphams Corner
Wellesley Sq.
Auburnville
Framingham
W. Natick
Morton St.
DETAIL
Fairmount
Quincy Center
To Grafton and WORCESTER
Endicott
Dedham Corp. Center
Readville
Islington
Route 128
Braintree
Norwood Depot
Norwood Central
Canton Junction
S. Weymouth
Windsor Gardens
Canton Center
Holbrook/Randolph
Abington
Plimptonville
Walpole
Norfolk
Sharon
Montello
Whitman
FORGE PARK/I-495
SLOUGHTON
Franklin/Dean College
Brockton
Hanson
CORDAGE/PLYMOUTH
Campello
Mansfield
Halifax
Bridgewater
KINGSTON/ROUTE 3

RHODE ISLAND

Attleboro
S. Attleboro
MIDDLEBOROUGH/LAKEVILLE
Providence
T.F. GREEN AIRPORT

KEY
○ End of rail line
—○— Rail line and stops

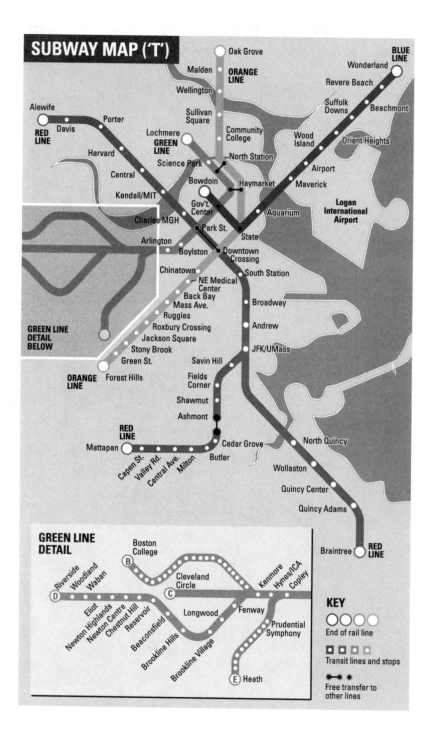

SUBWAY MAP ('T')

BLUE LINE
Wonderland
Revere Beach
Suffolk Downs
Beachmont
Wood Island
Orient Heights
Airport
Maverick
Logan International Airport

ORANGE LINE
Oak Grove
Malden
Wellington
Sullivan Square
Community College
North Station
Haymarket

RED LINE
Alewife
Davis
Porter
Harvard
Central
Kendall/MIT
Charles MGH
Arlington

GREEN LINE
Lochmere
Science Park
Bowdoin
Gov't. Center
Park St.
Boylston

Aquarium
State
Downtown Crossing
South Station
Broadway
Andrew
JFK/UMass

Chinatown
NE Medical Center
Back Bay
Mass Ave.
Ruggles
Roxbury Crossing
Jackson Square
Stony Brook
Green St.
ORANGE LINE
Forest Hills

Savin Hill
Fields Corner
Shawmut
Ashmont
Cedar Grove
Butler

GREEN LINE DETAIL BELOW

RED LINE
Mattapan
Capen St.
Valley Rd.
Central Ave.
Milton

North Quincy
Wollaston
Quincy Center
Quincy Adams
Braintree **RED LINE**

GREEN LINE DETAIL

Boston College
Riverside
Woodland
Waban
Eliot
Newton Highlands
Newton Centre
Chestnut Hill
Reservoir
Beaconsfield
Brookline Hills
Brookline Village
Cleveland Circle
Longwood
Fenway
Brookline Village
Heath

Kenmore
Hynes/ICA
Copley
Prudential
Symphony

B
D
C
E

KEY

End of rail line

Transit lines and stops

Free transfer to other lines

Places to Live

CHAPTER 1

Neighborhood Descriptions

It sounds like a cliché, but Boston really is a city of neighborhoods. In fact, outside of Boston Proper (basically the original settlement, today known as Beacon Hill, the North End and downtown), people don't even use "Boston" in their return address; they use Dorchester or West Roxbury or whatever their neighborhood happens to be. This gives Boston part of its charm as a place to live: You're part of a big city (major-league sports teams, world-renowned cultural attractions, and all of that), but when things just get too hectic, you can withdraw to the safety and quiet of your own little neighborhood.

The city of Boston is actually only a relatively small part of Greater Boston. Massachusetts's cities and towns have long had a strong tradition of home rule and antipathy toward central government (there was that little Revolution thing), so Boston was never able to grow by annexation to the same extent as other large cities. According to the U.S. Census Bureau, only 12 percent of what it considers Greater Boston's population of roughly five million actually lives in Boston. Now, the Census Bureau has a somewhat expansive view of the region—it considers the cities of Lawrence and Lowell and parts of southern New Hampshire as part of the Boston metropolitan area, which few Bostonians would—but even still, the result is that eastern Massachusetts is crowded with a huge number of communities. Each has its own government (many with that unique New England legislature, the town meeting), school system, police department, and individual character.

All of this means you'll have an incredibly varied choice of places to look for your new home, from urban (and urbane) townhouses on Beacon Hill to modern colonials on large pieces of land out in "the country" (all of fifteen miles away). You can live within sight (or even just scent) of the ocean or near a forest.

One of the things that makes the Boston area different is the omnipresent history and a respect for the past. You don't have to look hard to find history around here. It's everywhere, from the statue of Paul Revere in Boston's North End to the national historic sites in Lexington and Concord, from the colonial stone walls and mile markers that line many rural roads to the maritime sites along the North Shore (where George Washington commissioned his first navy ship). Many towns have official historic districts, where making alterations to the outside of your house is difficult or even impossible without the approval of a town historic or architectural commission. Such vigilance has helped preserve the charm of many a community in the face of onslaughts from megamalls, even if it does occasionally lead to some silliness. The Back Bay was one of the last neighborhoods in Boston to get cable television because of a dispute over the placement of cables in "historic" alleys.

Yet time is hardly standing still in the Boston area, which is home to world-renowned universities and research centers and burgeoning high-tech and biotech industries. The past ten years have seen some dramatic changes in the region, and there are more to come.

The most dramatic development is the "Big Dig," a project to build a tunnel to replace the antiquated, ugly, and clog-prone Central Artery, an elevated highway that runs through the heart of the city. Due to be completed in 2004, the $15 billion project (on a per-mile basis, the most expensive road project in U.S. history) has already changed the city skyline and become an important feature of the community. The Leonard Zakim Bunker Hill Bridge over the Charles River, at the project's northern end, is a stunning "cable stay" bridge that could become as much a signature for Boston as the Golden Gate is for San Francisco. You can buy Big Dig ice cream (sort of like rocky road, but with even more stuff thrown in) and Big Dig candy bars to eat as you gaze on all the Big Dig cranes while you're stuck in one of the ever-present traffic jams on the Central Artery.

Once the overhead highway is gone and replaced with parks and low-rise buildings, neighborhoods such as the North End and parts of South Boston will be knitted back into the city from which they've been separated for more than forty years. But will that mean an end to those unique neighborhoods as the well-to-do flock in and displace long-term residents? The changes could be profound: Billions of dollars are pouring into Boston to build new office buildings and luxury housing projects, in particular along the South Boston waterfront. But will the charm that attracts new residents disappear as the old-timers who provided that charm move?

A bit less expensive than the Big Dig, but in some ways just as dramatic, is the cleanup of Boston Harbor. Never again will a presidential candidate be able to stand on a boat in the harbor and complain about how dirty the water is. The cleanup has meant cleaner beaches and a healthier place for wildlife. Harbor seals and dolphins now routinely visit Boston, and scientists report fewer bizarre tumors on fish living in the harbor.

Meanwhile, Greater Boston's population is on the move. The 2000 census showed Boston increasing in population for the first time since the 1950s. Although some of the increase is due to suburbanites moving back into the city (itself an indication of how desirable Boston has become), a significant part of the increase is due to an influx of immigrants from places as diverse as Russia, Haiti, and Brazil. The city even has an Office of New Bostonians, aimed at helping new arrivals adjust to life in the city. The census figures also show that, for the first time, non-Hispanic whites have become a minority of Boston's total population (at roughly 49.5 percent).

In sheer numbers, however, the most dramatic population changes have occurred along the I-495 corridor that circles the city roughly twenty-six miles out. The communities along that highway have changed from sleepy rural towns to a booming high-tech belt that is building the next generation of computer and telephone networks. As the I-495 corridor's population explodes (the region is one of the fastest growing in the state) and becomes a series of "edge cities," it's beginning to experience some of the same woes as older areas closer in to Boston. I-495 now has traffic jams that rival those seen closer to Boston, and the towns along the corridor increasingly find themselves faced with thorny problems relating to everything from water supply to education.

Where to Live?

After you decide to move to the Boston area, your most important choice will be, obviously, where specifically to live. Among the factors you'll need to consider:

- Urban vs. suburban vs. rural (some people like the hustle and bustle of city life; some don't)
- Housing prices (pretty much all of the Boston area is really expensive; but some areas are astronomically so)
- The commute (how important is public transportation to you? Where is your job located? What is your tolerance for sitting in traffic?)
- Schools (we'll cover that in more detail in chapter 10)
- Taxes and water/sewer rates (some communities have higher property tax and water/sewer rates than others)

The location of your job might be a particularly important consideration. Although the Boston area overall is relatively small, some commutes can be killers. The Massachusetts Bay Transportation Authority (MBTA) provides decent subway and commuter-rail service to and from downtown Boston, but public transportation has failed to keep up with the rapid growth of jobs in the suburbs. It can be difficult or even impossible to use public transit to get from one suburb to another, so many people drive, which leads to ever-worsening congestion.

In very rough terms, you can look at the Boston area as a pie divided into slices. The commute within one "slice" generally won't be too bad, but commuting from one region to another could be an issue. The main areas are:

- The city of Boston. The city itself has a dramatic range of neighborhoods, from the expensive and tony brownstones of Beacon Hill and the Back Bay to the quiet single-family neighborhoods of West Roxbury and Roslindale, with virtually everything possible in between. Getting to or from downtown is really easy if you're near a subway or express-bus line. Going "crosstown" from, say, Roxbury or Roslindale to Cambridge is possible but more of a challenge. A major discussion among Boston transit planners is the development of a crosstown corridor that would loop around, rather than through, downtown.

- The inner suburbs. These are the suburbs that directly border Boston, or almost do, and have branches of the local subway, for example, Cambridge, Brookline, Newton, and Somerville. If you're working in downtown Boston and commuting time is important, some of these communities will be closer to your job than parts of Boston. Even if you're not, you might fall in love with one of them.

- The North Shore. These are the communities on Massachusetts Bay to the north of Boston. Many have commuter-rail service into Boston. If you don't want to drive to Logan Airport, there's an express bus from Woburn (off Route 128) to Logan Airport.

- The South Shore. The South Shore comprises the cities and towns south of Boston along Massachusetts Bay. The Red Line subway goes to Braintree; there is commuter-rail and ferry service to and from other South Shore communities. There's an express bus from Braintree (also off Route 128) to Logan Airport.

- The western and northern suburbs. These communities generally lie between Routes 128 and 495 to the west and northwest of Boston (the western suburbs are often called MetroWest). MetroWest also has express buses to and from Logan, from a terminal near Shoppers' World on the Natick/Framingham line (off Route 9).

Okay, so with all that in mind, if you get a job on the North Shore, you might not want to look for a house on the South Shore (or vice versa). The commute will be either incredibly long (looping all the way around Route 128 or I-495 in rush hour) or stressful (going right through downtown Boston on Route 93 at rush hour is not something even veteran Boston drivers prefer to do). The same might hold for a job in the western suburbs and a house on, say, the South Shore. Don't forget to factor in snow. A coworker of mine used to commute to our office in Southborough, in the western suburbs, from Quincy, just south of Boston. Normally, she could get here in under an hour (especially since she'd start work at 8 A.M.). But during or after a snowstorm? Her record was five hours from Southborough to Quincy (fortunately for her sanity, she's since moved to a town a bit closer to the office).

One vital tip no matter where you decide to move in Greater Boston: Invest in a good map book, one of those spiral-bound jobs you can get at any local bookstore. With the exception of a few small areas (the Back Bay and part of South Boston), there is little rhyme or reason to roads in the area. In fact, in many towns, main roads aren't even marked, so if you get lost on one, you could drive for miles before finding out what road you're on (hmm, can you tell my gender by that comment?). Also be aware that road names often change at town lines or former town lines, often with no notice. Lexington Street in Waltham becomes Waltham Street in Lexington; you're toodling along Poplar Street in Roslindale and all of a sudden you discover you're now on West Street because, unbeknownst to you, you've just crossed a municipal boundary line that hasn't actually existed since 1912. As they say around here, it's paht a the chahm.

Online Resources

There are several Web databases that can help you compare different neighborhoods and communities:

COMMONWEALTH COMMUNITIES

www.state.ma.us/cc/

This state Web site has detailed demographic, community, and tax statistics for all of Massachusetts's 351 cities and towns.

THE WARREN GROUP HOME SALES STATISTICS

www.thewarrengroup.com/home/ts

The publisher of *Banker and Tradesman* (a newspaper that focuses on Massachusetts real estate) provides median values for single-family home and condo sales in Massachusetts communities. Many of the values for communities listed in this chapter come from this site.

BOSTON REDEVELOPMENT AUTHORITY

www.cityofboston.com/bra/Neighborhoods.asp

The Neighborhoods page has overviews of Boston neighborhoods, including maps, census data, and summaries of current and pending large development projects.

MASSACHUSETTS BAY TRANSPORTATION AUTHORITY

www.mbta.com

If access to public transportation is important, use this site to look up subway, commuter-rail, bus, and ferry maps.

The Neighborhoods

What follows are brief descriptions of some neighborhoods and towns in the Boston area. It's far from complete; listing every city, town, and neighborhood in the area would take a book all by itself. Instead, I've tried to give a representative sampling of places to live around Boston.

Because most Massachusetts neighborhoods and communities are fairly small, real-estate brokers tend to cover several communities at once. So if you don't find what you're looking for in one of the places listed below, ask your broker about similar places nearby.

Because there are a number of cities and towns in a small area, it's often difficult to tell when you've left one community and entered another. If you're in Boston's Brighton neighborhood, you can easily walk into parts of Brookline without noticing the difference (until you look up and see that the street signs have changed from Boston's white on green to Brookline's black on silver). Ditto for some areas along the Cambridge/Somerville line. You can use this to your advantage while house hunting. If price is important, just a few feet's worth of difference can mean extremely different house prices. Of course, you'll have to balance that savings with other considerations; Brookline schools generally have a much better reputation than Boston ones, which is one of the reasons a house in Brookline will cost far more than an identical house just over the city line in Boston.

Conversely, if you don't find what you're looking for in a town you'd hoped to move to, don't give up hope quickly. Many communities in eastern Massachusetts have a diverse range of housing prices, housing styles, and neighborhoods. Brattle Street near Harvard Square in Cambridge is a neighborhood of million-dollar (plus!) homes that has almost nothing in common with the triple-decker, working- and middle-class neighborhoods of Cambridgeport and Inman Square just a couple of miles away.

The places discussed in this chapter are:

Boston Neighborhoods

- Allston/Brighton
- Back Bay
- Beacon Hill
- Dorchester
- Jamaica Plain
- North End
- Roslindale
- Roxbury
- South Boston
- South End
- West Roxbury

Inner Suburbs

- Brookline
- Cambridge
- Newton
- Quincy
- Somerville
- Watertown

Outer Suburbs

- Acton
- Arlington

- Beverly
- Braintree
- Cohasset
- Concord
- Framingham
- Franklin
- Hull
- Lexington
- Natick
- Needham
- Norwood
- Salem
- Wakefield
- Wellesley
- Weston
- Weymouth

A note on parking: Parking can be quite a challenge in Boston and the inner suburbs. I've tried to give an indication of what to expect if you decide to bring your car with you (it's possible to live here without a car; look in your local bookstore for the Association for Public Transportation's *Car Free in Boston,* which is regularly updated every few years). The situation is better in the outer suburbs. Be aware, though, that many towns ban overnight parking. Some towns relax the restriction in summer months, but get tough starting in the fall— they want to keep the streets clear for snow plowing.

City Neighborhoods

ALLSTON/BRIGHTON

Technically two neighborhoods, but nobody's really sure where the boundary is and most people don't mention one without the other.

Its greatest strength is also possibly its biggest drawback: students. Sandwiched between Boston College and Boston University,

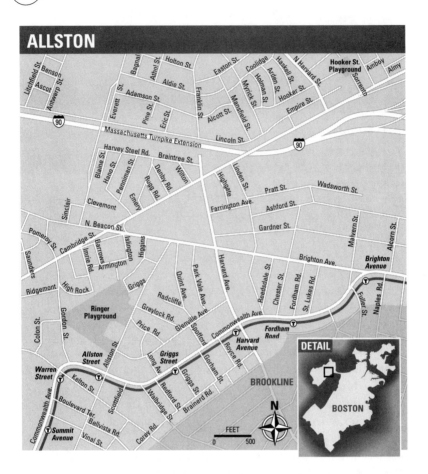

ALLSTON

Allston/Brighton is home to thousands of undergraduates, grad students, and recent graduates, living in the relatively inexpensive apartments and condos that line and surround Commonwealth Avenue (in the Boston area, "inexpensive" generally means "slightly less than frightfully expensive"). They help make the area vibrant with numerous clubs, bars, and good, low-priced ethnic restaurants (in particular along and just off Harvard Avenue). The problem is that once you've joined the working world, the joys of being awakened at 2 A.M. on a Wednesday by the party upstairs begin to pale.

The rents also attract immigrants; along Commonwealth Avenue, you're more likely to hear Russian, Haitian Creole, or Brazilian Portuguese than Boston English.

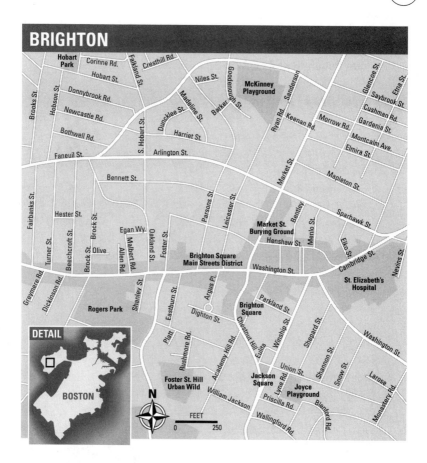

Most of the apartments are in pre-war buildings. In the few newer luxury apartment and condo buildings, don't be surprised if you find many of your neighbors are students; some parents spare no expense in making sure their offspring have only the best.

Away from the student ghettos of Commonwealth Avenue, you'll find Brighton Center and Oak Square. Brighton Center has relatively large populations of native Irish (i.e., people actually born in Ireland; pick up your Irish newspapers and food at the Palace Spa) and orthodox Jews, mostly living in solid single-family homes with some two-families, triple-deckers, and small apartment buildings. Oak Square is an unassuming, quiet neighborhood of one- and two-family homes, convenient to the Massachusetts Turnpike.

Neighborhood Statistical Profile

Total Population: 69,648

Population by Ethnicity

White:	47,835	(69%)
Black	3,110	(4%)
Hispanic:	6,336	(9%)
Asian/Pacific Islander:	9,611	(14%)
Native American:	105	(<1%)
Other single race:	828	(1%)
Multiracial:	1,823	(3%)

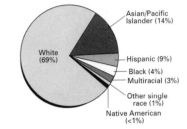

Population by Gender

Female:	51.2%
Male:	48.8%

Population by Age

Median age:	29.1
Under 18:	8.4%
18–24:	26.5%
25–44:	38.3%
45–64:	14.4%
65+:	12.4%

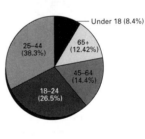

Median home sale $280,500

Median condo sale $160,000

Average rent $1,200

Average Housing Costs

Median home sale:	$280,500
Median condo sale:	$160,000
Average rent:	$1,200

Other Statistics

Crime: A generally safe neighborhood.

Income: A mix of working class, college students, and very young professionals.

Parking: On-street parking is possible, but count on a long search if you get home much past 7 P.M. Resident parking permit required for on-street parking in most areas.

The Commute

The commute to downtown Boston is relatively easy, if somewhat slow; the Boston College branch of the Green Line inches along Commonwealth Avenue at a glacial pace. If you can get to them, the Beacon Street and Riverside branches in nearby Brookline will get you downtown much faster. The best way to get downtown by car from Allston is to get on the Massachusetts Turnpike at the Allston/Cambridge entrance; you'll be in Back Bay in five to ten minutes. From the western end of Brighton, the Newton Corner entrance might make more sense. It's another five minutes farther from downtown, but you don't have to fight morning traffic in Brighton Center. Brighton Center and Oak Square have no ready subway access; from those points, you'd need to take a bus to Commonwealth Avenue or Newton Corner for an express bus to downtown.

Noteworthy in the Neighborhood

Allston is one of the few places in the country named for an artist: Washington Allston, who painted scenes of the stockyards that once existed in the area.

A park along the Charles River offers everything from volleyball to picnic tables to prime spots for watching boats go by on the river. A walking/jogging path lets you get to the Back Bay and Beacon Hill entirely on foot. There's plenty of free parking off Soldiers Field Road.

As you might expect from a student-oriented neighborhood, Allston/Brighton has more late-night dining options than most Boston-area neighborhoods. Redneck's, a roast-beef joint on Harvard Avenue, is open until 3 A.M.

Supermarkets

Bread & Circus
15 Washington Street
(617) 738-8187

Natural-food supermarket.

Star Market
1065 Commonwealth Avenue
(617) 783-5878

Stop & Shop
60 Everett Street
(617) 779-9116

Pharmacies

CVS
1266 Commonwealth Avenue
(617) 277-2953

Melvin Pharmacy
1558 Commonwealth Avenue
(617) 566-2281

Hardware Stores

Model Hardware
22 Harvard Avenue
(617) 782-5131

Hospitals/ Emergency Rooms

St. Elizabeth's Medical Center
736 Cambridge Street
(617) 789-3000

www.semc.org

BACK BAY

With its classic, elegant nineteenth-century brownstones (along with a few scattered high-rises), the Back Bay vies with Beacon Hill for the title of most prestigious Boston address. This is definitely a place to consider if you have lots of money and want to be in the center of it all.

As its name implies, the neighborhood was once mostly under-water (in fact, it was a brackish, smelly tidal swamp on the Charles River). A massive twenty-three-year project started in 1857 turned it into a stylish neighborhood with one of the few street grids in Boston (the streets ascend in alphabetical order from the Public Garden). Many of the Back Bay's buildings, including the massive Trinity Church, sit on wooden pilings sunk into the former bay. Most of the residential buildings were constructed under one of the first zoning codes in the country, an early example of the care with which residents have long treated the neighborhood.

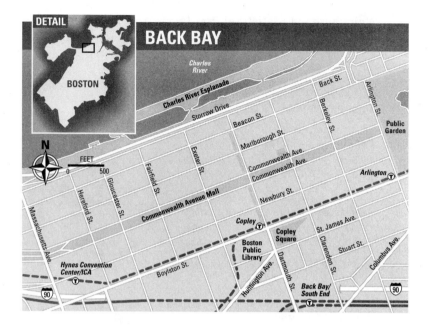

Today Commonwealth Avenue is a boulevard that rivals any in Europe and features a large collection of statues. They start with George Washington looking out from the Public Garden and end with, incongruously, Leif Ericsson looking back toward Washington from Charlesgate (the latter statue was built by a nineteenth-century Bostonian who believed that Vikings had sailed up the Charles). If you have a dog, you'll quickly become friends with fellow dog walkers on the Commonwealth Avenue Mall (the grassy strip that runs down the center of the boulevard). Newbury Street is the most hoity-toity of Boston's shopping streets, although the Massachusetts Avenue end has some funkier stores, including the original Newbury Comics (the place for punk and alternative CDs).

If you can afford the Back Bay, chances are you can afford parking for your car, which is a good thing because on-street parking is woefully inadequate, and spaces in some of the neighborhood's car condos (yep!) have gone for six figures.

Neighborhood Statistical Profile

Note: The city groups the Back Bay with Beacon Hill; these figures represent both neighborhoods (the Back Bay represents about two-thirds of the combined population).

Total Population: 26,721

Population by Ethnicity

White:	*22,654*	*(84.79%)*
Black:	*792*	*(2.96%)*
Hispanic:	*1,099*	*(4.11%)*
Asian/Pacific Islander:	*1,620*	*(6.1%)*
Native American:	*38*	*(0.1%)*
Other single race:	*79*	*(0.3%)*
Multiracial:	*439*	*(1.64%)*

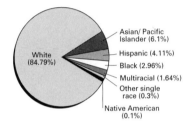

Population by Gender

(Note: Figures are for both Beacon Hill and the Back Bay; numbers are affected by the presence of the Suffolk County House of Corrections.)

Female:	*48.8%*
Male:	*51.2%*

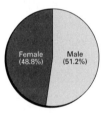

Population by Age

Median age:	*33.5*
Under 18:	*5.59%*
18–24:	*19.34%*
25–44:	*44.12%*
45–64:	*20.38%*
65+:	*10.57%*

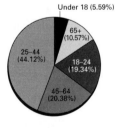

Median home sale $1,405,000

Median condo sale $365,000

Average rent $1,650

Average Housing Costs

Median home sale:	*$1,405,000*
Median condo sale:	*$365,000*
Average rent:	*$1,650*

Other Statistics

Crime: A safe neighborhood, but a car alarm wouldn't hurt.
Income: Solidly upper class.
Parking: Rough. Resident parking permit required.

The Commute

The Back Bay is pretty much in the center of things. On nice days, you could easily walk to your downtown office. The Back Bay entrance to the Massachusetts Turnpike gives speedy car access to points west and south; several entrances on Storrow Drive give ready access to points north and south (much slower at rush hour, of course). Amtrak and commuter-rail lines stop at Back Bay Station, where you can also get on the Orange Line subway (there are Green Line stops on Boylston Street at Massachusetts Avenue and Dartmouth Street).

Noteworthy in the Neighborhood

- Back Bay cross streets are named for British dukes.
- In case Newbury and Boylston Streets don't satisfy your shopping urge, the Copley Square and Prudential Center malls offer an upscale suburban-mall shopping experience. They're connected by human hamster tubes, so you never have to worry about getting sullied on the city streets.
- Copley Square offers a number of unique experiences, from the splendor of Trinity Church and the Mother Church to the views from the observatory atop the Prudential Building.

• For a beautiful view of downtown Boston, walk across the Massachusetts Avenue Bridge into Cambridge.

Supermarkets

Star Market
800 Boylston Street
(Prudential Center)
(617) 262-4688

Pharmacies

CVS
240 Newbury Street
(617) 236-2210

Hardware Stores

Parks Paint & Hardware
233 Newbury Street
(617) 536-0913

Hospitals/Emergency Rooms

Massachusetts General Hospital
55 Fruit Street
(off Cambridge Street)
(617) 726-2000

www.mgh.harvard.edu

BEACON HILL

Beacon Hill is one of Boston's smallest neighborhoods (only about one square mile), but to many outsiders, it *is* Boston: stately brownstones on narrow cobblestone streets lit by gaslight lamps. Throw in some top-hatted Brahmins strolling past Swan Boats in the Public Garden and the picture is complete.

The Brahmin presence has waned over the years as the city's Protestant elite left for greener quarters in horsey towns such as Dover. And Beacon Hill was never totally Brahmin; the hill's "North Slope" was home to Boston's first black neighborhood and then to successive waves of immigrants. Still, there's no argument that Beacon Hill is one of Boston's premier addresses—and one of its most expensive.

Perhaps the epicenter of Brahmin Beacon Hill is Louisburg Square, a small, charming square that is privately owned. (Once a year, the owners of the homes around the square close it off to assert their ownership.) Most homes on Beacon Hill are covered by strict city ordinances that forbid exterior alteration without the approval of the architectural commission.

Beacon Hill's main shopping street—the five-block long Charles Street—is lined with intimate restaurants and a variety of shops, many locally owned. Charles Street is particularly noteworthy for its antique and decorating shops—there are more than forty on Charles or intersecting side streets.

Neighborhood Statistical Profile

Note: The city groups the Back Bay with Beacon Hill; these figures represent both neighborhoods (Beacon Hill represents about one-third of the combined population).

Total Population: 26,721

Population by Ethnicity

White:	22,654	(84.79%)
Black:	792	(2.96%)
Hispanic:	1,099	(4.11%)
Asian/Pacific Islander:	1,620	(6.1%)
Native American:	38	(0.1%)
Other single race:	79	(0.3%)
Multiracial:	439	(1.64%)

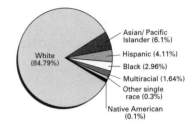

Population by Gender

(Note: Figures are for both Beacon Hill and the Back Bay; numbers are affected by the presence of the Suffolk County House of Corrections.)

Female:	48.8%
Male:	51.2%

Population by Age

Median age:	33.5
Under 18:	5.59%
18–24:	19.34%
25–44:	44.12%
45–64:	20.38%
65+:	10.57%

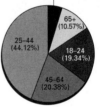

Average Housing Costs

Median home sale:	$1,405,000
Median condo sale:	$365,000
Average rent:	$1,650

Other Statistics

Crime: *A safe neighborhood.*

Income   *As upper-class as you can get in Boston.*

Parking: *Rough. Resident parking permit required.*

The Commute

Like the Back Bay, Beacon Hill is at Boston's epicenter; you can easily walk to your downtown office. The Back Bay entrance to the Massachusetts Turnpike gives speedy car access to points west and south; Leverett Circle has an on-ramp to I-93 for points north and south. Back Bay Station offers Amtrak and commuter-rail service.

Noteworthy in the Neighborhood

- You can tell the really old homes on Beacon Hill by the panes of purple glass. Originally regarded as an imperfection (the panes were supposed to stay clear), today they mark the historic houses in a neighborhood where age is regarded as a virtue.
- Architect Charles Bullfinch laid out several Beacon Hill streets and designed the State House on Beacon Hill. His name also lives on at the Bull & Finch Pub, which became the inspiration for the TV show *Cheers.*
- There are few more quintessentially Boston experiences than strolling in the Public Garden or ice-skating on the Frog Pond on the Common in the winter. Every Mother's Day, Mt. Vernon and Charles Streets are closed for the "Make Way for Ducklings" parade, in which scores of little kids dressed like ducklings (with the odd Officer Mike thrown in) stroll down the route taken by Mrs. Mallard and her brood in the classic children's book.
- An eagle-topped flagpole in the State House's rear parking lot is all that's left of the estate of former governor John Hancock.

Supermarkets	Hardware Stores
DeLuca's Market *11 Charles Street* *(617) 523-4343*	**Charles Street Supply** *54 Charles Street* *(617) 367-9046*

Stop & Shop
181 Cambridge Street
(617) 742-6094

Hospitals/
Emergency Rooms

Pharmacies

Massachusetts
General Hospital
55 Fruit Street

CVS
155 Charles Street
(617) 227-0437

(off Cambridge Street)
(617) 726-2000

Open 24 hours.

www.mgh.harvard.edu

DORCHESTER

Both in size and population, Dorchester is Boston's largest neighborhood. It's really subdivided into a number of smaller neighborhoods, with names such as Ashmont, Fields Corner, Upham's Corner, Savin Hill, and Codman Square. You can find everything from large remodeled Victorians to start-up triple-deckers. Many of the smaller neighborhoods are clustered around particular squares and parishes.

Dorchester is one of Boston's most ethnically diverse neighborhoods, an increasing source of pride in the neighborhood. Many residents retain this pride even when they move to the suburbs; you can buy bumper stickers reading "OFD" ("Originally from Dorchester").

A trip along Dorchester Avenue ("Dot Av" to the locals) will quickly satisfy your need for Vietnamese food and Irish pub grub. Meeting House Hill has everything from Cape Verdean to Jamaican restaurants and bakeries. Dorchester also has a sizable Haitian community. The annual Dorchester Days celebration in June (culminating in the Dorchester Day Parade) commemorates the neighborhood's diversity and history, as does the Ronan Park Multicultural Festival in August.

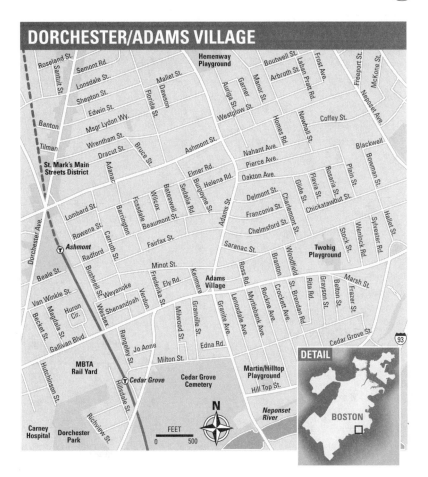

DORCHESTER/ADAMS VILLAGE

The neighborhood also features an impressive range of recreational activities, from the new John Paul II park on the shores of the Neponset River to the golf courses, zoo, and open fields of Franklin Park to twenty-four-hour bowling at the Boston Bowl Family Fun Center.

Neighborhood Statistical Profile

Total Population: 92,115

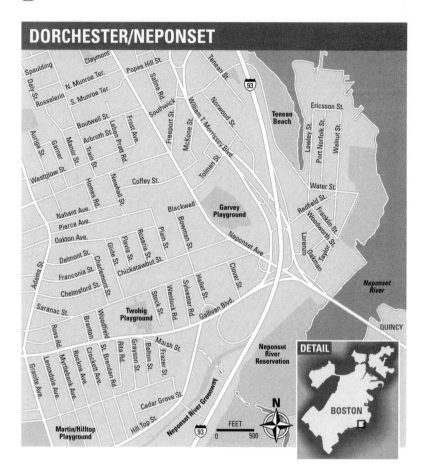

DORCHESTER/NEPONSET

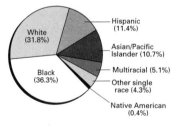

Population by Ethnicity

White:	29,253	(31.8%)
Black:	33,435	(36.3%)
Hispanic:	10,568	(11.4%)
Asian/Pacific Islander:	9,854	(10.7%)
Native American:	350	(0.4%)
Other single race:	3,941	(4.3%)
Multiracial:	4,714	(5.1%)

White (31.8%)
Hispanic (11.4%)
Asian/Pacific Islander (10.7%)
Multiracial (5.1%)
Black (36.3%)
Other single race (4.3%)
Native American (0.4%)

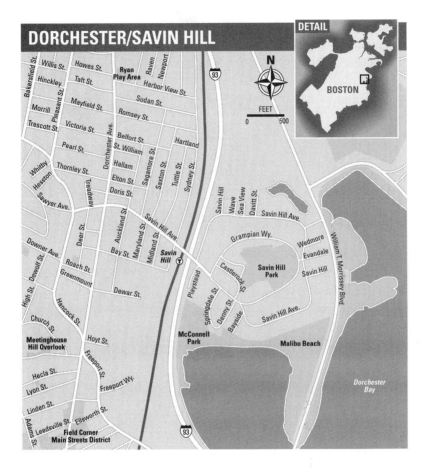

DORCHESTER/SAVIN HILL

DETAIL

BOSTON

N

FEET
0   500

Population by Gender

Female:	*51.8%*
Male:	*48.2%*

Female
(51.8%)

Male
(48.2%)

Population by Age

Median age:	30.7
Under 18:	27.99%
18–24:	11.1%
25–44:	33.56%
45–64:	18.68%
65+:	8.67%

65+ (8.67%)

18–24 (11.1%)

25–44 (33.56%)

45–64 (18.68%)

Under 18 (27.99%)

Median home sale $196,500

Median condo sale $131,250

Average rent $1,000

Average Housing Costs

Median home sale:	$196,500
Median condo sale:	$131,250
Average rent:	$1,000

Other Statistics

Crime: Most parts of Dorchester are safe, but there are some dicey areas.

Income: From working class to yuppie.

Parking: On-street parking available in most areas. Resident parking permits not needed everywhere.

The Commute

Parts of Dorchester are served by the Red Line subway, which will get you downtown in fifteen minutes or so. Other parts rely on buses feeding into the Red Line, which can take a bit longer. Main car access downtown is via the Southeast Expressway (I-93), which is one of the Boston area's most congested highways during rush hour.

Noteworthy in the Neighborhood

- The town of Dorchester was founded a few days before the Puritans established Boston in 1630. Dorchester held the first town meeting and was the first town to vote tax money to pay for a local school. You can read more about the local history at www.dotnews.com/history.html.

- Baker's Chocolate is named for James Baker, who started the country's first chocolate mill in 1765 on the Neponset River.
- The *Dorchester News* provides extensive local news coverage and history, both in a weekly print edition and on the Web at www.dotnews.com.
- The Emerald Necklace ends (or begins, depending on your orientation), at Franklin Park, which has numerous walking trails, the Franklin Park Zoo, a public golf course, and an annual kite-flying competition.

Supermarkets

Star Market
45 Morrissey Boulevard
(617) 265-1776

Stop & Shop
545 Freeport Street
(617) 287-9193

Pharmacies

CVS
2235 Dorchester Avenue
(617) 296-1027

Walgreens
757 Gallivan Boulevard
(617) 282-3889

Hardware Stores

Franklin Field Lumber & True Value Hardware
28 Talbot Avenue
(617) 282-1740

Hamilton True Value Hardware
259 Bowdoin Street
(617) 825-7340

Hospitals/ Emergency Rooms

Carney Hospital
2100 Dorchester Avenue
(617) 296-4000

www.carneyhospital.org

JAMAICA PLAIN

J. P., as everybody calls it, rivals Cambridge as the most eclectic area in Greater Boston—only without the tourists taking up all the parking spaces. J. P. boasts an incredibly varied population, from Central American and Dominican immigrants (Hyde Square boasts several Hispanic restaurants and markets; don't be surprised if you see the Red Sox's Pedro Martinez wandering around) to artists, gays (lesbians

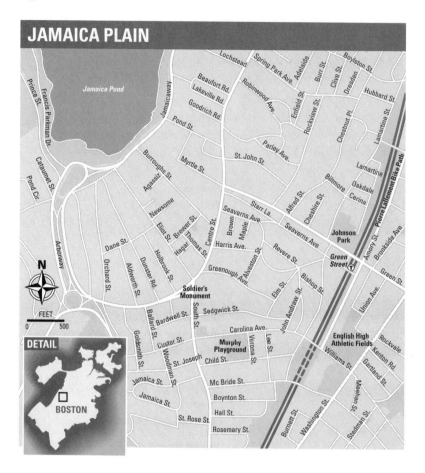

JAMAICA PLAIN

in particular), and young professionals. Unfortunately, J. P.'s popularity has meant rapidly rising housing prices—to the point that some people who wanted to live in the neighborhood are now moving to neighboring Roslindale instead.

J. P.'s character is reflected on the main shopping street, Centre Street. It's lined with small, ethnic restaurants and locally owned shops and boutiques. Thai and Hispanic restaurants mingle with classic Boston Irish pubs. Centre Street also boasts the city's only giant fiberglass cow's head (atop the J. P. Licks ice cream shop in a former firehouse) and the unique melding of bowling and live music at the Milky

Way Lounge and Lanes. The urban funkiness is counterbalanced by some surprising rural touches, for example, the Arnold Arboretum (home of one of the world's largest collections of trees) and Allandale Farm, the only working farm left within Boston city limits.

J. P. has one of the highest concentrations of Victorian homes of any Boston neighborhood. In recent years, many of the larger Victorians have been subdivided into condominiums. This lets you live in an elegant house while sharing the cost of maintenance with others.

Neighborhood Statistical Profile

Total Population: 38,196

Population by Ethnicity

White:	19,030	(50%)
Black:	6,390	(17%)
Hispanic:	8,958	(23%)
Asian/Pacific Islander:	2,485	(7%)
Native American:	100	(<1%)
Other single race:	180	(<1%)
Multiracial:	1,053	(3%)

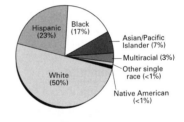

Population by Gender

Female:	53.1%
Male:	46.8%

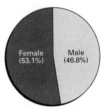

Population by Age

Median age:	34.3
Under 18:	16.54%
18–24:	22.17%
25–44:	35.31%
45–64:	16.87%
65+:	9.11%

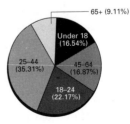

Median home sale $395,000

Median condo sale $212,500

Average rent $1,250

Average Housing Costs

Median home sale:	*$395,000*
Median condo sale:	*$212,500*
Average rent:	*$1,250*

Other Statistics

Crime: *Generally safe, but be careful getting off the subway at night.*

Income: *From working class to yuppie, but increasingly tending toward the well heeled.*

Parking: *On-street parking available in most areas, but can be hard to find along the Centre Street corridor. Resident parking permits needed in many areas.*

The Commute

J. P. has a number of stops on the Orange Line subway, which will get you downtown in ten minutes. Getting anywhere by car quickly can be a problem; the area's major road, the Jamaicaway, is narrow and twisty and completely jammed at rush hour.

Noteworthy in the Neighborhood

- Jamaica Pond, part of the Emerald Necklace, is a great place to jog (there's a path around the pond) or just hang out (a small grassy area near the boathouse is a popular spot). In the summer, you can rent a sailboat, listen to a free concert, or even do a little fishing. Every spring, the city releases a pair of swans onto the pond.

- The Arnold Arboretum, also part of the Emerald Necklace, features tree-lined paths and a bonsai garden. Spring brings Lilac Sunday to "the Arb." On this day thousands take sniffs of the large collection of lilacs and then sit down for picnics (it's the only day picnicking is allowed). (617) 524-1718 or www.arboretum.harvard.edu.

- James Michael Curley, the "Rascal King" mayor made famous in the book and movie *The Last Hurrah,* held court in his home on the Jamaicaway. The house is now owned by a trust, which periodically opens it for public tours.

Supermarkets

Stop & Shop
301 Centre Street
(617) 522-4300

Tropical Market
280 Centre Street
(617) 524-1312

Pharmacies

CVS
704 Centre Street
(617) 525-3933

Hardware Stores

Yumont True Value
702 Centre Street
(617) 524-4572

Hospitals/ Emergency Rooms

Faulkner Hospital
1153 Centre Street
(617) 983-7000

www.faulknerhospital.org

THE NORTH END

For hundreds of years, the North End has been an immigrant neighborhood. First the Irish, then the Jews, then the Italians stepped off the boat, looked around, and stayed.

Today, the neighborhood is possibly the most European in the entire country; it feels a lot like a small town in Italy. The streets are narrow and lined with old apartment buildings. Grandmothers hang out windows watching the kids play, while old guys in fedoras sip expresso outside the Caffe dello Sport and chat in Italian. Of course, what would an Italian town be without an endless number of excellent restaurants? Oh, and don't forget the weekend saints' festivals in the summer.

Enjoy it while you can. The Italians are slowly being replaced by well-off Financial District types who like being right next to the water. Recent years have seen a number of former wharves on the harbor converted into pricey condos. Expect the transformation to

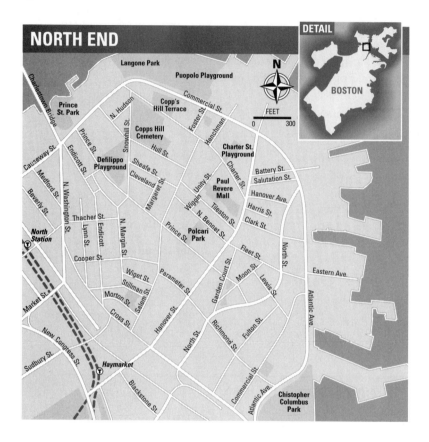

NORTH END

DETAIL

BOSTON

Langone Park

Puopolo Playground

Charlestown Bridge

Prince St. Park

N. Hudson St.

Copp's Hill Terrace

Commercial St.

Foster St.

Henchman St.

Prince St.

N. Illinois St.

Copps Hill Cemetery

Hull St.

Charter St. Playground

Endicott St.

Defilippo Playground

Sheafe St.

Cleveland St.

Margaret St.

Unity St.

Charter St.

Paul Revere Mall

Battery St.

Salutation St.

Causeway St.

Medford St.

Beverly St.

N. Washington St.

Thacher St.

Endicott St.

N. Margin St.

Wiggin St.

Tileston St.

Hanover Ave.

Harris St.

Clark St.

North Station

Lynn St.

Cooper St.

Prince St.

Polcari Park

N. Bennet St.

Fleet St.

North St.

Eastern Ave.

Market St.

Wiget St.

Stillman St.

Parameter St.

Garden Court St.

Moon St.

Lewis St.

Atlantic Ave.

New Congress St.

Morton St.

Salem St.

Cross St.

Hanover St.

North St.

Richmond St.

Fulton St.

Sudbury St.

Haymarket

Blackstone St.

Commercial St.

Atlantic Ave.

Chistopher Columbus Park

FEET

0   300

N

hasten over the next decade as the Central Artery—that hulking green elevated highway that cuts the North End from the rest of the city—is torn down.

Neighborhood Statistical Profile

Total Population: 8,617

Population by Ethnicity

White:	7,735	(89.8%)
Black:	187	(2.2%)
Hispanic:	289	(3.41%)
Asian/Pacific Islander:	296	(3.44%)
Native American:	8	(0.01%)
Other single race:	5	(0.01%)
Multiracial:	97	(1.13%)

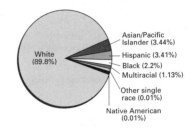

Population by Gender

Female:	66%
Male:	34%

Population by Age

Median age:	35.5
Under 18:	4.19%
18–24:	13.54%
25–44:	55.01%
45–64:	14.89%
65+:	12.37%

Median home sale $425,000
Median condo sale $343,000

Average rent $1,450

Average Housing Costs

Median home sale:	$425,000
Median condo sale:	$343,000
Average rent:	$1,450

Other Statistics

Crime: *Very safe.*

Income: *Working and middle class, although housing prices range toward the very expensive immediately along the waterfront.*

Parking: *Forget about it! There are virtually no on-street spaces, ever. Resident parking permits required.*

The Commute

If you work downtown, you can walk to work. Subway access is via the Haymarket stop on the Orange and Green Lines. If by some miracle you do find a parking space, you can get to points north, south, and west fairly easily via the Central Artery and the Massachusetts Turnpike. Commuter rail to the north and northwest is a short walk away at North Station.

Noteworthy in the Neighborhood

- Almost every weekend in the summer brings a different saint's festival. Hanover Street, the main street, is closed off for the celebrations, which typically include the parading of a statue of whichever saint is being honored.
- Old North Church is where those famous lanterns were hung to alert Paul Revere to start his famous ride. Revere's North End house still stands (with extensive renovations over the centuries); today, it's the oldest house still standing in Boston. Some of the tombstones in Copps Hill Cemetery still bear pockmarks from the Revolution, when British soldiers used them for target practice.
- Every weekend, Haymarket is the place to buy fresh fruits and vegetables and watch a little street theater as the vendors hawk their wares.
- Boccie is the Italian version of lawn bowling, only it's not played on lawns. Watch it played with intensity at the boccie courts at Puopolo Park on Commercial Street.

Supermarkets

Brothers Supermarket
46 Washington Street
(617) 445-2962

Stop & Shop
181 Cambridge Street
(617) 742-6094

Pharmacies

CVS
230–238 Hanover Street
(617) 720-2688

Hospitals/ Emergency Rooms

Massachusetts General Hospital
55 Fruit Street
(off Cambridge Street)
(617) 726-2000

www.mgh.harvard.edu

ROSLINDALE

Roslindale was long a forgotten neighborhood—a quiet blue-collar enclave that few outsiders had heard of or had any reason to visit, except as a way to get to the George Wright Golf Course in neighboring Hyde Park. The neighborhood was popular among Boston city employees, such as police officers and firefighters, who are required by law to live in the city. The center of the neighborhood, once a bustling commercial center, had slowly declined over the decades.

Over the last few years, though, "Rozzie" has become Boston's "next hot neighborhood" (which residents know because they keep reading about the renaissance in the *Boston Globe*). Priced out of neighborhoods like the South End and Jamaica Plain, young professionals and gays have flocked to Roslindale, where they find large houses in a variety of styles and an easy commute downtown via the Orange Line subway and commuter rail. Boutiques have sprouted in Roslindale Square, along with a gourmet bread shop, a fancy wine store, and restaurants (not to mention Ali's Roti Wraps, where you can get several types of curry, including goat). The square is also home to a pita bakery and a meat market that complies with Islamic religious strictures to serve the area's Lebanese residents. Roslindale has sizable Hispanic and Greek communities; a bust of Alexander the Great sits in a tiny park in the square, across from a Greek Orthodox church.

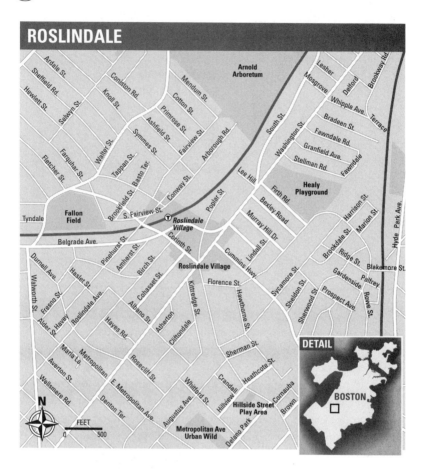

ROSLINDALE

Arnold Arboretum

Healy Playground

Roslindale Village

Fallon Field

Roslindale Village

Hillside Street Play Area

Metropolitan Ave Urban Wild

DETAIL

BOSTON

N

FEET
0   500

The area between Roslindale Square and the Arnold Arboretum in particular has become popular—to the point where housing prices there are no longer the bargain that they are in such areas as Jamaica Plain. Like J.P., Roslindale manages to shift from the urban to the suburban in just a few blocks. Washington Street is lined with low-rise apartment buildings and triple-deckers. But Grew Hill and Metropolitan Hill feel more like suburbs than part of the largest city in New England. Not only are the streets lined with trees (and kids), they also offer great views of the downtown skyline and the surrounding countryside. Take a ride to the top of Metropolitan Avenue and look out—you'll swear you're entering Vermont.

Neighborhood Statistical Profile

Total Population: 34,618

Population by Ethnicity

White:	19,317	*(56%)*
Black:	5,667	*(16%)*
Hispanic:	6,904	*(20%)*
Asian/Pacific Islander:	1,346	*(4%)*
Native American:	69	*(<1%)*
Other single race:	156	*(<1%)*
Multiracial:	1,159	*(3%)*

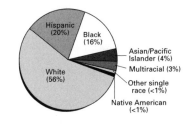

Population by Gender

Female:	53%
Male:	47%

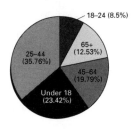

Population by Age

Median age:	35
Under 18:	23.42%
18–24:	8.5%
25–44:	35.76%
45–64:	19.79%
65+:	12.53%

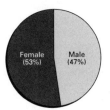

Median home sale $225,000

Median condo sale $167,500

Average rent $1,225

Average Housing Costs

Median home sale:	$225,000
Median condo sale:	$167,500
Average rent:	$1,225

Other Statistics

Crime: Generally safe.

Income: Solidly middle class, although housing prices are veering toward the expensive in the Arboretum area.

Parking: On-street parking available in most areas. Resident parking permits generally not needed.

The Commute

A commuter-rail stop in Roslindale Square will get you downtown in twelve minutes. Frequent bus service along Washington Street gets you to the Forest Hills stop on the Orange Line subway, which is also about twelve minutes from downtown. Driving downtown can be a major pain; there is no direct route and the main road, the VFW Parkway, turns into the Jamaicaway, which is narrow, twisty, and jammed with traffic during rush hour.

Noteworthy in the Neighborhood

- In the early part of the twentieth century, William Fox, as in 20th-Century Fox, built a Victorian mansion in Roslindale, where he'd summer after taking the train up from New York City. He lost the house and almost everything else during the Depression. Today the house still stands on Metropolitan Avenue, although a third of it has been carved away and moved a few hundred feet to make a second, smaller house.

- Adams Park in Roslindale Square has free evening concerts in the summer as well as an Easter egg hunt in the spring.

- If you like gardening, chances are you'll be making many trips to American Legion Highway, home to a number of gardening centers.

- My personal favorite: You'll find the neighborhood's best Chinese food at Ton Chiu, 4403 Washington Street, at the corner of Metropolitan at (617) 323-8239. It's mostly a take-out business, though there are three tiny tables for dining in.

Supermarkets

Stop & Shop
950 American Legion Highway
(617) 327-2160

Village Market
26 Corinth Street
(617) 327-2588

Pharmacies

Sullivan's Pharmacy
& Medical Supply
1 Corinth Street
(617) 323-6544

Hardware Stores

Roslindale Hardware
4407 Washington Street
(617) 323-8639

Wallpaper City
732 South Street
(617) 327-3200

Hospitals/Emergency Rooms

Faulkner Hospital
1153 Centre Street
Jamaica Plain
(617) 983-7000

www.faulknerhospital.org

ROXBURY

The heart of Boston's black community, Roxbury is experiencing a revival. Although it still has some of Boston's highest crime statistics, it also has rapidly rising housing prices. Members of the black middle class, who fled the city along with whites in earlier decades, are moving back in increasing numbers, drawn by a sense of community as well as some solid housing choices, all in an area practically on top of downtown. Fort Hill, near the South End, has a number of 100-year-old Victorians that have rapidly escalated in price. Meanwhile, areas such as Dudley Square and Grove Hall have seen new commercial development.

Named for the towering Mission Church on Tremont Street, Mission Hill is a multiethnic community in Roxbury's northeastern corner. Tension has grown in recent years as students from nearby colleges have moved into apartments in the area, reducing the supply (and increasing the rents) for longtime residents. A monthly rent of $1,500 is no longer unheard of for two-bedroom apartments.

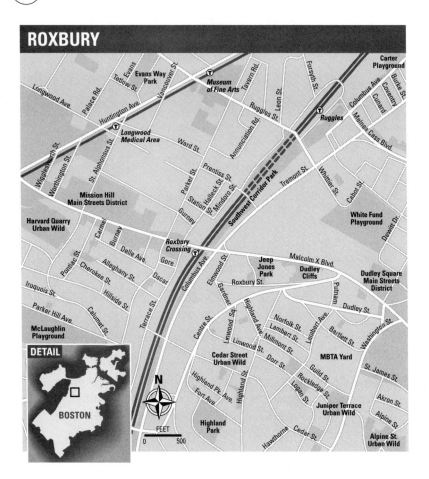

Much of Roxbury avoided demolition in the 1960s when, at the last minute, the state canceled plans to build a new interstate through the heart of Boston and Cambridge. Today, the right of way is taken up by the Orange Line subway and a series of lineal parks and a bike path.

Neighborhood Statistical Profile

Total Population: 56,658

Population by Ethnicity

White:	2,742	(5%)
Black:	35,441	(63%)
Hispanic:	13,827	(24%)
Asian/Pacific Islander:	355	(1%)
Native American:	239	(<1%)
Other single race:	1,725	(3%)
Multiracial:	2,329	(4%)

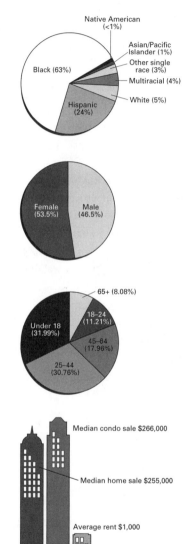

Population by Gender

Female:	53.5%
Male:	46.5%

Population by Age

Median age:	28.7
Under 18:	31.99%
18–24:	11.21%
25–44:	30.76%
45–64:	17.96%
65+:	8.08%

Average Housing Costs

Median home sale:	$255,000
Median condo sale:	$266,000
Average rent:	$1,000

Other Statistics

Crime: Has some rough areas.

Income: Lower to middle class.

Parking: On-street parking available in most areas. Resident parking permits required in some areas.

The Commute

The Orange Line has several Roxbury stops; you can be downtown in ten minutes. Driving will take you fifteen to twenty minutes.

Noteworthy in the Neighborhood

- Dudley Square has New England's largest collection of Afrocentric stores, selling everything from jewelry to hand-carved musical instruments. It has fifteen sites on the National Register of Historic Sites, many dating back to colonial days, when Roxbury was an independent town. They include the Eliot Cemetery, established in 1630, and Frederick Douglass Square, a series of 19th-century row houses.

- Egleston Square has a number of Hispanic markets and restaurants. It's also home to Doyle's Café, one of Boston's oldest pubs and is within walking distance of the Franklin Park Zoo.

Supermarkets

Stop & Shop
301 Centre Street
Jamaica Plain
(617) 522-4300

Pharmacies

Egleston Square Pharmacy
3090 Washington Street
(617) 442-6070

Ruggles Square Pharmacy
1123 Tremont Street
(617) 536-1890

Walgreens
1890 Columbus Avenue
(617) 442-7810

Hardware Stores

Bloom Hardware
1578 Tremont Street
(617) 566-4568

**Egleston Square
True Value Hardware**
3121 Washington Street
(617) 522-4001

Hospitals/ Emergency Rooms

Brigham and Women's Hospital
75 Francis Street
Longwood Medical Area
(617) 732-5500

www.brighamandwomens.org

SOUTH BOSTON

Feisty and proud of its heritage as a blue-collar, Irish-American (and Lithuanian) enclave, South Boston is slowly yielding to the forces of gentrification. (Not that the area hasn't resisted gentrification; local politicians got an ordinance to ban sidewalk cafes and rooftop bars.) The yuppies have discovered how close it is to the Financial District (you can walk to it on a nice day) and what great views of the water you can get here. Plans on the books call for more than $1 billion in new development on the South Boston waterfront, including a new convention center and a nonstop "new city" of apartments, offices, and cultural attractions.

"Southie" has a complex and sometimes antagonistic relationship with the rest of the city. Boston's infamous busing crisis of the 1970s was sparked here, when a federal judge (who lived safely outside the city) ordered busing to end segregation in Boston schools. For a time, Boston police had to escort black students bused into South Boston High School. Although tensions have long since eased, the neighborhood remains one of the most segregated in the city, along with West Roxbury (and, surprisingly, Beacon Hill and the Back Bay). More recently, the neighborhood has faced off against the rest of the city on the issue of "linkage" payments made by commercial developers for local housing projects. (Such payments are supposed to go into a citywide pool. South Boston politicians managed to get all the money from one particularly large project dedicated to South Boston, at least until it became a front-page story.)

Surrounded by water on three sides, South Boston has a number of beaches. The Fort Point Channel area is home to many artists, who live in lofts in former commercial buildings. However, they are being driven out as the buildings are torn down or renovated for use as office buildings.

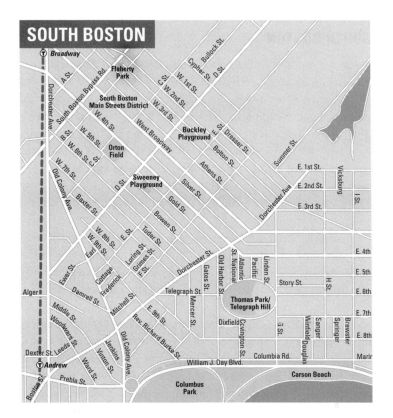

Neighborhood Statistical Profile

Total Population: 29,965

Population by Ethnicity

White:	25,327	(85%)
Black:	741	(2%)
Hispanic:	2,244	(7%)
Asian/Pacific Islander:	1,166	(4%)
Native American:	79	(<1%)
Other single race:	41	(<1%)
Multiracial:	367	(1%)

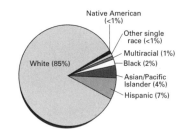

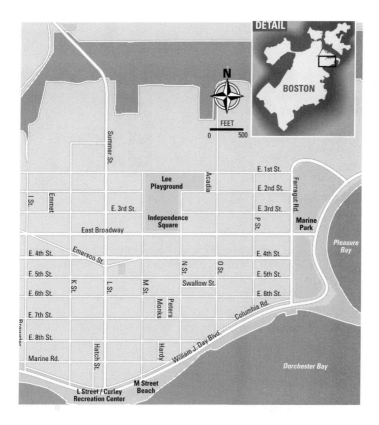

Population by Gender

Female: 52.9%

Male: 47.1%

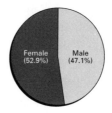

Population by Age

Median age: 33.6

Under 18: 18.26%

18–24: 9.44%

25–44: 39.1%

45–64: 20%

65+: 13.19%

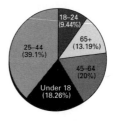

Median condo sale $242,000

Median home sale $211,500

Average rent $1,275

Average Housing Costs

Median home sale: *$211,500*
Median condo sale: *$242,000*
Average rent: *$1,275*

Other Statistics

Crime: *Safe.*

Income: *Working and middle class.*

Parking: *On-street parking available in most areas, although finding a space can be difficult sometimes. Resident parking permits not needed.*

The Commute

The Red Line stop at Andrews will get you downtown in a few minutes.

Noteworthy in the Neighborhood

- Among Southie's beaches and bathing facilities is the L Street Bathhouse, from which the L Street Brownies take their annual run into Dorchester Bay on New Year's Day.

- Colonial cannons stealthily placed atop South Boston's hills helped convince the Redcoats to evacuate Boston on March 17, 1776—a date still celebrated in Boston as Evacuation Day.

- The annual South Boston St. Patrick's Day parade is one of the largest in the world.

- *Good Will Hunting* made the L Street Tavern famous. And it remains much the way it was shown in the movie.

Supermarkets

Blue Ocean Grocery
305 West Broadway
(617) 464-4373

Stop & Shop
713 East Broadway
(617) 269-7989

Pharmacies

CVS
423 West Broadway
(617) 269-3604

Hardware Stores

Old Time Hardware
389 West Broadway
(617) 268-3634

**Hospitals/
Emergency Rooms**

**Massachusetts
General Hospital**
55 Fruit Street
(off Cambridge Street)
(617) 726-2000

www.mgh.harvard.edu

THE SOUTH END

The South End is like a livelier, more multicultural Back Bay. Like the Back Bay, from which it is separated by the Massachusetts Turnpike and the suburban-style shopping fortress known as Copley Place, the South End is full of Victorian-era brick row houses or brownstones on tree-lined streets, many following the old English model of residential squares around small parks.

But where the Back Bay is, well, basically staid, the South End is trendy. It has art galleries to match those in the Back Bay—and artists in residence. The Boston Center for the Arts sponsors a variety of performances and exhibits in South End buildings, including the historic Cyclorama: (617) 426-5000 or www.bcaonline.org. The United South End Artists has a Web site listing members throughout the neighborhood: www.useaboston.org.

The South End is the center of gay life in Boston. One of the country's first gay-pride parades took place in the South End in 1971. Add in all the trendy restaurants that have opened up along Tremont Street and Columbus Avenue in recent years, and you've got a neighborhood that knows how to keep ahead of the times.

Residents take great pride in their neighborhood and their blocks. The fairly small neighborhood is divided into eighteen block associations: www.southend.org.

Important note: Outsiders sometimes get the South End and South Boston mixed up. They are worlds apart, although, oddly, they share the same city councillor.

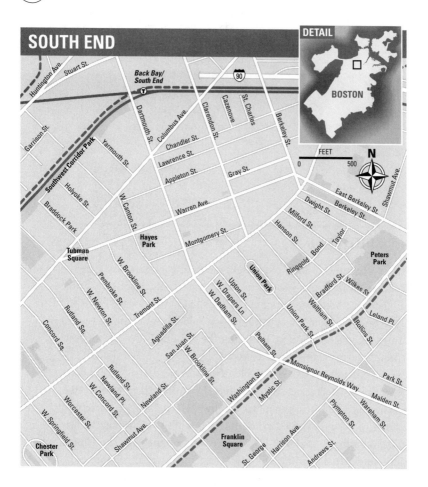

Neighborhood Statistical Profile

Total Population: 28,239

Population by Ethnicity

White:	12,780	(45.3%)
Black:	6,422	(23%)
Hispanic:	4,773	(17%)
Asian/Pacific Islander:	3,358	(12%)
Native American:	94	(0.3%)
Other single race:	117	(0.4%)
Multiracial:	695	(2%)

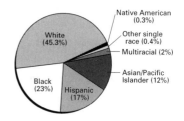

Population by Gender

Female: *46.1%*
Male: *53.9%*

Female (46.1%)   Male (53.9%)

Population by Age

Median age: *33.8*
Under 18:   *15.64%*
18–24:   *11.58%*
25–44:   *44.25%*
45–64:   *20.17%*
65+:   *8.36%*

65+ (8.36%)
18–24 (11.58%)
25–44 (44.25%)
Under 18 (15.64%)
45–64 (20.17%)

Median home sale $727,500

Median condo sale $319,000

Average rent $1,600

Average Housing Costs

Median home sale: *$727,500*
Median condo sale: *$319,000*
Average rent: *$1,600*

Other Statistics

Crime: *Generally safe, although car theft can be a problem.*
Income: *Mixture of poor and very rich.*
Parking: *Right. Resident permits required on most streets.*

The Commute

The neighborhood is served by the Orange Line subway—five minutes to downtown. Back Bay Station, which is right next to the South End, is the place to get on board commuter-rail and Amtrak trains. The Back Bay entrance on the Massachusetts Turnpike provides a quick getaway to points west.

Noteworthy in the Neighborhood

- The Cyclorama was built in the late 1800s to house a giant mural commemorating the Civil War. Today it's home to the Boston Center for the Arts, which runs and sponsors a variety of cultural programs, from theater to art exhibits.
- Many of the streets that run parallel to Massachusetts Avenue were named for cities served by the old Boston and Albany Railroad.
- One of the problems of living in a city is where to let your dog roam. There's a dog park at Peters Park.

Supermarkets

Alves Market
77 Stoughton Street
(617) 825-8267

Pharmacies

CVS
231 Massachusetts Avenue
(617) 266-5022

Hardware Stores

Warren Hardware
470 Tremont Street
(617) 426-7525

Hospitals/Emergency Rooms

New England Medical Center
750 Washington Street
(617) 636-5000

www.nemc.org

WEST ROXBURY

If you had to sum up West Roxbury in one word, it would be "quiet." Not much ever happens here, and residents like it that way.

Most of West Roxbury feels more like a quiet suburb than part of a large city. The neighborhood consists mainly of single-family homes (with some suburban-style apartment and condo complexes along Washington and Spring Streets). Driving down the West Roxbury Parkway, you might be forgiven for thinking you made a wrong turn and wound up in Brookline or Dedham instead. Don't move here if innovative dining or nightlife or ethnic diversity is important; there is none.

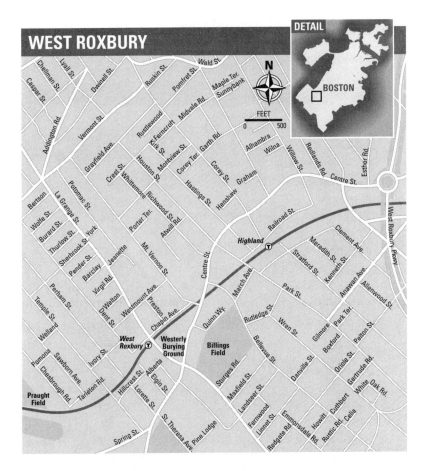

West Roxbury is a family-oriented neighborhood. The YMCA and the Roche Community Center provide extensive programs for children of all ages, and West Roxbury has excellent playgrounds. It's also possibly the most heavily Irish-Catholic neighborhood in Boston (more so than even South Boston). Be sure to visit the West Roxbury Pub to take a look at the dining room. The walls are covered with murals celebrating the life of Boston's most famous Irish mayor, James Michael Curley. There is a small international enclave in Hancock Village on the West Roxbury/Brookline line.

Neighborhood Statistical Profile

Total Population: 28,753

Population by Ethnicity

White:	*24,029*	*(83.5%)*
Black:	*1,718*	*(6%)*
Hispanic:	*1,309*	*(4.5%)*
Asian/Pacific Islander:	*1,090*	*(4%)*
Native American:	*58*	*(<1%)*
Other single race:	*75*	*(<1%)*
Multiracial:	*474*	*(2%)*

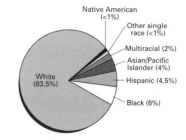

Population by Gender

Female:	*54.5%*
Male:	*45.5%*

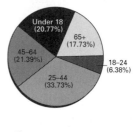

Population by Age

Median age:	*41.1*
Under 18:	*20.77%*
18–24:	*6.38%*
25–44:	*33.73%*
45–64:	*21.39%*
65+:	*17.73%*

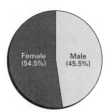

Median home sale $265,000

Median condo sale $150,000

Average rent $1,300

Average Housing Costs

Median home sale:	*$265,000*
Median condo sale:	*$150,000*
Average rent:	*$1,300*

Other Statistics

Crime: *A safe neighborhood.*

Income: *Middle and upper middle class.*

Parking: *Piece of cake. Resident parking permits needed for on-street parking only near the LaGrange Street commuter-rail stop.*

The Commute

The easiest way to get downtown is via commuter rail. West Roxbury has three stops on the Needham line that will get you to South Station in twenty-five minutes or less. There's no easy way to get downtown by car. The VFW Parkway and the Jamaicaway (the same road, actually) is a twisty, narrow route that quickly clogs during rush hour. Depending on where you are in the neighborhood and where you're heading, it might be easier to take Route 1 to Route 128 and then loop north on to Route 93. Ditto for getting to Amtrak: It might be easier to drive to the Route 128 station than battle the traffic to get to South Station.

Noteworthy in the Neighborhood

- Millennium Park, dedicated in November 2000, is the city's newest. It sits atop a former city landfill, but once you get used to that idea, you'll love the panoramic views, from the Great Blue Hill to the south to the tops of the Hancock and Prudential skyscrapers to the north. The park also features a couple of nice playgrounds for the kids, a canoe-launching area on the Charles River, and running and walking paths.

- Nearby is Gethsemane Cemetery, built on the grounds of Brook Farm, a famous transcendentalist utopian community founded in 1841.

- One of Boston's most unusual landmarks is the giant neon chicken that waves at motorists on the VFW Parkway to advertise Fontaine's Topsy's Restaurant (which specializes in—big surprise—chicken).

Supermarkets

Roche Bros.
1931 Centre Street
(617) 327-7666

Star Market
75 Spring Street
(617) 327-0564

Stop & Shop
1230 VFW Parkway
(617) 327-3766

Pharmacies

CVS
1918 Centre Street
(617) 469-2222

West Roxbury Pharmacy
1868 Centre Street
(617) 325-0017

Hardware Stores

Home Depot
1213 VFW Parkway
(617) 327-5000

True Value Atlas
1871 Centre Street
(617) 325-9494

Hospitals/Emergency Rooms

Faulkner Hospital
1153 Centre Street
Jamaica Plain
(617) 983-7000

www.faulknerhospital.org

The Suburbs

Suburb or city? It's not quite the absolute, either/or decision you might have to make in areas such as New York or San Francisco. As noted above, the town lines in the Boston area are sometimes indistinguishable. Parts of some suburbs are actually closer or more convenient to downtown Boston than parts of the city itself. So it's possible to live a suburban lifestyle while still taking advantage of everything the city has to offer. It's even possible to live an urban lifestyle in some suburbs (in particular, some of the inner suburbs) while taking advantage of their school systems or other unique attributes. If ethnic diversity is important to you, you'll want to look closer in to Boston. Of the communities discussed below, only Framingham has anything remotely near the diversity you'll find in Boston or Cambridge. And if public transportation is important, you'll need to keep that in mind as well.

A Word on Suburban Government

Few things typify New England more than the town meeting (besides lobster, perhaps). Many Massachusetts communities are still run by these sessions. Although town meetings don't have the independence they once did (due to state mandates on how to spend education and highway funds), they can still be a stirring example of the ultimate in democracy and provide a chance to catch up with your neighbors as well. Residents get their say and town officials don't always get their way.

In general, towns of up to about 20,000 residents have periodic "open" town meetings, which means that any registered voter can attend and vote (it's the Norman Rockwell school of government). On town meeting nights, be careful about skipping out. Many towns have quorums, and moderators (elected officials who run the meetings) have been known to send the police out to round up residents at local bowling alleys and stores when not enough people show up.

Larger towns have gone to either "representative" town meetings (any registered voter can speak his mind, but only elected town meeting members, of which there are typically 200 or so, can actually vote) or town councils, which function more like city councils, right down to the weekly meetings.

Towns that hold town meetings also have elected boards of selectmen, who act as a collective mayoral body between meetings. In reality, towns with either open or representative town meetings are run by boards largely made up of volunteers, who often spend long hours deciding no-win situations (no matter how they vote, somebody will get upset. That's often not easy for town officials, most of whom have their home numbers listed in the phone book).

In either type of town meeting, the outline of action is similar: The moderator stands at a podium in the high school auditorium, calling up the issues and trying to keep the meeting in order (the meetings are often confrontational democracy in action; things sometimes get very heated). Selectmen sit at the front, as does the finance committee, an appointed board that makes recommendations on any votes with financial ramifications. The town meeting votes on articles that have been published in a warrant circulated around the town in the weeks before the meeting.

In the audience, every town seems to have a similar group of characters. There's always at least one woman who faithfully attends every session with her knitting. At least one gadfly rises on every issue to contest whatever it is town officials want to do (larger towns sometimes have dueling gadflies who argue with each other). In some towns, wise town officials know the quickest way to silence a gadfly is to appoint him to the finance committee. Controversial issues (such as leash laws) always produce a huge turnout of people, most of whom leave as soon as their issue has been voted on.

Parking

A number of the inner suburbs are so build up they have the same sort of parking issues as Boston. Parking situations are noted in the descriptions for each town. In the outer suburbs, parking is usually less of an issue. However, be aware that most towns have overnight parking bans. While some generally do not enforce these in the summer, you'll need to get your car off the street on winter nights because the towns want to keep the streets clear for snow plowing.

Inner Suburbs

BROOKLINE

On a map, this town looks like it should be part of Boston; it's surrounded by the city on three sides. But when Boston was gobbling up surrounding towns in the nineteenth century, Brookline resisted. Today it offers a mix of urbanized and suburban living within an easy commute to downtown Boston. It is also the heart of the Boston area's Jewish community. Harvard Avenue in particular is home to numerous Jewish and Israeli shops, including Ruth's Kitchen, one of the world's few kosher Korean take-out restaurants.

Route 9 splits the town—and not just geographically. North of the route, Brookline feels like a small city, full of apartment buildings and homes on small lots (the one exception is stately Fisher Hill), most within an easy walk of a trolley or bus line. Beacon Street is lined with some particularly striking pre-war apartment buildings and brownstones. Coolidge Corner is an increasingly hip area to shop and stroll. Chain stores have failed to dislodge homegrown shops in this area (Brookline Booksmith remains in business several years after a Barnes & Noble opened a couple of blocks away). It's also a great place for dinner and a movie (at the old-fashioned Coolidge Corner Theater, now run by a nonprofit group). Brookline Village, a few miles to the south, has a number of restaurants and boutiques.

South of Route 9, Brookline feels more like a ritzy suburb, with large single-family homes on big lots and golf courses (including the Country Club, home to the 2000 Ryder Cup). A key problem on either side of the divide is housing prices: Whether you rent or plan to buy, Brookline can be very expensive.

Politics is more than a spectator sport in Brookline. John F. Kennedy was born here (the house, at 83 Beals Street, is maintained by the National Park Service), and Michael Dukakis still lives here (when he was governor, he'd often take the Beacon Street trolley to work at the State House). Local elections are lively and often pit homeowners against apartment dwellers.

If you don't smoke—and don't like secondhand smoke—you'll love Brookline: All its restaurants and bars are smoke-free.

Neighborhood Statistical Profile

Total Population: 57,107

Population by Ethnicity

White:	44,922	(78.7%)
Black:	1,501	(2.63%)
Hispanic:	2,018	(3.5%)
Asian/Pacific Islander:	7,317	(12.8%)
Native American:	44	(0.07%)
Other single race:	212	(0.4%)
Multiracial:	1093	(1.9%)

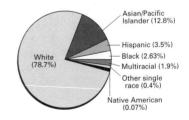

Population by Gender

Female:	*54.8%*
Male:	*45.2%*

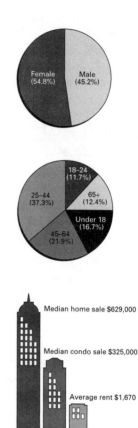

Population by Age

Median age:	*34.5*
Under 18:	*16.7%*
18–24:	*11.7%*
25–44:	*37.3%*
45–64:	*21.9%*
65+:	*12.4%*

Median home sale $629,000

Median condo sale $325,000

Average rent $1,670

Average Housing Costs

Median home sale:	*$629,000*
Median condo sale:	*$325,000*
Average rent:	*$1,670*

Other Statistics

Crime: A safe town.

Income: Middle and upper middle class.

Parking: Overnight parking is banned, and you're not even supposed to park for more than two hours during the day except on a few streets and with a resident parking permit. The town rents overnight spaces in municipal lots for $80 a month (in three-month increments), but there's often a waiting list. So if you're renting, count on another $100 to $200 a month for a space.

Type of Government

Representative town meeting.

The Commute

Brookline is served by two branches of the Green Line trolley—Beacon Street and Riverside. Route 9 provides quick access to the Back Bay; Coolidge Corner is an easy walk to the Longwood Medical Area. The Massachusetts Turnpike is about ten minutes away in Allston.

Noteworthy in the Neighborhood

- The Coolidge Corner Theater, 290 Harvard Street, runs a variety of film series in a facility lovingly maintained by a nonprofit group: (617) 734-2500 or www.coolidge.org.
- Harvard Avenue was originally named Road to the Colleges.
- A popular place to jog is the Brookline Reservoir just off Route 9.
- Brookline's original name was Muddy River, for the creek that still separates it from Boston.

Supermarkets

Star Market
1717 Beacon Street
(617) 566-1802

Stop & Shop
155 Harvard Avenue
(617) 566-4559

Trader Joe's
1317 Beacon Street
(617) 278-9997

Pharmacies

CVS
255 Washington Street
(617) 734-7335

Village Pharmacy
1 Brookline Place
(617) 735-9094

Hardware Stores

Atlas Paint & Supply
294 Washington Street
(617) 277-2095

Connelly Hardware
706 Washington Street
(617) 277-7349

Hospitals/Emergency Rooms

Brigham and Women's Hospital
75 Francis Street, Roxbury
(617) 732-5500

www.brighamandwomens.org

CAMBRIDGE

Cambridge is to Boston as Berkeley is to San Francisco. It's the smaller, feistier cousin across the water ("across the river" is faint praise in both Cambridge and Boston).

One could make a good case for Cambridge being the intellectual capital of New England. It's home to both Harvard University and MIT, along with Leslie College and any number of high-tech and biotech startups. Harvard Square, just outside Harvard Yard (yes, it's true: You can't pahk ya cah in Hahvid Yahd), has one of the country's highest concentrations of bookstores, many specializing in specific genres (such as mystery, foreign language, and history). On weekends, it's a great place to people watch. Thousands of college students from across Greater Boston flood in, joining the street punks, tweedy Harvard profs, tourists, and street performers.

Cambridge has a number of distinct neighborhoods. The area around Harvard Yard, for example, tends toward the upper middle class and outright rich, especially along Brattle Street. East Cambridge and Inman Square are solid working-class areas. Central Square, which has more Indian restaurants than anywhere else in New England, is undergoing rapid gentrification, which happened in Porter Square a few years ago.

Cambridge is still home to large working-class and immigrant communities, although they are increasingly being forced out by rapidly rising rents and real-estate prices. It's no longer news when a home goes for $3 million or even $4 million in the area around Harvard Square (take a look at the average home and condo prices that follows).

Cambridge's politics tend toward the left. It once funded a full-time peace commissioner, and a few years ago somebody posted "Welcome to the People's Republic of Cambridge" signs at the end of one of the bridge crossings into the city from Boston. Unusual for Massachusetts, Cambridge has local parties (roughly, conservatives and progressives) that vie for a majority on the city council in each election. Unusual for the United States, Cambridge elects its officials through proportional representation, in which voters rank candidates in order of preference. The goal is to ensure that all voices are heard in city government, but it means that tallying votes can take days.

There's occasional friction between residents and the colleges, particularly Harvard. Take, for example, the reason a main street into Harvard Square is now officially JFK Street. The mayor got wind of a (false) rumor that Harvard was about to change the name of the John F. Kennedy School of Government and convinced the city council to rename the street in front of the school to JFK Street to make sure there was always a Kennedy presence in the Square. The move came despite denials from Harvard that it had any plans to change the name of the school—the council acted just in case (the school, by the way, remains named after Kennedy).

Cambridge is also notable for its high percentage of single people: More than 40 percent of city households consist of just one person. Partly, this is due to the high number of students living in the city; but partly because Cambridge is particularly amenable to the singles' lifestyle, with its heavy concentration of clubs and cultural attractions.

Neighborhood Statistical Profile

Total Population: 101,355

Population by Ethnicity

White:	*65,425*	*(64.55%)*
Black:	*11,627*	*(11.48%)*
Hispanic:	*7,455*	*(7.36%)*
Asian/Pacific Islander:	*12,055*	*(11.9%)*
Native American:	*213*	*(0.2%)*
Other single race:	*713*	*(0.7%)*
Multiracial:	*3,867*	*(3.81%)*

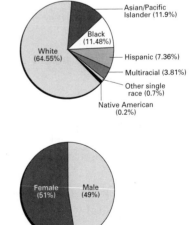

Population by Gender

Female:	*51%*
Male:	*49%*

Population by Age

Median age:	30.4
Under 18:	13.3%
18–24:	21.1%
25–44:	38.6%
45–64:	17.8%
65+:	9.2%

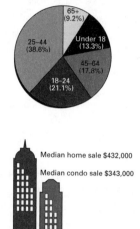

Median home sale $432,000

Median condo sale $343,000

Average rent $1,850

Average Housing Costs

Median home sale:	$432,000
Median condo sale:	$343,000
Average rent:	$1,850

Other Statistics

Crime: Most neighborhoods are safe.

Income: Lower to upper income.

Parking: Resident parking permits cost $8 a year. Expect to drive around a bit looking for a space in most parts of the city after dark. Unlike in Boston, residents can get temporary permits for visitors to use.

Type of Government

City.

The Commute

Most parts of Cambridge are just a short subway or car ride away from downtown Boston. The Red Line subway gets you to downtown Boston from Harvard or Porter Squares in less than fifteen minutes. Route 2 provides a getaway to the north and west, but count on a slow ride getting to it.

Noteworthy in the Neighborhood

- On summer Sunday afternoons, the state shuts down a 1.5-mile stretch of Memorial Drive near Harvard so pedestrians, skaters, and bicyclists can use it.
- The annual River Festival in June brings folk, jazz, gospel, and children's music performers to Cambridge for free concerts along the Charles River: www.ci.cambridge.ma.us/~CAC/.
- Good places to jog: Fresh Pond and along the Charles River.

Supermarkets

Bread & Circus
115 Prospect Street
(617) 492-0070

Natural foods.

Star Market
49 White Street
(617) 492-5566

Pharmacies

Ciampa Apothecary
425 Cambridge Street
(617) 547-0322

CVS
1013 Massachusetts Avenue
(617) 547-7434

Hardware Stores

Dickson Brothers True Value
26 Brattle Street
(617) 876-6760

Inman Square Hardware
1337 Cambridge Street
(617) 491-3405

Hospitals/ Emergency Rooms

Mount Auburn Hospital
330 Mount Auburn Street
(617) 492-3500

www.mountauburn.
caregroup.org

NEWTON

If you can afford it and like the suburban lifestyle but still want to be near the city, this is the place for you. Newton has many big houses on large lots, a good school system, and easy access downtown via trolley, commuter rail, and car. It's called "the Garden City" for good reason.

Just to the west of Boston, Newton is divided into thirteen "villages," each of which has its own center and feel (read more at www.tiac.net/users/unnewton/villages.html). As in Boston, most residents use the name of their neighborhood in their return address rather than the name of the city. One of the most unusual neighborhoods is Nonantum, where residents have their own variant of English that borrows extensively from the Italian of the area's dwellers. Only in Nonantum, for example, do people refer to a friend as a "moosh" or a crazy person as a "divvia."

Auburndale boasts a number of stone houses (and was originally named Pigeonville, after one of its founders, C. D. Pigeon). Newton Centre is home to weekly ethnic festivals in the summertime. Nonantum was founded in 1647 as a settlement of Indians converted to Christianity by John Eliot (who later also founded Natick). Some of the most exclusive homes in Newton are in Chestnut Hill, a neighborhood that crosses over into Brookline.

Commonwealth Avenue, which runs the length of the city, has some stunning mansions and is best known for "Heartbreak Hill," a long, slow upgrade that tests runners in the annual Boston Marathon. Just as they're running out of reserves, the runners hit this incline that doesn't seem to end.

Neighborhood Statistical Profile

Total Population: 83,829

Population by Ethnicity

White:	72,388	(86.35%)
Black:	1,584	(1.9%)
Hispanic:	2,111	(2.52%)
Asian/Pacific Islander:	6,433	(7.67%)
Native American:	43	(0.05%)
Other single race:	213	(0.25%)
Multiracial:	1,057	(1.26%)

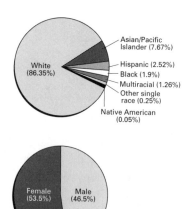

Population by Gender

Female:	53.5%
Male:	46.5%

Population by Age

Median age:	*38.7*
Under 18:	*21.2%*
18–24:	*10.3%*
25–44:	*28.2%*
45–64:	*25.2%*
65+:	*15.1%*

Median home sale $558,000

Median condo sale $349,000

Average rent $1,275

Average Housing Costs

Median home sale:	*$558,000*
Median condo sale:	*$349,000*
Average rent:	*$1,275*

Other Statistics

Crime: *Safe.*
Income: *Middle and upper middle class.*
Parking: *Overnight parking is prohibited.*

Type of Government

City.

The Commute

The Riverside branch of the Green Line trolley offers fast service into downtown Boston. There are also commuter-rail stops along the Massachusetts Turnpike in Newtonville, West Newton, and Auburndale. The city also has its own local bus system for intra-town travel, called Nexus (www.ci.newton.ma.us/Nexus/nexus.htm for information and schedules). The Underground Newton Transportation Site has detailed information on all manner of public transit in the city: geocities.com/newtontransit/unts.html. Two entrances on the Massachusetts Turnpike (one at the Weston line, the other in West Newton) mean you can be downtown in fifteen minutes.

Noteworthy in the Neighborhood

- The Hemlock Gorge is a twenty-three-acre reservation along the Charles River that features dramatic evidence of glacial action: the beautiful Echo Bridge. You can hear yourself echo while standing under the bridge, one of the largest stone arches in the world (www.channel1.com/users/hemlock).

- The Newton Mothers' Forum provides resources for local parents, including helping mothers get to know each other and a monthly mothers' night out: www.newtonmoms.com.

- The Jackson Homestead is an 1809 Federalist-style farmhouse that houses paintings, costumes, toys, photographs, and other items from Newton's past: (617) 552-7238 or www.ci.newton. ma.us/jackson.

- Rent canoes and kayaks for meandering down the Charles River at Charles River Canoe & Kayak, 2401 Commonwealth Avenue, just off Route 128: (617) 965-5110 or www.ski-paddle.com/ cano/canoe.shtml.

Supermarkets

Bread & Circus
916 Walnut Street
(617) 969-1141

Natural foods.

Omni Foods Supermarket
200 Boylston Street (Route 9)
(617) 558-3364

Star Market
2040 Commonwealth Avenue
(617) 965-1793

Stop & Shop
978 Boylston Street
(617) 964-7341

Pharmacies

CVS
1195 Boylston Street
(617) 731-5228

Eaton Apothecary
425 Centre Street
(617) 244-3700

Fox Pharmacy of Newton
416 Watertown Street
(617) 527-2310

Hubbard Drug
425 Centre Street
(617) 244-3700

Walgreens
1101 Beacon Street
(617) 332-4410

Hardware Stores

Donato Tools & Hardware
41 Los Angeles Street
(617) 969-1785

Swartz True Value Hardware
353 Watertown Street
(617) 244-4580

Waban Hardware
1641 Beacon Street
(617) 244-4566

**Hospitals/
Emergency Rooms**

Newton-Wellesley Hospital
2014 Washington Street
(617) 243-6000

www.nwh.org

QUINCY

Birthplace of two presidents (John Adams and John Quincy Adams), Quincy is a bustling city to Boston's immediate south that also offers easy access to the rest of the South Shore. Quincy has everything from large apartment complexes to single-family homes. Like Boston, Quincy is a city of older homes: Close to half of all the units in the city were built before 1950, almost three-quarters before 1970. The Wollaston neighborhood consists largely of colonials and Victorians built around the turn of the century (the twentieth century, that is), especially up on the hill. Marina Bay is a condo community right on the harbor with a boardwalk that offers views of the Boston skyline, along with a variety of pubs and restaurants.

Quincy generally remains more affordable than surrounding communities. Recent years, however, have seen an explosion in local housing prices, especially for homes in waterfront areas, such as Squantum, but also for apartments. Quincy's apartment vacancy rate is comparable to Boston's, which is to say almost nonexistent.

Recent years have also seen Quincy become more of a multieth-nic community. The Asian community, the Chinese in particular, has grown dramatically.

Quincy has a number of beaches on Quincy Bay. They're all swim-mable most of the time now, thanks to a suit by the city against the state in 1982 that led to a multibillion-dollar cleanup of Boston Harbor.

Neighborhood Statistical Profile

Total Population: 88,025

Population by Ethnicity

White:	68,980	*(78.36%)*
Black:	1,846	*(2.1%)*
Hispanic:	1,835	*(2.08%)*
Asian/Pacific Islander:	13,538	*(15.4%)*
Native American:	129	*(0.14%)*
Other single race:	290	*(0.32%)*
Multiracial:	1,407	*(1.6%)*

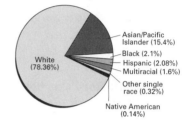

Population by Gender

Female:	52.3%
Male:	47.7%

Population by Age

Median age:	37.6
Under 18:	17.5%
18–24:	8.1%
25–44:	36.1%
45–64:	22.1%
65+:	16.2%

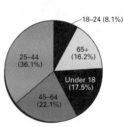

Median home sale $240,000

Median condo sale $175,000

Average rent $1,700

Average Housing Costs

Median home sale:	*$240,000*
Median condo sale:	*$175,000*
Average rent:	*$1,700*

Other Statistics

Crime: *A generally safe city.*
Income: *Middle class.*
Parking: *Overnight parking is prohibited.*

Type of Government

City.

The Commute

Quincy has four stops on the Red Line subway, getting you to downtown Boston in twenty-two minutes or less. There's also a commuter-rail stop in Quincy Center. Route 93 connects Quincy with downtown Boston as well. If the traffic cooperates, you can be downtown in fifteen minutes. Frequently, however, it doesn't, so bring something to read or plenty of CDs. There is also a ferry service from the Quincy Shipyard to Logan Airport and Long Wharf, near the Financial District; it's a forty-minute ride.

Noteworthy in the Neighborhood

- The name of the city is pronounced "Quin-zee" (see ci.quincy.ma .us/htm/quincy.htm for a detailed explanation). Quincy was named for Colonel John Quincy, the great-grandfather of John Quincy Adams. All other U.S. towns called Quincy were named for John Quincy Adams. The Adams National Historic Site (www.nps.gov/adam) commemorates five generations of Adamses. You can now take "trolley" tours of the city's various historic sites.

- One of the results of the multibillion-dollar cleanup of Boston Harbor is that Quincy has regained its place as a prime fishing spot. Quincy Bay is particularly noted for striped bass and bluefish.

- Quincy Shore Drive has plenty of clam shacks, ice-cream stands, and bars along the beach. It's a popular people-watching spot. Look for the muscle guys and their babes with the halter tops.

Supermarkets

Fuyang Supermarket
49 Billings Road
(617) 479-9516

Star Market
130 Granite Street
(617) 770-0841

Victory Supermarket
475 Hancock Street
(617) 769-0088

Pharmacies

Brooks Pharmacy
316 Washington
(781) 331-7997

CVS
108 Main Street
(781) 843-7770

Hardware Stores

Curry Hardware
370 Copeland Street
(617) 472-8250

O'Malley Ace Hardware
53 Billings Road
(617) 773-0808

Hospitals/Emergency Rooms

Quincy Medical Center
114 Whitwell Street
(617) 773-6100

SOMERVILLE

Once considered Cambridge's poor relation, Somerville has come into its own over the past decade. (The two cities have long shared mutual disrespect: Cantabrigians diss "Slummaville"; Somerville residents complain about Cambridge "Barnies.")

The extension of the Red Line subway opened up neighborhoods such as Davis Square to the rest of greater Boston. Mix in coffeehouses, restaurants, and nightclubs, sprinkle in a hefty dose of undergrads from Tufts University (on the Somerville/Medford line) and MIT grad students, and suddenly Somerville has become the place to be, only with lower rents than Cambridge. Artists have flocked to the city, which has an active arts council. The Vernon Street Studios (www.vernonstreet.com), for example, is a former foam factory now home to artists who work in a variety of media, and the Brickbottom Artists Building (www.brickbottomartists.com)was originally a supermarket warehouse. The Washington Street Art Center is a community arts center and workspace run by an artists' collective (www.kickball.com/wsac).

Most of the gentrification has occurred in the western part of the city, around Porter and Davis Squares. The Winter Hill and Union Square areas are packed with row after row of triple-deckers. They help make Somerville one of the most densely populated cities in the country, with more than 18,000 people per square mile.

Neighborhood Statistical Profile

Total Population: 77,478

Population by Ethnicity

White:	56,320	*(72.7%)*
Black:	4,868	*(6.29%)*
Hispanic:	6,786	*(8.77%)*
Asian/Pacific Islander:	5,005	*(6.47%)*
Native American:	128	*(0.17%)*
Other single race:	1,197	*(1.5%)*
Multiracial:	3,174	*(4.1%)*

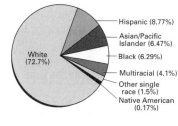

Population by Gender

Female:	52.3%
Male:	47.7%

Population by Age

Median age:	37.6
Under 18:	17.5%
18–24:	8.1%
25–44:	36.1%
45–64:	22%
65+:	16.3%

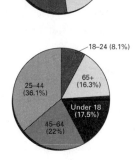

Median home sale $240,000

Median condo sale $175,000

Average rent $1,300

Average Housing Costs

Median home sale: *$240,000*
Median condo sale: *$175,000*
Average rent: *$1,300*

Other Statistics

Crime: *A generally safe city.*
Income: *Working and middle class.*
Parking: *It can be tight. Resident parking permits cost $1 a year.*

Type of Government

City.

The Commute

Somerville has a Red Line subway stop at Davis Square, providing quick access to Cambridge and downtown, roughly sixteen minutes to Park Street. The Porter Square and Alewife stops on the Red Line are closer to some parts of the city. By car, Somerville is a relatively short drive from downtown via I-93 and the McGrath and O'Brien Highways. However, you'll be sharing those roads with plenty of company from the north, so expect a harried ride at rush hour.

Noteworthy in the Neighborhood

- Somerville was once one of the world's largest producers of bricks.
- A former Ford assembly plant was converted into a shopping mall, which failed. Redevelopment of this land, now known as Assembly Square, is a major issue for the city.
- The Somerville Museum, owned by the Somerville Historical Society, frequently has exhibits of artwork by Somerville residents: (617) 666-9810.

Supermarkets

Star Market
299 Broadway
(617) 776-7733

275 Beacon Street
(617) 354-7023

Pharmacies

Brooks Pharmacy
622 Somerville Avenue
(617) 625-5513

Osco
8 McGrath Highway
(617) 776-3003

Walgreens
345 Broadway
(617) 776-4914

Hardware Stores

A. Grace Hardware
531 Medford Street
(617) 776-7090

Builders Specialty & Hardware
26 Weston Avenue
(617) 666-3000

Hospitals/Emergency Rooms

Somerville Hospital
230 Highland Avenue
(617) 591-4500

WATERTOWN

A former Charles River mill town, Watertown today blends proximity to Cambridge and Boston with quiet neighborhoods. Parts of Watertown will remind you of Cambridge; others of your basic split-level-ranch suburb. Apartment and condo buildings have sprouted along Main Street and along the Charles River near the Arsenal Mall. Recent years have seen the once-somnolent Watertown Square transformed into a restaurant hot spot, where you can take an after-dinner stroll along the Charles River.

The town is the center of the Boston area's Armenian community, one of the largest in the United States. East Watertown is sometimes called "Little Armenia," and Coolidge Square is where you'll find several Armenian markets, selling everything from pomegranate juice to lamajuns (thin, pita-like bread covered in meat).

Neighborhood Statistical Profile

Total Population: 32,986

Population by Ethnicity

White:	29,591	(89.7%)
Black:	556	(1.7%)
Hispanic:	883	(2.7%)
Asian/Pacific Islander:	1,279	(3.9%)
Native American:	42	(0.1%)
Other single race:	62	(0.2%)
Multiracial:	573	(1.7%)

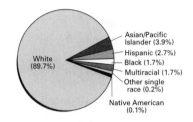

Population by Gender

Female:	53.7%
Male:	46.3%

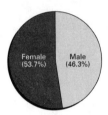

Population by Age

Median age:	36.7
Under 18:	14.1%
18–24:	9.4%
25–44:	39.8%
45–64:	20%
65+:	16.7%

Average Housing Costs

Median home sale:	$312,350
Median condo sale:	$249,000
Average rent:	$1,030

Other Statistics

Crime:	A generally safe town.
Income:	Working and middle class.
Parking:	No overnight parking.

Type of Government
Town council.

The Commute
Watertown Square is the local transportation hub, with local and express buses to Cambridge and downtown Boston. You can be in Harvard Square or downtown via bus in fifteen minutes. There's an entrance to the Massachusetts Turnpike nearby in Newton Corner. Once there, you're ten to fifteen minutes from downtown.

Noteworthy in the Neighborhood
- Stanley Steamers were built in Watertown.
- The Perkins School for the Blind, established in 1829, was the first such school in the country: www.perkins.pvt.k12.ma.us.
- Watertown Square is connected to Harvard Square in Cambridge by "trackless trolleys"—electric buses powered by overhead electric lines.
- Founded in 1816, the Watertown Arsenal was one of the country's oldest producers of military weapons. Its buildings were eventually converted into a mall, senior-citizen housing, and offices.

Supermarkets
Stop & Shop
171 Watertown Street
(617) 969-6410

Pharmacies
CVS
189 Watertown Street
(617) 332-2861

Hardware Stores
Coolidge Hardware
622 Mount Auburn Street
(617) 924-6122

Hospitals/Emergency Rooms
Mount Auburn Hospital
330 Mount Auburn Street
(617) 492-3500

www.mountauburn.
caregroup.org

Outer Suburbs

ACTON

Acton is a mirror image to the neighboring (and better known) Concord (see below). Sure, it has the Revolutionary history. And it has the similarly pricey estate-style homes. But where Concord can be stand-offish and snooty, Acton is more relaxed. And unlike Concord, it has plenty of mini-malls and low-slung apartment and condo complexes, mostly along Route 2A.

Aside from Route 2A, much of Acton has a semirural or rural feel (particularly North Acton), right down to the stone walls along the narrow, winding roads. Acton has small villagelike centers in West and South Acton and Acton Center.

Many people move to Acton because of its unique elementary school system. Instead of neighborhood schools, the town has an educational campus that lets parents choose among a strict three-Rs curriculum, a more flexible "progressive" curriculum, and one that falls in between.

Neighborhood Statistical Profile

Total Population: 20,331

Population by Ethnicity

White:	17,729	(87.2%)
Black:	142	(0.68%)
Hispanic:	360	(1.8%)
Asian/Pacific Islander:	1,745	(8.58%)
Native American:	15	(0.07%)
Other single race:	55	(0.27%)
Multiracial:	285	(1.4%)

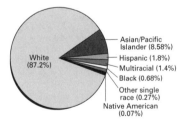

Population by Gender

Female: 50.7%
Male: 49.3%

Population by Age

Median age: 37.9
Under 18:   29.5%
18–24:   4.3%
25–44:   31.4%
45–64:   26.4%
65+:   8.4%

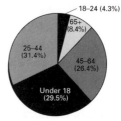

Average Housing Costs

Median home sale: $441,000
Median condo sale: $140,500
Average rent: $1,060

Other Statistics

Crime: A safe town.
Income: Upper middle class.

Type of Government

Open town meeting.

The Commute

Acton is fifty minutes out of downtown via the South Acton commuter-rail stop. It's forty-five to fifty minutes from downtown by car via Route 2. Route 495 is ten to fifteen minutes to the west.

Noteworthy in the Neighborhood

- The famous Minuteman statue at Old North Bridge in Concord depicts Isaac Davis of Acton, one of the first to die at the battle at the bridge, one of the opening battles in the Revolution. Davis, who led the Acton contingent of Minutemen, was the youngest commander at the battle. Traditionally, that meant his men would be the last to see battle, but older commanders declined to face the Redcoats. Davis yelled, "I have not a man who is afraid to fight!" and charged to the front, where he was promptly killed. The plow he dropped in his field to lead his men to battle is on display at Acton Town Hall.

- Acton has some of the cleanest drinking water in the country. The discovery in 1978 of potentially carcinogenic chemicals in Acton's water from a local plastics plant led to a revolution in the town government in which environmentalists took control and enacted water-quality standards that are much stricter than most federal and state standards.

- The Children's Discovery Museum and Science Discovery Museum are filled with interactive exhibits for toddlers to school-aged children. Just look for the green dinosaur on Main Street: (978) 264-0030 or www.ultranet.com/~discover.

Supermarkets

Roche Bros.
387 Massachusetts Avenue
(978) 263-0404

Stop & Shop
100 Powder Mill Road
(978) 897-6449

Pharmacies

Acton Pharmacy
563 Massachusetts Avenue
(978) 263-3901

CVS
344 Great Road
(978) 264-9130

Hardware Stores

Acton Ace Hardware
210 Main Street
(978) 263-7754

Hospitals/Emergency Rooms

Emerson Hospital
133 Old Road to Nine Acre Corner
Concord
(978) 369-1400

www.emersonhospital.org

ARLINGTON

Arlington is sort of a transition town between city and 'burbs: On one side, it borders Cambridge; on the other, the distinctly suburban Lexington is its neighbor. Arlington has enough going on to keep you in town many evenings, including the Capitol Theater (one of the Boston area's few remaining "classic" movie theaters), the neighboring Quebrada Baking Company (classic European pastries and coffee), and any number of ethnic restaurants (all Arlington restaurants are smoke-free).

Every Patriots' Day (the Monday closest to April 19), the town hosts a large parade in which Minutemen troops from across the region march down Massachusetts Avenue. Also notable is the Minuteman Commuter Bike Trail, which starts in Arlington and follows an abandoned railway line into Lexington and Bedford.

When the MBTA began planning to expand the Red Line beyond Harvard Square in the 1980s, the original idea was to have it run down Massachusetts Avenue into Arlington. Arlington didn't want the subway, though, so the Red Line stops at Alewife, just before Arlington. If you drive to the stop, get there early, because the parking garage often fills up. Once on the train, you'll be downtown in fifteen minutes or so. Getting to downtown Boston by car is a twenty to twenty-five-minute ride on Route 2 and one of the "river roads" (either Memorial Drive in Cambridge or Storrow Drive in Boston).

Neighborhood Statistical Profile

Total Population: 42,389

Population by Ethnicity

White:	38,058	(89.8%)
Black:	690	(1.6%)
Hispanic:	787	(1.85%)
Asian/Pacific Islander:	2,100	(4.95%)
Native American:	46	(0.1%)
Other single race:	112	(0.3%)
Multiracial:	596	(1%)

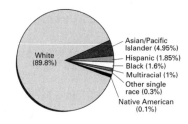

Population by Gender

Female:	*53.6%*
Male:	*46.4%*

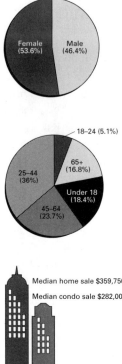

Population by Age

Median age:	*39.5*
Under 18:	*18.4%*
18–24:	*5.1%*
25–44:	*36%*
45–64:	*23.7%*
65+:	*16.8%*

Average Housing Costs

Median home sale:	*$359,750*
Median condo sale:	*$282,000*
Average rent:	*$1,360*

Other Statistics

Crime:	*A safe town.*
Income:	*Middle and upper middle class.*

Type of Government

Representative town meeting.

The Commute

Arlington is a short drive from the Alewife stop on the Red Line, which is fifteen to twenty minutes from downtown Boston. Access to downtown is via Route 2 and Memorial and Storrow Drives.

Noteworthy in the Neighborhood

- Arlington has both a community theater (Arlington Friends of the Drama, www.afdtheatre.org) and an orchestra (the Arlington Philharmonic Society, www.psarlington.org).
- Spy Pond and the Mystic Lakes are "kettle hole" ponds, formed by melting glaciers about 15,000 years ago.
- Uncle Sam, a.k.a. Samuel Wilson, was born in Arlington (then known as Menotomy) in 1766. There's a statue of him near the corner of Mystic Street and Massachusetts Avenue. Arlington changed its name from Menotomy 100 years later to honor fallen Civil War soldiers buried in Arlington National Cemetery.

Supermarkets

Stop & Shop
905 Massachusetts Avenue
(781) 646-8072

Trader Joe's
1427 Massachusetts Avenue
(781) 646-9138

Pharmacies

CVS
319 Broadway
(781) 648-7019

Maida Pharmacy Inc.
121 Massachusetts Avenue
(781) 643-7840

Menotomy Pharmacy
1332 Massachusetts Avenue
(781) 643-1247

Hardware Stores

R.W. Shattuck & Company
24 Mill Street
(781) 643-0114

Wanamaker Hardware True Value
1298 Massachusetts Avenue
(781) 643-1900

Hospitals/ Emergency Rooms

Somerville Hospital
230 Highland Avenue
Somerville
(617) 591-4500

BEVERLY

Founded in 1626, Beverly is one of the state's oldest communities. Over the years, it's changed from an industrial powerhouse (it used to be a leading shoe manufacturer) to a largely residential community with a dose of high-tech and biotech startups (many in the former United Shoe Manufacturing plant).

The northern end of the town is still home to the mansions and estates built in the late 1800s. Tuck Point is a condo project right on the harbor. There are also single-family homes of all types.

Neighborhood Statistical Profile

Total Population: 39,862

Population by Ethnicity

White:	37,781	(94.8%)
Black:	391	(1%)
Hispanic:	720	(1.8%)
Asian/Pacific Islander:	517	(1.3%)
Native American:	58	(0.1%)
Other single race:	43	(0.1%)
Multiracial:	352	(0.9%)

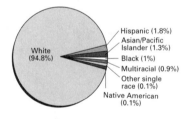

Population by Gender

Female:	52.7%
Male:	47.3%

Population by Age

Median age:	38.3
Under 18:	21.7%
18–24:	9%
25–44:	30.9%
45–64:	22.8%
65+:	15.6%

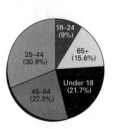

Median home sale $278,250

Median condo sale $150,500

Average rent $1,500

Average Housing Costs

Median home sale:	*$278,250*
Median condo sale:	*$150,500*
Average rent:	*$1,500*

Other Statistics

Crime:	*Safe.*
Income:	*Middle and upper middle class.*

Type of Government

City.

The Commute

Beverly's about thirty-five minutes from downtown Boston by commuter rail, about forty minutes by car.

Noteworthy in the Neighborhood

- William Howard Taft's summer White House was on Woodbury Point in Beverly. He chose Beverly in part because it was "comfortable Republican territory."
- The schooner Hannah was the first naval vessel commissioned by George Washington, in 1775. A local group is now working to rebuild the schooner: (800) 276-1775 or www.thehannah.org.
- The city has a number of ocean beaches for residents: www.beverlychamber.com/Beaches.shtml.
- The big local celebration is Beverly Homecoming, held over several days in mid-summer. Events run from concerts to walking tours to a carnival: www.beverlyhomecoming.com.

Supermarkets

Henry's of North Beverly
588 Cabot Street
(978) 922-3885

Stop & Shop
37 Enon Street
(978) 921-0920

Pharmacies

CVS
446 Rantoul Street
(978) 921-0402

Medicine Shoppe
409 Cabot Street
(978) 927-9075

Hardware Stores

Dawson's True Value Hardware
50 Enon Street
(978) 927-1320

P. J. Hansbury Hardware & General Store
95 Rantoul Street
(978) 927-3145

Hospitals/Emergency Rooms

Beverly Hospital
85 Herrick Street
South Weymouth
(978) 922-3000

www.beverlyhospital.org

BRAINTREE

Home to the regional mega-mall, the South Shore Plaza, and the place where major commuter roads Route 3 and I-93 come together, Braintree still manages to be a quiet residential area that offers both single-family homes and condominiums.

In 2001, Braintree Square was renovated—benches, brick sidewalks, and antique lighting fixtures were added—to give it the feel of a small village.

Braintree boasts some of the lowest property-tax rates in the area, although that has also meant growing concerns about the condition of local roads and school buildings. It's bordered by the Blue Hills Reservation with its thousands of acres of woods and trails, and features a number of town parks and beaches. Electricity and high-speed Internet access are provided by a town department.

Neighborhood Statistical Profile

Total Population: 33,698

Population by Ethnicity

White:	31,438	(93.3%)
Black:	377	(1.1%)
Hispanic:	394	(1.2%)
Asian/Pacific Islander:	1,051	(3.1%)
Native American:	31	(0.09%)
Other single race:	128	(0.38%)
Multiracial:	279	(0.83%)

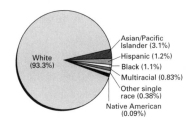

Population by Gender

Female:	52.9%
Male:	47.1%

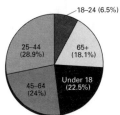

Population by Age

Median age:	40
Under 18:	22.5%
18–24:	6.5%
25–44:	28.9%
45–64:	24%
65+:	18.1%

Median home sale $249,500

Median condo sale $179,000

Average rent $1,050

Average Housing Costs

Median home sale:	$249,500
Median condo sale:	$179,000
Average rent:	$1,050

Other Statistics

Crime: A safe town.

Income: Middle and upper middle class.

Type of Government

Representative town meeting.

The Commute

You can be downtown in about twenty-five minutes after boarding the Red Line subway, whose terminus is in Braintree. It'll take you twenty to twenty-five minutes to drive into town on I-93.

Noteworthy in the Neighborhood

- A town department supplies electricity, cable television, and broadband Internet access.
- Sunset Lake has a town beach and is the site of the town's Fourth of July celebrations and fireworks.
- Although the city of Quincy (see above) now claims presidents John Adams and John Quincy Adams as native sons, their home was actually part of Braintree when they were born (Quincy wasn't founded until 1792, 25 years after John Quincy Adams was born).

Supermarkets

Shaws
125 Pearl Street
(781) 356-4467

Stop & Shop
316 Grove Street
(781) 356-1730

Pharmacies

CVS
884 Washington Street
(781) 356-4325

Osco
11 Pearl Street
(781) 356-3337

Hardware Stores

Ashmont Discount Home Center
464 Quincy Avenue
(781) 848-7350

Curry Hardware
190 Quincy Avenue
(781) 843-1616

Hospitals/ Emergency Rooms

South Shore Hospital
55 Fogg Road
South Weymouth
(781) 340-8000

www.southshorehospital.org

COHASSET

The center of this South Shore town about twenty-five miles south of Boston is classic seacoast New England: a large common surrounded by white steeple-topped churches and fishing boats bobbing in the harbor. Away from the common, large colonials sit on hills with sweeping views of the Atlantic Ocean (only the Minot Lighthouse stands between Cohasset and Europe). The town also has some "cluster" homes: houses that are built closer together than would otherwise be allowed and that are bought and sold like condominiums.

Bring plenty of money if you're serious about moving here. A vacant lot can cost upwards of $1 million in this town with little buildable land left.

Neighborhood Statistical Profile

Total Population: 7,261

Population by Ethnicity

White:	7,099	(97.77%)
Black:	13	(0.18%)
Hispanic:	50	(0.69%)
Asian/Pacific Islander:	53	(0.73%)
Native American:	5	(0.07%)
Other single race:	0	(0%)
Multiracial:	41	(0.56%)

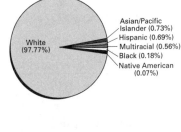

Population by Gender

Female:	51.8%
Male:	48.2%

Population by Age

Median age:	40.9
Under 18:	27.9%
18–24:	3.5%
25–44:	26.6%
45–64:	26.6%
65+:	15.4%

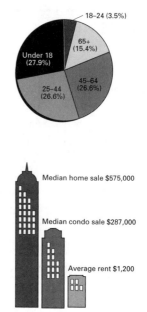

18–24 (3.5%)

65+ (15.4%)

Under 18 (27.9%)

45–64 (26.6%)

25–44 (26.6%)

Median home sale $575,000

Median condo sale $287,000

Average rent $1,200

Average Housing Costs

Median home sale:	$575,000
Median condo sale:	$287,000
Average rent:	$1,200

Other Statistics

Crime: Very safe.

Income: Upper middle class, rich.

Type of Government

Open town meeting.

The Commute

Expect a ride of about forty-five minutes into downtown via Route 3A and I-93. Ferry service from neighboring Hingham takes thirty-five minutes to get to Rowes Wharf near the Financial District. The state is currently planning the revival of a long-dormant commuter-rail line that would pass through Cohasset.

Noteworthy in the Neighborhood

- St. Stephen's Church has had Sunday carillon concerts since 1824.
- The South Shore Art Center has galleries and teaching studios: (781) 383-2787 or www.ssac.org.

- The Cohasset Sailing Club, open to town residents only, offers sailing lessons to both children and adults: www. cohassetsailingclub.com.

Supermarkets

Stop & Shop
400 Chief Justice Cushing Highway
(781) 383-6614

Pharmacies

CVS
790 Chief Justice Cushing Highway
(781) 383-6240

Walgreens
767 Chief Justice Cushing Highway
(781) 383-1773

Hardware Stores

Hingham Lumber
190 Summer Street
(781) 749-4200

Hospitals/ Emergency Rooms

South Shore Hospital
55 Fogg Road
South Weymouth
(781) 340-8000
www.southshorehospital.org

CONCORD

Who hasn't heard of Concord, the midnight ride of Paul Revere, and the shot heard 'round the world? Or the city's later contributions to American life: the transcendentalists, Louisa May Alcott, and Henry David Thoreau?

They all combine to make Concord one of the most visited places in the country. Yet unlike other tourist destinations, Concord has managed to remain largely unsullied by crass commercialism. There are no strip malls here (Concordians do their grocery shopping and movie going next door in Acton); the only lodging is the suitably quaint Colonial Inn and a nearby B&B (the Concordian Motel is actually in Acton). The town looks and feels exactly like what you'd expect from an exclusive, semirural New England town: lots of grand old houses on meandering country roads, with a quaint town center filled with boutiques, fancy cheese shops, and the grounds of an exclusive prep school (Concord Academy).

Outsiders can be forgiven if they find all this more than a wee bit stuffy, as did Thoreau, who rebelled against Concord conformity by fleeing to Walden Pond (the town responded by building the town dump right across the road from the pond). The town meeting once banned the serving of food on paper plates in an attempt to keep a pizza chain from opening up in town; the chain came in anyway, by replacing its paper plates with china.

West Concord, home to a medium-security prison and a prison farm, is far less snooty; its "downtown" is dominated by stores selling everyday goods. The West Concord 5 and 10 is one of five five-and-dimes left in the state.

Neighborhood Statistical Profile

Total Population:16,993

Population by Ethnicity

White:	15,428	(90.8%)
Black:	373	(2.2%)
Hispanic:	474	(2.9%)
Asian/Pacific Islander:	493	(2.9%)
Native American:	16	(0.09%)
Other single race:	56	(0.3%)
Multiracial:	153	(0.9%)

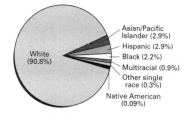

Population by Gender

Female:	49.9%
Male:	50.1%

Population by Age

Median age:	42.2
Under 18:	25.1%
18–24:	4.2%
25–44:	25.8%
45–64:	28.4%
65+:	16.5%

Median home sale $540,000

Median condo sale $375,000

Average rent $1,700

Average Housing Costs

Median home sale:	*$540,000*
Median condo sale:	*$375,000*
Average rent:	*$1,700*

Other Statistics

Crime:	*Very safe.*
Income:	*Upper middle class, rich.*

Type of Government

Open town meeting.

The Commute

There are commuter-rail stops in West Concord and Thoreau Street in Concord Center; North Station in Boston is about forty minutes away. Route 2 is the main road through town toward Boston (thirty-five to forty-five minutes) and I-495 (ten to fifteen minutes).

Noteworthy in the Neighborhood

- In the rest of the country, Massachusetts' Patriots' Day holiday is known mostly for the running of the Boston Marathon. In Concord, it's a day to celebrate the initial battles of the Revolution. Concord Minutemen get up before dawn to re-create the "Line of March" to the Old North Bridge. There, joined by Minutemen from surrounding towns, they stage a mock battle with a troop of Redcoats. Darned if the Redcoats don't always lose. Patriots' Day is celebrated on the Monday closest to April 19.

- Daniel Chester French of Concord sculpted the Minuteman statue at the Old North Bridge. He later became famous for the statue of Abraham Lincoln at the Lincoln Memorial in Washington, D.C.

- Concord has three rivers, several "great" ponds, and a large part of the Great Meadows National Wildlife Sanctuary. Canoeing is a popular pastime on the Sudbury and Concord Rivers. For more information, see www.concordma.com/nature/toc.html.
- Walden Pond is a state park. In addition to its connection to Thoreau, it's a popular swimming hole in the summer. Parking is limited, so get there early (crisp, quiet fall days might be a better time to appreciate the pond as Thoreau did).

Supermarkets

Donelan's Supermarket
248 Great Road
Acton
(978) 635-9893

Pharmacies

Brooks Pharmacy
49 Main Street
(781) 259-0028

West Concord Pharmacy
1212 Main Street
(978) 369-3100

Hardware Stores

Rocky's Ace Hardware
203 Sudbury Road
(978) 369-5181

Vanderhoof Hardware
28 Main Street
(978) 369-2243

Hospitals/Emergency Rooms

Emerson Hospital
133 Old Road to Nine Acre Corner
(978) 369-1400

www.emersonhospital.org

FRAMINGHAM

Mention Framingham to most people in the Boston area, and their first (and maybe only) thought will be "shopping malls." Although the "Golden Triangle" made up of Route 9, Route 30, and Speen Street on the Natick/Framingham line is New England's second-largest retail area, there is a lot more to this town twenty miles west of Boston than just stores and bad Christmastime traffic.

Beyond the malls is a complex and sprawling community that spans run-down tenements downtown to million-dollar-plus homes on oversized lots in North Framingham. Like Brookline, Framingham is split by Route 9. Those on the North Side sometimes look down on the South Side, but outside the fairly small area just south of the downtown train tracks, there are some lovely family-oriented neighborhoods south of the highway.

Although Framingham now pays considerable attention to land-use issues, the effects of fifty years of laissez-faire zoning are evident along Route 9, which is lined with large apartment complexes and where there is virtually no buffer between the commercial strips and residential areas right behind them. Despite this congestion, Framingham has a beautiful town common just off Route 9, along with a wide variety of housing types, from Victorians to split-level ranches.

With 67,000 residents, Framingham is larger than many Massachusetts cities, but residents have rebuffed numerous attempts to change their town meeting form of government; they feel it gives them more of a say in how the community is run.

The town used to be a major industrial center, but over the past twenty years, many of its larger facilities have shut down (including a General Motors assembly plant and a Dennison printing plant). Today local jobs are far more likely to be in the service sector: at those malls on Route 9 and the high-tech startups to the west of town.

Neighborhood Statistical Profile

Total Population: 66,910

Population by Ethnicity

White:	*50,293*	*(75.2%)*
Black:	*2,991*	*(4.47%)*
Hispanic:	*7,265*	*(10.86%)*
Asian/Pacific Islander:	*3,523*	*(5.27%)*
Native American:	*79*	*(0.1%)*
Other single race:	*1,148*	*(1.7%)*
Multiracial:	*1,.611*	*(2.4%)*

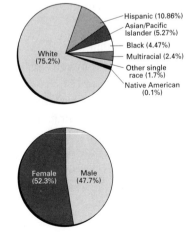

Population by Gender

Female:	*52.3%*
Male:	*47.7%*

Population by Age

Median age:	*36.2*
Under 18:	*21.4%*
18–24:	*9%*
25–44:	*34.5%*
45–64:	*22.1%*
65+:	*13%*

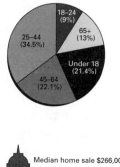

Average Housing Costs

Median home sale:	*$266,000*
Median condo sale:	*$87,950*
Average rent:	*$1,000*

Median home sale $266,000

Median condo sale $87,950

Average rent $1,000

Other Statistics

Crime: *Generally very safe except for a few blocks near the downtown train station.*

Income: *Working, middle, upper middle class.*

Type of Government

Representative town meeting.

The Commute

There's a commuter-rail stop in downtown Framingham, though the stop in West Natick is closer to some parts of town. South Station is about fifty minutes away (there are a couple of express trains that will get you there in thirty-five minutes). Framingham has two entrances on the Massachusetts Turnpike; downtown Boston is about thirty minutes away once you get on the highway. (The hardest part might be getting through local traffic to get to them.) I-495 is fifteen minutes to the west. Framingham has its own local bus system, which connects downtown with the malls, the Framingham Industrial Park, and some surrounding communities.

Noteworthy in the Neighborhood

- Framingham is the largest community in the United States run by a town meeting.
- In most Massachusetts towns, "downtown" and "the center" are synonymous. Only Framingham has a separate downtown (the intersection of Routes 126 and 135) and center (off Route 9 a few miles to the north). Downtown Framingham feels like part of a small city. Framingham Center is a classic New England town center, complete with a tree-lined common, churches, and historic buildings. Why are they separate? In the 1800s, the railroad was originally slated to run through Framingham Center; when residents objected, the railroad was reconfigured further south. In Framingham the big summertime holiday is Flag Day, commemorated with a parade.
- Salem End Road commemorates the place where refugees from the Salem witch trials settled. Old Connecticut Path is named for a route some early colonists took to walk from Boston to Connecticut.
- Framingham has one of Greater Boston's oldest black communities. Crispus Attucks, the first man to die in the Boston Massacre, was from Framingham.

Supermarkets

Asian Groceries
169 Concord Street
(508) 872-8746

Stop & Shop
19 Temple Street
(508) 879-4044

235 Old Connecticut Path
(508) 820-0900

Pharmacies

CVS
121 Worcester Road (Route 9)
(508) 875-7211

390 Union Avenue
(508) 881-5475

Lincoln Discount Drugs
20 Nicholas Road
(508) 877-0300

Hardware Stores

South Middlesex Supply
541 Concord Street
(617) 244-6521

White True Value Hardware
428 Franklin Street
(508) 872-8828

Hospitals/Emergency Rooms

MetroWest Medical Center
115 Lincoln Street
(508) 271-2000

www.mwmc.com

FRANKLIN

Old-timers remember when this was a sleepy farm hamlet (with a 19th-century industrial core centered on felt and shoe making). The construction of I-495 and the development of a high-tech corridor along that highway, though, has transformed this town twenty-two miles southwest of Boston into a bustling commuter town that's particularly popular with families. As you can see from the following statistics, it has a lower median age and a higher percentage of children in its population than many surrounding towns. The boom means more kids for yours to play with, but also growing traffic congestion on local roads and the once rural I-495.

You can find everything from antique and modern colonials to Capes, condos, and luxury townhouses, from High Victorian Gothic to Queen Ann.

Despite the massive development, rural touches still abound in Franklin. The Charles River forms one of the town's boundaries. The town also has an 800-acre state forest and two large town parks with nature trails, boating, and fishing.

Neighborhood Statistical Profile

Total Population: 29,560

Population by Ethnicity

White:	28,165	(95.3%)
Black:	305	(1%)
Hispanic:	318	(1.1%)
Asian/Pacific Islander:	493	(1.7%)
Native American:	36	(0.1%)
Other single race:	32	(0.1%)
Multiracial:	211	(0.7%)

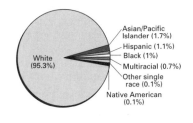

Population by Gender

Female:	51%
Male:	49%

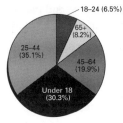

Population by Age

Median age:	34.8
Under 18:	30.3%
18–24:	6.5%
25–44:	35.1%
45–64:	19.9%
65+:	8.2%

Average Housing Costs

Median home sale:	$280,000
Median condo sale:	$147,050
Average rent:	$900

Other Statistics

Crime:	Safe.
Income:	Middle class, professional.

Type of Government

Town council.

The Commute

South Station is about an hour away by commuter rail. Route 495 crosses the town, providing quick access to points north and south. By car, downtown Boston is about an hour away.

Noteworthy in the Neighborhood

- Franklin was originally named Exeter; it became the first community in the United States to rename itself after Benjamin Franklin. Franklin responded to the honor by sending the town some books with which to start a public library.
- The Franklin Zeotrope Theater, 34 East Central Street, shows second-run movies for just $4 a ticket ($1 if you're unemployed)—and uses real butter on its popcorn.
- Franklin is home to Dean College, a two-year school with a fair number of foreign students.

Supermarkets

Star Market
221 East Central Street
(508) 520-6880

Stop & Shop
West Central Street
New Franklin Plaza
(508) 520-4102

Pharmacies

Brooks Pharmacy
250 East Central Street
(508) 528-7627

CVS
272 East Central Street
(508) 528-0794

Hardware Stores

Aubuchon Hardware
240 Cottage Street
(508) 528-8484

D. G. Ranieri Supply
438 West Central Street
(508) 528-8150

Hospitals/Emergency Rooms

Milford-Whitinsville Regional Hospital
14 Prospect Street
Milford
(508) 473-1190

www.mwrh.com

HULL

Like living on the water? Smell the salt air in Hull, a narrow peninsula surrounded by Boston Harbor twenty miles south of Boston (seven miles by sea), where most homes are no more than a few blocks from the water. Sure, sometimes this is a problem, like during the famous Blizzard of '78, when the town was transformed into three temporary islands. But it also means the town has water views galore, a seawall walk, Nantasket Beach, and the still-operating Paragon Carousel, a merry-go-round that's the last remnant of the Paragon Park amusement park. Ferry service to downtown Boston increasingly attracts financial types and other professionals who work downtown.

Neighborhood Statistical Profile

Total Population:11,050

Population by Ethnicity

White:	*10,642*	*(96.3%)*
Black:	*39*	*(0.4%)*
Hispanic:	*120*	*(1.1%)*
Asian/Pacific Islander:	*100*	*(0.9%)*
Native American:	*32*	*(0.25%)*
Other single race:	*28*	*(0.25%)*
Multiracial:	*89*	*(0.8%)*

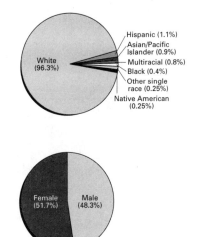

Population by Gender

Female:	*51.7%*
Male:	*48.3%*

Population by Age

Median age:	*40.2*
Under 18:	*22.1%*
18–24:	*6%*
25–44:	*31.6%*
45–64:	*28.3%*
65+:	*12%*

Median home sale $225,000
Median condo sale $191,000

Average rent $1,200

Average Housing Costs

Median home sale:	*$225,000*
Median condo sale:	*$191,000*
Average rent:	*$1,200*

Other Statistics

Crime: *Safe.*
Income: *Middle to upper middle class.*

Type of Government

Open town meeting.

The Commute

Ferry service gets you to Long Wharf near the Financial District in an hour (the ferry also stops at Logan Airport). Boston is about forty minutes away via Route 3A and I-93.

Noteworthy in the Neighborhood

- During the Revolution, a fort on the harbor helped harass the British and later sheltered a French fleet. Boston Light is the oldest continuously operated lighthouse in the United States.
- Hull High School is located at the very tip of the Hull peninsula, where the Atlantic Ocean meets Massachusetts Bay.

- Locals are known as Hullonians. Drowned Hogs are a group of Hullonians who dive into the ocean the Saturday before Ground Hog Day (www.drownedhogs.com). If they all submerge completely before coming out, then spring is just around the corner.
- The Town Light Plant provides power to local residents.

Supermarket

Stop & Shop
400 Lincoln Street
Hingham
(781) 749-1143

Pharmacies

Nantasket Pharmacy
480 Nantasket Avenue
(781) 925-1270

Hardware Stores

Anastos Hardware Store
259 Nantasket Avenue
(781) 925-0978

Hospitals/Emergency Rooms

South Shore Hospital
55 Fogg Road
South Weymouth
(781) 340-8000

www.southshorehospital.org

LEXINGTON

Like neighboring Concord, Lexington has managed to retain its basic residential character despite being one of the most visited tourist spots in the country. Lexington has a more suburban feel in general than Concord, but the town also has extensive parkland and conservation areas. It's also relatively less expensive than Concord and is closer to Cambridge and Boston and to Route 128. Nearby is Hanscom Field, where you can catch a commuter plane to the New York area (although residents in Lexington and surrounding towns continue to fight commercial air service at the field, saying it is helping to ruin the area's national monuments).

Homes in Lexington run from centuries-old Colonials to more modern designs.

The town center focuses on historic Lexington Green, scene of the first major battle in the Revolution. The Minuteman Commuter Bikeway lets you ride your bike all the way to the Alewife subway stop in Cambridge.

Neighborhood Statistical Profile

Total Population: 30,355

Population by Ethnicity

White:	*25,822*	*(85.1%)*
Black:	*337*	*(1.11%)*
Hispanic:	*428*	*(1.4%)*
Asian/Pacific Islander:	*3,307*	*(10.88%)*
Native American:	*20*	*(0.07%)*
Other single race:	*61*	*(0.2%)*
Multiracial:	*380*	*(1.24%)*

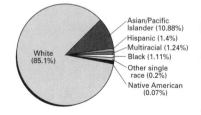

Population by Gender

Female:	53%
Male:	47%

Population by Age

Median age:	43.7
Under 18:	26.4%
18–24:	3.5%
25–44:	22.7%
45–64:	28.4%
65+:	19%

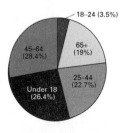

Average Housing Costs

Median home sale:	*$463,750*
Median condo sale:	*$280,000*
Average rent:	*$1,400*

Other Statistics

Crime: *A safe town.*

Income: *Upper middle class.*

Type of Government

Representative town meeting.

The Commute

Lexington is just off Routes 2 and 128. Boston is about thirty minutes away by car. There's no commuter-rail stop in town, but there is bus service to the Alewife Red Line station in Arlington. The trip takes about twenty minutes to the station. The town has its own local bus service, called Lexpress, which has six routes around the town (one of which also goes to the Burlington Mall in nearby Burlington): www.lexingtonma.org/LEXPRESS.

Noteworthy in the Neighborhood

- The Lexington Newcomers Club is a way for new residents to get to know each other. Activities include a book club, a child-care co-op, and historical tours: www.lexingtonnewcomers. homestead.com.

- As you'd expect, Patriots' Day, which commemorates the Battles of Lexington and Concord in 1775, is a popular holiday in town. The Lexington Minute Men Company is a group of residents who re-create the activities of the original Minutemen (Lexington was one of the first towns to organize a militia): www.lexingtonminutemen.com.

- The town has a number of Revolutionary sites in addition to the ones maintained by the Minuteman National Historic Park: people.ne.mediaone.net/wrcmc/BuckmanTxt.html.

Supermarkets

Stop & Shop

36 Bedford Street

(781) 861-0457

Pharmacies

CVS

1735 Massachusetts Avenue

(781) 863-0912

Theatre Pharmacy
1784 Massachusetts Avenue
(781) 862-4480

Hardware Stores

Wanamaker's True Value Hardware
1298 Massachusetts Avenue
Arlington
(781) 643-1900

Hospitals/Emergency Rooms

Emerson Hospital
133 Old Road to Nine Acre Corner
Concord
(978) 369-1400

www.emersonhospital.org

NATICK

True Natickites don't like to admit it, but the town has some things in common with neighboring Framingham, with which it has had a longtime football rivalry. Like Framingham, Natick sometimes suffers the unfair reputation of being just a series of shopping malls. But Walnut Hill and the Henry Wilson Historic District downtown both offer stately Victorians a short walk away from commuter rail and from the brick charms and classic New England town common of Natick Center. South Natick, for its part, has a distinct rural feel that almost makes it seem more like neighboring Dover than the rest of Natick. South Natick also has a history that goes back to its founding in 1651 as a town for "praying Indians" converted to Christianity.

Wethersfield, north of Route 9, is named for the Wethersfield Capes that were built there by the hundreds after World War II. After fifty years, the once near-identical houses now stand under towering trees and have become unique statements of their owners' individuality. West Natick has your basic split-level ranches, along with four giant apartment complexes (which are sometimes collectively called "Yuppie Gulch").

The town has a fierce pride, evidenced by the "Home of Champions" sign downtown. The motto is sometimes taken to extremes. If you go to any Natick town meetings, expect to hear it used as a rhetorical argument akin to the "If we can put a man on the moon, why can't we . . ." argument you might hear elsewhere ("If we're the

Home of Champions, why can't we repave that road?"). The slogan became widely known during Doug Flutie's days as a quarterback for Natick High School and Boston College, but it actually goes back to the late 1800s, when Natick's fire department routinely won "muster" competitions with other towns and cities.

Neighborhood Statistical Profile

Total Population: 31,868

Population by Ethnicity

White:	28,970	(90.9%)
Black:	505	(1.58%)
Hispanic:	624	(1.96%)
Asian/Pacific Islander:	1,215	(3.8%)
Native American:	30	(0.09%)
Other single race:	79	(0.25%)
Multiracial:	445	(1.42%)

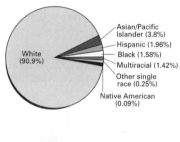

Population by Gender

Female:	52.7%
Male:	47.3%

Population by Age

Median age:	38.2
Under 18:	23%
18–24:	5.1%
25–44:	34.3%
45–64:	23.3%
65+:	14.3%

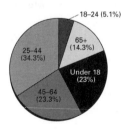

Median home sale $300,000

Median condo sale $148,500

Average rent $1,300

Average Housing Costs

Median home sale: *$300,000*
Median condo sale: *$148,500*
Average rent: *$1,300*

Other Statistics

Crime: *Safe.*
Income: *Middle to upper middle class.*

Type of Government

Representative town meeting.

The Commute

There are commuter-rail stops in Natick Center and West Natick, roughly forty minutes from South Station. By car, Natick is about forty minutes from downtown Boston and twenty minutes from Route 495 by way of the Massachusetts Turnpike.

Noteworthy in the Neighborhood

- Natick has two working farms: the town-owned Natick Community Farm, which functions as a sort of living museum, and Marino's Lookout Farm, whose owners raise exotic animals for their Cambridge restaurant and where you can pick your own fruits.
- Downtown Natick boasts a number of large brick buildings, many erected after an 1872 fire that destroyed much of the area. For the true Natick experience, get an "all around" at Casey's Diner on South Street after a Natick High School football game.
- The Fourth of July brings the annual parade down Main Street as well as a visit from the circus.

- The first Bible printed in British North America was one in the Natick Indian language shortly after the town's 1651 founding. Although the tribe has vanished, victims of colonial oppression (the Indians were exiled to the barren Deer Island after King Philip's War even though they fought on the side of the British), their names survive locally. A main thoroughfare is Speen Street, named for Joseph Speen, one of the early converts. Captain Tom's Hill on the Framingham line is also named for one of the town's Indian inhabitants (who worked as a scout for the British).

Supermarkets

Roche Bros.
150 West Central Street
(508) 655-5540

Stop & Shop
829 Worcester Street (Route 9)
(508) 650-4050

Tilly & Salvy's Bacon Street Farm
100 Bacon Street
(508) 653-4851

Pharmacies

Jones Drug
7 Main Street
(508) 653-1820
www.jonesdrug.com

South Natick Pharmacy
57 Eliot Street
(508) 653-5131

Hardware Stores

Town Paint & Supply
23 South Main Street
(508) 653-6932

Hospitals/ Emergency Rooms

MetroWest Medical Center— Leonard Morse
67 Union Street
(508) 650-7000

www.mwmc.com

NEEDHAM

In the 1800s Needham was a country getaway for Boston's rich; many of their large homes still stand. Today Needham is one of those well-heeled commuter suburbs where not much ever seems to happen. It's popular among professionals who work downtown, such as lawyers and Boston TV types (one Boston TV station, Channel 5, is headquartered in Needham).

Needham Center has some restaurants, along with such essentials as a hardware store. The Charles River loops around the town, providing numerous opportunities for recreation. A variety of high- and low-tech facilities (including a Coca Cola bottling plant) line Route 128, which splits Needham, and which most outsiders think is all there is to the town.

Neighborhood Statistical Profile

Total Population: 28,911

Population by Ethnicity

White:	27,140	*(93.9%)*
Black:	187	*(0.65%)*
Hispanic:	341	*(1.18%)*
Asian/Pacific Islander:	1,023	*(3.54%)*
Native American:	7	*(0.02%)*
Other single race:	34	*(0.12%)*
Multiracial:	179	*(0.61%)*

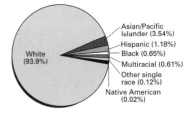

Population by Gender

Female:	52.6%
Male:	47.4%

Population by Age

Median age:	40.8
Under 18:	26.2%
18–24:	5.3%
25–44:	25.8%
45–64:	24.7%
65+:	18%

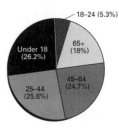

Average Housing Costs

Median home sale: *$443,500*
Median condo sale: *$256,000*
Average rent: *$1,250*

Other Statistics

Crime: *Safe.*
Income: *Middle to upper middle class.*

Type of Government

Representative town meeting.

The Commute

Four commuter-rail stations mean South Station isn't more than forty minutes away. Take Route 128 to the nearby Massachusetts Turnpike for a twenty- to twenty-five-minute ride to downtown Boston.

Noteworthy in the Neighborhood

- The town "dump" (the real dump was closed years ago) is a great place to catch up with neighbors and to swap your unused items and books for other people's stuff.
- The Needham Children's Museum lets children learn about their surroundings and the world through hands-on exhibits: (781) 455-8114.

Supermarkets

Bread & Circus
63 Kendrick Street
(781) 444-0700

Natural foods.

Roche Bros.
377 Chestnut Street
(781) 444-0411

Sudbury Farms
1177 Highland Avenue
(781) 449-9180

Pharmacies

Birds Hill Pharmacy
401 Great Plain Avenue
(781) 449-0550

Walgreens
1478 Highland Avenue
(781) 444-5814

Hardware Stores

Aubuchon Hardware
1068 Great Plain Avenue
(781) 453-0051

Harvey's Ace Hardware
1004 Great Plain Avenue
(781) 444-4515

Hospitals/Emergency Rooms

Deaconess-Glover Hospital
148 Chestnut Street
(781) 453-3000

www.glover.caregroup.org

NORWOOD

When people in Boston neighborhoods such as Roslindale and West Roxbury want to move to the suburbs, Norwood is one of the first places they often look. A quiet suburb with a quaint downtown (a common with summertime concerts at the bandstand, plus a good second-run movie theater), Norwood is just down the road from the old neighborhood. It features a plentiful supply of apartments and condos in addition to single-family homes. Route 1 features an endless supply of car dealerships as it branches off from and runs parallel to Route 128 a mile or so from the center of town.

Neighborhood Statistical Profile

Total Population: 28,587

Population by Ethnicity

White:	25,606	(89.6%)
Black:	643	(2.25%)
Hispanic:	473	(1.65%)
Asian/Pacific Islander:	1,445	(5.05%)
Native American:	23	(0.08%)
Other single race:	90	(0.31%)
Multiracial:	307	(1.06%)

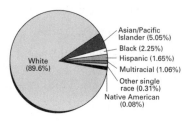

Population by Gender

Female:	52.7%
Male:	47.3%

Population by Age

Median age:	38.6
Under 18:	20.8%
18–24:	6.4%
25–44:	33.2%
45–64:	22.1%
65+:	17.5%

Median home sale $255,000

Median condo sale $147,500

Average rent $1,300

Average Housing Costs

Median home sale:	$255,000
Median condo sale:	$147,500
Average rent:	$1,300

Other Statistics

Crime:	Safe.
Income:	Middle class.

Type of Government

Representative town meeting.

The Commute

Commuter rail gets you to South Station in thirty-five minutes via one of three Norwood stops. Route 128 skirts the town; you can be downtown in thirty to forty minutes. There's also bus service to the Forest Hill subway stop.

Noteworthy in the Neighborhood

- Nobody knows how the town founders chose Norwood as the town name in 1882. Among the rejected names: Balch, Cedarville, and Queertown.
- Norwood is one of several Massachusetts communities served by a town power department instead of by a private utility.

Supermarkets

Victory Super Market
434 Walpole Street
(781) 769-0905

Pharmacies

Brooks Pharmacy
991 Providence Highway (Route 1)
(781) 762-4979

CVS

136 Nahatan Street
(781) 769-8336

Hospitals/Emergency Rooms

Caritas/Norwood Hospital
800 Washington Street
(781) 769-2950

www.caritasnorwood.org

SALEM

It's hard to avoid the witches in Salem. What other city has an official witch? A witch flies from the masthead of the local paper, the *Salem Evening News*. A witch on a broomstick emblazons police cruisers. Yes, Salem is overflowing with overhyped, often hokey witch attractions.

But if you can get beyond that, you'll find a charming New England seaport that retains many of its original houses and buildings from the colonial era and the nineteenth century. Chestnut Street, for example, is part of a federal historic district and is home to numerous beautiful examples of nineteenth-century architecture on brick-lined sidewalks.

Salem is also a multicultural community: More than twenty languages are spoken by students in the local school system.

Neighborhood Statistical Profile

Total Population: 40,407

Population by Ethnicity

White:	33,277	(82.4%)
Black:	966	(2.4%)
Hispanic:	4,541	(11.2%)
Asian/Pacific Islander:	814	(2%)
Native American:	59	(0.15%)
Other single race:	132	(0.33%)
Multiracial:	618	(1.52%)

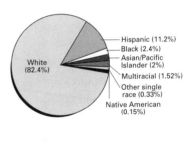

Population by Gender

Female:	53.6%
Male:	46.4%

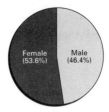

Population by Age

Median age:	36.4
Under 18:	20.2%
18–24:	10.4%
25–44:	33.4%
45–64:	21.9%
65+:	14.1%

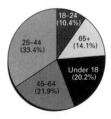

Average Housing Costs

Median home sale:	$225,000
Median condo sale:	$169,900
Average rent:	$1,100

Other Statistics

Crime:	Safe.
Income:	Middle class.

Type of Government
City.

The Commute.
Salem is thirty minutes from North Station on commuter rail and about a similar distance by car.

Noteworthy in the Neighborhood
- Nathaniel Hawthorne was a Salem resident. The House of the Seven Gables is open to tourists today: (978) 744-0991.
- The city motto is, translated from Latin, "To the farthest port of the rich east," which commemorates Salem's long-standing trade with the Far East, in particular its trade in pepper with what is now Indonesia (to this day, whole peppercorns are called "Salem peppers" in Australia).
- More examples of Salem's maritime past can be found at the Peabody Essex Museum, which commemorates the city's colonial and trading history: (800) 745-4054. Also noteworthy is the Salem Maritime National Historic Site on Derby Street: (978) 740-1680.
- The Pickering Wharf area has a number of restaurants and bars.

Supermarkets

Los Amigos Supermarket
122 Lafayette Street
(978) 740-9114

Shaws
Highlander Plaza
(978) 741-8660

Pharmacies

Eaton Apothecary
111 Canal Street
(978) 744-0161

Walgreens
29 Derby Street
(978) 744-5592

Hardware Stores

Sears Hardware
10 Traders Way
(978) 825-1714

Hospitals/Emergency Rooms

Salem Hospital
81 Highland Avenue
(978) 741-1215

WAKEFIELD

Convenience is a good reason to move to Wakefield. Route 128 (a.k.a. I-95) passes through town and connects nearby with I-93, providing easy access to both Boston and points north (like New Hampshire). The town also has two commuter-rail stops.

In addition to good auto access, Wakefield has an excellent local park system, along with a 640-acre state forest on the Saugus line. Wakefield has an annual town tennis tournament. Lake Quannapowitt is a focus of local recreation; it has a "yacht" club and is popular for walks along its three-mile-long shoreline.

Neighborhood Statistical Profile

Total Population: 24,804

Population by Ethnicity

White:	23,902	*(96.4%)*
Black:	106	*(0.43%)*
Hispanic:	204	*(0.8%)*
Asian/Pacific Islander:	355	*(1.4%)*
Native American:	15	*(0.07%)*
Other single race:	22	*(0.09%)*
Multiracial:	200	*(0.81%)*

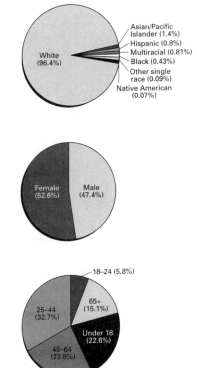

Population by Gender

Female:	52.6%
Male:	47.4%

Population by Age

Median age:	38.9
Under 18:	22.6%
18–24:	5.8%
25–44:	32.7%
45–64:	23.8%
65+:	15.1%

Median home sale $289,900

Median condo sale $167,000

Average rent $1,300

Average Housing Costs

Median home sale: *$289,900*
Median condo sale: *$167,000*
Average rent: *$1,300*

Other Statistics

Crime: *A safe town.*
Income: *Middle and upper middle class.*

Type of Government

Open town meeting.

The Commute

Wakefield is twenty-three minutes from North Station by commuter rail. It's about twenty-five miles to Boston by car.

Noteworthy in the Neighborhood

- The Wakefield Arts and Crafts Society has been promoting the arts and artists since 1915. Prospective members must have at least two of their works approved by a jury of members: www.wakefield.org/artsandcraftssociety.
- The Friends of Lake Quannapowitt seeks to protect and improve the lake and surrounding land: (781) 979-2400 or www.wakefield.org/folq.

Supermarkets

Shaw's
99 Main Street
Stoneham
(781) 438-7533

Pharmacies

Medicine Shoppe
409 Lowell Street
(781) 246-3527

Smith Drug Store
390 Main Street
(781) 245-0380

Walgreens
572 Main Street
(781) 246-2498

Hardware Stores

L. R. Hart Hardware
442 Main Street
(781) 245-0989

Hospitals/Emergency Rooms

Hallmark Health/Melrose-Wakefield Campus
585 Lebanon Street
Melrose
(781) 979-3000

www.lmh.edu/memhospitals/melrose.html

WELLESLEY

Wellesley is a rarity in Greater Boston: It's solidly Republican (with the exception of a small area just outside the center of town that's home to Democratic professor types).

Populated by the well heeled, Wellesley is what the *Boston Globe* often refers to as a "leafy suburb." Although there are some apartments along Washington Street, most of the town consists of large, single-family homes on tree-lined streets. Still, Wellesley doesn't have a lot of really large lots; in recent years, a number of houses have been torn down to make way for large "McMansions" on these small lots.

Wellesley's main shopping area is quaint; stores are allowed to use only hand-carved wooden signs—even the chain stores. Wellesley is home to three colleges: the all-women's Wellesley College, the business-oriented Babson College, and Massachusetts Bay Community College.

Neighborhood Statistical Profile

Total Population: 26,613

Population by Ethnicity

White:	23,509	(88%)
Black:	409	(1.5%)
Hispanic:	617	(2%)
Asian/Pacific Islander:	1,690	(6%)
Native American:	16	(<1%)
Other single race:	37	(<1%)
Multiracial:	335	(1%)

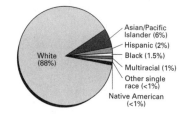

Population by Gender

Female:	56.2%
Male:	43.8%

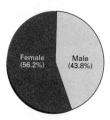

Population by Age

Median age:	37.6
Under 18:	25.1%
18–24:	13.9%
25–44:	22.9%
45–64:	24.2%
65+:	13.9%

Average Housing Costs

Median home sale:	$852,500
Median condo sale:	$540,000
Average rent:	$1,650

Other Statistics

Crime:	Safe.
Income:	Rich.

Type of Government

Representative town meeting.

The Commute

Wellesley's about thirty minutes from South Station by commuter rail (the town has three stops). By car, Boston is thirty to forty-five minutes from downtown. The malls of Natick and Framingham are ten minutes away.

Noteworthy in the Neighborhood

- Wellesley gets its name from the mansion of H. Hollis Hunnewell, a local businessman who named his estate after his wife's maiden name, Welles. The Hunnewell family remains prominent in town affairs; you can see the Hunnewell estate (and the family cows) on Route 16 near the Natick line.
- Katherine Lee Bates, a Wellesley College professor, wrote "America the Beautiful" in 1893.
- Wellesley's town hall is an architectural gem, modeled after a French chateau. A park at Town Hall features a small, fenced-in creek for feeding ducks and geese.
- A marker on Route 135 marks the nation's oldest football rivalry: Wellesley and Needham have faced each other on Thanksgiving every year since 1882.

Supermarkets

Bread & Circus
278 Washington Street
(781) 235-7262

Natural foods.

Star Market
448 Washington Street
(781) 237-9680

Pharmacies

Andrews Pharmacy
324 Weston Road
(781) 235-1001

Belvedere Pharmacy
266 Washington Street
(781) 235-1464

CVS
65 Central Street
(781) 237-7034

Hardware Stores

F. Diehl
180 Linden Street
(781) 235-1530

**Richmond Hardware &
Plumbing Supply**
899 Washington Street
(781) 843-0066

Hospitals/Emergency Rooms

**MetroWest Medical Center—
Leonard Morse**
67 Union Street
Natick
(508) 650-7000

www.mwmc.com

WESTON

Unless you're a corporate executive or successful surgeon, don't spend much time looking for a home in this western suburb; you won't be able to afford it. Weston vies with Dover for the title of the most expensive community in Massachusetts.

But if you do have the money and you're looking for an exclusive address, lots of peace, and plenty of room to have somebody landscape, then Weston's for you. Large houses nestle on large wooded lots in this quiet rural suburb that tries to fend off incursions from the outside world (in 2001, the town voted against a state plan to turn an abandoned rail line that runs through the town into a bicycle path). Minimum zoning is one acre per lot, so you won't feel hemmed in by neighbors. Weston Center has the basic neighborhood stores, and you're not far from the malls of Chestnut Hill, Natick, and Framingham.

Neighborhood Statistical Profile

Total Population: 11,469

Population by Ethnicity

White:	10,167	(89%)
Black:	132	(1%)
Hispanic:	218	(2%)
Asian/Pacific Islander:	788	(7%)
Native American:	6	(<1%)
Other single race:	22	(<1%)
Multiracial:	136	(1%)

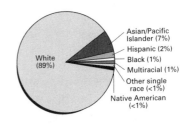

Population by Gender

Female:	53.6%
Male:	46.4%

Population by Age

Median age:	41.9
Under 18:	28%
18–24:	7.3%
25–44:	20.4%
45–64:	27.8%
65+:	16.5%

Average Housing Costs

Median home sale:	$887,000
Median condo sale:	$767,500
Average rent:	$1,700

Other Statistics

Crime:	Safe.
Income:	Rich.

Type of Government
Open town meeting.

The Commute
The Massachusetts Turnpike and Route 128 come together in one corner of the town, so you can be downtown in twenty minutes or less. The train will get you to North Station in thirty minutes.

Noteworthy in the Neighborhood
- The town has an extensive system of forest trails. Get more information at www.weston-forest-trail.org.
- The Weston Friendly Society of the Performing Arts is the second-oldest theater group in Massachusetts: (781) 893-9883.

Supermarkets

Omni Foods
21 Center Street
(781) 894-0675

Pharmacies

Eaton Apothecary
397 Boston Post Road
(781) 894-3785

Richardson Drug
37 Center Street
(781) 891-1440

Hardware Stores

Puopolo Hardware
450 Boston Post Road
(781) 899-4000

Hospitals/Emergency Rooms

Deaconess-Waltham Hospital
Hope Avenue
Waltham
(781) 647-6000

www.waltham.caregroup.org

WEYMOUTH

Founded in 1622, this South Shore town is the second oldest in Massachusetts, although it got off to a rocky start. Within a year of its founding, all the settlers (including Myles Standish) had either fled or been killed by Indians, from whom they kept stealing food. Today, Weymouth is a largely residential suburb about twelve miles south of Boston, nestled on Hingham Bay. There are town beaches on both the bay and at Whitman's Pond.

A major issue in town is what to do with the 1,400-acre former South Weymouth Naval Air Station. Should it become a giant mall, an industrial park, or some combination of retail, housing, and recreational projects? Although major development would bring new tax revenue, some residents express concern about such issues as traffic.

Neighborhood Statistical Profile

Total Population: 53,988

Population by Ethnicity

White:	50,758	(94%)
Black:	759	(1.3%)
Hispanic:	721	(1.3%)
Asian/Pacific Islander:	860	(2%)
Native American:	96	(<1%)
Other single race:	206	(0.4%)
Multiracial:	588	(1%)

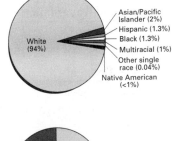

Population by Gender

Female:	52.5%
Male:	47.5%

Population by Age

Median age:	38.4
Under 18:	22%
18–24:	6.6%
25–44:	32.7%
45–64:	23.3%
65+:	15.4%

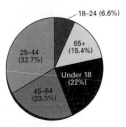

Median home sale $223,000

Median condo sale $123,500

Average rent $1,020

Average Housing Costs

Median home sale: *$236,000*
Median condo sale: *$123,500*
Average rent: *$1,020*

Other Statistics

Crime: Safe.
Income: Middle class.

Type of Government

Town council.

The Commute

Boston is about twenty-five minutes away by commuter rail (there's a stop in South Weymouth) or car (Route 3, which runs right through the town, to I-93).

Noteworthy in the Neighborhood

- A noted local event is the springtime herring run up the Weymouth Back River. The silvery fish return from the sea to spawn in Whitman's Pond. The town has been taking measures to protect the fish since the 1700s.
- Great Esker Park runs along the river. The annual Great Esker Day in mid- to late summer celebrates the park with tours, music, and canoe rides.
- Abigail Adams, wife of president John Adams, was born in Weymouth.

Supermarkets

Shaw's
610 Middle Street
(781) 331-5108

Pharmacies

Brooks Pharmacy
316 Washington
(781) 331-7997

CVS
108 Main Street
(781) 843-7770

Hardware Stores

J. T. Cazeault and Sons
286 Bridge Street
North Weymouth
(781) 335-4000

Park Avenue Market & Hardware
46 Park Avenue
South Weymouth
(781) 335-3338

Hospitals/ Emergency Rooms

South Shore Hospital
55 Fogg Road
South Weymouth
(781) 340-8000

www.southshorehospital.org

Farther Out

A general Boston axiom is that the farther out you go, the more house you get for the money. Although you have to go really far away to get housing prices comparable to most of the rest of the country, some relatively distant areas offer somewhat lower prices and are not an insurmountable distance from Boston.

SOUTHERN NEW HAMPSHIRE

These days, southern New Hampshire is more like an annex to Massachusetts than a part of the flinty Granite State (similar to the relationship between Fairfield County, Connecticut, and New York City). Attracted by lower housing prices and the absence of a state income tax, fairly large numbers of Boston-area residents have migrated to an area extending roughly twenty miles north of the Massachusetts line, from the suburbs of Nashua in the west to Portsmouth on the coast.

You can see many of these people heading south in their cars every morning, clogging Route 3 and I-93 as they head to their jobs in the Boston area or along I-495 (Massachusetts is currently widening Route 3 to handle all the extra traffic). Plan on ninety minutes to two hours to get into Boston.

The fairly short New Hampshire seacoast has numerous beaches and beach-related attractions. If you do look at a New Hampshire seacoast town, be aware you'll face maddening traffic jams in the summer as you battle for a spot on the road with beachgoers. There's nothing like coming to a complete standstill on Route 1 as you gaze at the Seabrook nuclear plant and wonder how in the world they would ever evacuate the area on a hot July day.

In addition to somewhat lower housing prices, advantages include more space, no state income tax, cheap booze at the well-stocked state liquor stores, and being that much closer to skiing. For basic city amenities, you have Nashua and Portsmouth. The latter has a revitalized waterfront area filled with restaurants and shops.

The disadvantages of life in New Hampshire: the increasingly long commute to jobs in Massachusetts and high property taxes (which is largely how the state funds local schools).

A fact that's either a disadvantage or advantage depending on your point of view: Whereas Massachusetts is generally considered a liberal, Democratic state (even though it currently has a Republican governor), New Hampshire is generally considered a conservative, Republican state (even though it currently has a Democratic governor). After all, this is the state that puts "Live free or die" on its license plates.

WORCESTER AND ITS SUBURBS

Like southern New Hampshire, towns such as Auburn, Westborough, Millbury, Shrewsbury, and Grafton to the west of I-495 have become popular among people who work along that highway but who want a bit more house or land for their money. Some of these towns have become so popular that they are as expensive as areas closer to Boston. Median sales prices for homes in Westborough, for example, topped $300,000 in early 2001. Increasingly, Worcester itself is becoming a desirable place to live. Although it has its rough spots, it also has a number of museums, including the Worcester Art

Museum, which has some world-class exhibits, and the Higgins Armory Museum, which is devoted entirely to arms and suits of armor.

Commuting into Boston from these towns can take forty-five to sixty minutes by car, depending on how close you are to the Massachusetts Turnpike. There are commuter-rail stops in Worcester and Grafton (with one planned for Westborough); the trip takes about an hour. If you're getting a job along I-495, at least along its westernmost stretch, though, these could be places to seriously consider because that highway is right at your doorstep.

THE MERRIMACK VALLEY

Towns such as Tewksbury, Chelmsford, and Andover to Boston's north offer quick car access to employment along I-495's northern stretch. They're all generally quiet suburbs not notable for anything particularly interesting (unless you count the fact that Jay Leno is from North Andover), but there's something to be said for peace and quiet, too. The Lowell and Haverhill commuter-rail lines provide access to North Station; it's thirty-seven minutes there from North Billerica and forty-six minutes from Andover.

GLOUCESTER AND ROCKPORT

Both of these sea towns to Boston's north have their own charm and history. Gloucester is famous for the Gloucester mariner statue (think Gorton's of Gloucester); Rockport for Motif No. 1, a red lobster shanty that is possibly the country's most popular subject for painters.

More recently, Gloucester has become famous as the home port of the *Andrea Gail*, the fishing boat that went down in the movie *The Perfect Storm*. The city very much remains a working port; despite the decline of the fisheries off the Massachusetts coast, fishing and fish processing remain important local industries.

The best word to describe Rockport is "quaint." Bearskin Neck, a small peninsula in charming Rockport harbor, consists mainly of small boutiques, restaurants, and cottages.

Both towns have a strong local identity. Residents sometimes talk about something being "over the bridge," a reference to the Piatt Andrew Bridge, which connects Cape Ann to the mainland.

Commuter rail gets you from Rockport to North Station in about an hour and ten minutes; from Gloucester, in a little over an hour.

FALL RIVER, NEW BEDFORD, AND PROVIDENCE

Fall River and New Bedford, in southeastern Massachusetts near the Rhode Island line, share a history of whaling and fishing. Both are rebounding from economic difficulties in recent decades and offer good housing values. The problem is that they are not particularly convenient to Boston; count on a commute of more than an hour by car. They're much closer to Providence, Rhode Island, which actually offers many large-city attractions, in particular, excellent Italian dining, and is located just a short trip away from the area on I-195.

In fact, Providence and some of its suburbs might be worth looking into if your job is along the southern stretch of I-495. Federal Hill in Providence is a particularly charming neighborhood. Rhode Island is the smallest state in the country, but it has its own unique character and even language (it's also one of the most densely populated states in the country). Only in Rhode Island do people drink "coffee milk" (look for Autocrat coffee syrup in supermarkets) and Del's lemonade (lemony syrup poured over crushed ice). And what non–New Englanders call milk shakes and Bostonians call frappes, Rhode Islanders call cabinets. Both Rhode Island and the Fall River/New Bedford area (now sometimes called the Southcoast) offer plenty of opportunities for water activities (think Newport, Rhode Island, and its mansions, not to mention its summertime jazz festival). It's still possible to get a house on a large lot.

From Providence, you can take either Amtrak or an MBTA commuter train into Boston. Amtrak's faster (fifty-five minutes versus seventy-three minutes on commuter rail), but it costs more. The state plans to extend a commuter-rail line to the New Bedford/Fall River area by 2004.

CHAPTER 2

Advice on Finding
an Apartment

The good news is that Boston has apartments to suit every taste, from modern units in high-rises to cozy floors in two-family houses on tree-lined streets.

The bad news is that finding an apartment in Boston can be both time-consuming and expensive. Demand far outpaces supply; in recent years, Boston has had an average vacancy rate of 2 percent or lower. One of the few advantages of the recent slowdown in the local economy has been that vacancy rates are creeping up. This means apartment prices are unlikely to increase at the double-digit rate increases common in the 1990s and that finding a place to live might become a bit easier. Between 1995 and 2000, the cost of an average two-bedroom apartment increased 59 percent—from $909 a month to $1,448—according to a report by the Mayor's Housing Advisory Committee.

In a seller's market, don't be surprised if you're asked to pony up three or even four months' worth of rent when you sign a lease (first and last months' rent, a security deposit equal to one month's rent, and a broker's fee also equal to one month's rent). In 2001, these demands were sometimes reduced, though, as the housing market cooled. Add to this the fact that Boston-area leases often run

MOVING TIP

When you first move into your new apartment, take a few minutes to walk around with a pad of paper and a pen, noting anything that needs work. It'll help when you call the super—and protect you when you move out from having any of your security deposit withheld.

September 1 through August 31, thanks to the 130,000 or so students who flood the area (about half of whom will be competing with you for apartments in many neighborhoods). So unless you get really lucky, count on spending a couple of weeks, at a minimum, looking for an apartment. July is a good time to look for apartments opening up on September 1.

Even as the apartment shortage eases somewhat, some brokers might try to rush you through apartments or pressure you into signing a lease when you're not really ready. Don't let them; you're going to be spending an awful lot on rent. Even in a tight market like Boston, you can still afford to look around. Still, take your checkbook just in case you find a place to die for that you want to hold while you get the certified checks the landlord and broker will insist on.

Unlike some cities, such as New York, the Boston area offers apartments in a wide variety of buildings:

- *Apartment buildings.* Range from three-story buildings to skyscrapers. Don't be surprised if you're asked to pay extra for parking.

- *Apartment complexes.* Typically found in the outer suburbs (although West Roxbury and Brookline have some), these consist of a large number of low-rise buildings, each with a few units. Usually surrounded by free parking.

- *Two-family houses.* Found everywhere outside of the North End, the Back Bay, Beacon Hill, and the South End.

- *Triple-deckers.* Unique to eastern Massachusetts, these are three-story buildings in which each floor is a separate apartment (there are also some "double-wides," or triple-deckers wide enough to have two apartments on each floor). These are typically a bit less expensive than other options, in part because they're more commonly found in less desirable areas.

Large complexes or buildings and owner-occupied buildings each have their pros and cons.

Pros and Cons of Living in a Large Complex or Building

PROS

- Typically have a live-in superintendent or a large maintenance staff, which can mean big problems get fixed quickly.
- You have more freedom to come and go and to entertain without worrying about what the landlord living right below you might think.
- More likely to have amenities, such as laundry rooms, workout rooms, or even a pool.

CONS

- You're more likely to deal with a faceless bureaucracy if something goes wrong.
- More expensive.
- You never really get to meet your neighbors.

Pros and Cons of Living in an Owner-Occupied Two-Family Home or Triple-Decker:

PROS

- Typically less expensive.
- If something does go wrong, the landlord is right there.
- You can find one on a quiet, tree-lined street, where you get to know your neighbors.

CONS

- If you like to entertain or stay out late, there could be problems: The floors aren't soundproofed.
- Owner-occupied two-families are exempt from many state tenant-protection laws.
- Parking can be a problem.

Living in a house could also mean things get fixed quickly because major problems will affect not just you but the owner. But living right above or below your landlord might mean problems if you like music louder than he or she does. I once shared the second floor of a three-story house that was often freezing because the landlord had set the thermostat (in a locked case) too low. We fixed that by wrapping the case in ice—at least until he noticed his heating bills had gone way up. That's not a problem that would happen in an apartment building. In Massachusetts, there are two kinds of leases: a standard one-year contract lease and "tenancy-at-will." A contract lease gives you stability, notably a guarantee that your rent won't go up for at least one year. However, if you move out early, you could be held liable for the remaining rent on your lease if the landlord can't find somebody to replace you (given the state of the Boston apartment market, though, this often is not a problem).

When you sign the contract, check to see if it's "fixed" (that is, it really does run out after a year) or "self-extending" (that is, it will stay in force as long as neither you nor the landlord says anything about terminating the lease). If it's self-extending, you'll need to give thirty days' notice at the end of the lease before moving out. Also check the lease's sublet provisions. Many leases allow subletting (handy if you need to move out quickly) but only with landlord approval. If your lease doesn't allow subletting but you do it anyway, the landlord could come after you for the remaining rent on the lease.

In a tenancy-at-will arrangement, your lease basically runs month to month (you may or may not have a formal contract specifying this condition). You only have to give the landlord thirty days' notice before you move out; the flip side is that the landlord only has to give you thirty days' notice before kicking you out too.

Also note that even though Massachusetts and Boston have fairly strong tenant-protection laws, many of these laws do not apply to owner-occupied two-family homes. You can get more tips on leases from the state Office of Consumer Affairs and Business Regulation at www.state.ma.us/consumer/Pubs/tenant.htm. Real-estate attorney A. Joseph Ross has an online guide, "How to Be a Tenant in Massachusetts and Avoid Getting Ripped Off," at world.std.com/~lawyer/tenant.html.

Although Boston apartment prices overall are high (don't count on getting even an unfurnished studio for less than $900 a month), they are considerably varied. A luxury apartment in the Back Bay is going to cost you far more than a similar unit in West Roxbury or Dorchester. Count on $1,000 to $2,000 for a one-bedroom apartment, depending on location. Among the considerations you'll have to take into account:

- The size of the apartment
- The type of building you wish to live in
- Cost
- Neighborhood
- Safety
- Proximity to your job and/or public transit
- Location of shopping, houses of worship, and other services

Outside Boston, most communities have at least a small number of apartments in two-family homes and the like. Some suburban towns are noted for their large apartment complexes, which can be a good value if you're looking for a place to stay while you figure out your long-term housing goals. Waltham, Natick, and Framingham to the west, Acton and Boxborough to the northwest, and Quincy to the south are all places to consider if you're set on an apartment but don't want to pay Back Bay prices. Natick has four large complexes right across the street from a commuter-rail stop. Acton and Boxborough's complexes are an easy drive from commuter rail, and Quincy has Red Line subway service.

Brookline, Cambridge, and Somerville also have large numbers of apartments, but their rents tend to be much closer to Boston's (and in Brookline you have to worry about where to park your car, because the town bans overnight street parking).

Renting vs. Buying

RENTING PROS

- Renting lets you get to know the area before you really commit to buying a house or condo.
- Even with all the deposits and fees, renting is still less expensive up front than buying.
- You have more freedom to move, especially with a tenancy-at-will lease.
- It's a good option for young people, especially if you go in with a roommate to share costs.
- You don't have to worry about things like repairs or shoveling sidewalks in the winter.
- You can deduct half your rent (up to $2,500 a year) from your Massachusetts income tax.

RENTING CONS

- All that money goes right to the landlord; you don't build up any equity.
- Even with the renter's deduction, you still won't make out as well on taxes as those who deduct their mortgage interest from their federal income tax.
- If you have (or are planning to have) two or more kids, it's a lot easier to find a house with a lot of bedrooms than an apartment.
- You're limited in how you can decorate or renovate your living quarters.
- With the current tight market, it can be hard to find a landlord that allows pets (you're more likely to get permission for a cat than a dog).
- In crowded downtown neighborhoods, you may face an additional charge for a parking space.

• Lugging your laundry to the laundry room or a nearby coin laundry gets tiring after a while, as does feeding quarters into dryers that never seem to work quite right.

RENT CONTROL

Until 1994, Boston, Brookline, and Cambridge had various rent-control and rent-stabilization programs in place to protect lower- and middle-income families from excessive rent increases. That year, however, voters statewide approved a referendum question to eliminate rent control and rent stabilization. Landlords argued that repealing rent control would lead to rent reductions by spurring the development of more housing units, but that wasn't the case.

APARTMENT JARGON

"One-bedroom" and "two-bedroom" are self-explanatory phrases when it comes to apartments. Here are some other terms you might see or hear while apartment hunting:

• *Studio.* This is a single-room apartment with both living and sleeping space in the same area. The kitchen is often in a small nook.

• *Alcove studio.* A studio with a small area off to one side that has enough room for a small bed and dresser, but no actual doorway (otherwise, it would be a one-bedroom apartment).

• *Hkup.* The apartment has facilities for putting in a washer and dryer.

• *Reasonable wear and tear.* It's a common phrase in rental agreements and relates to security deposits. If you

CITY FACT

Bostonians call their public-transit system the T. What does that stand for? Nothing specific; it was intended to symbolize such terms as "transportation," "tunnel," and "train."

punch a hole in the wall, the landlord can deduct the cost of repair from your deposit. But he can't deduct the cost of reasonable wear and tear (for example, if he routinely paints apartments between tenants, he can't charge you for that).

- *On T.* Within an easy walk of the subway (which Bostonians call "the T").
- *Sunny.* The apartment has windows.

Things to Ask and Consider While Looking

The first thing, obviously, is to figure out how much you can afford for rent. However, that's not a simple question of subtracting your other expenses from your income. Renting an apartment in the Boston area could involve quite a few other costs, from parking to furniture.

If you have a car and have your heart set on downtown neighborhoods, such as the Back Bay, Beacon Hill, or the North End, on Brookline, or even on some apartment-heavy neighborhoods such as Allston/Brighton, consider whether you can set aside another $100 to $200 a month for parking.

Most Boston apartments come unfurnished—some don't even come with a refrigerator—so you'll need to figure out how to furnish your new place.

If you're looking at a unit in a two-family or triple-decker, add another $80 to $120 a month for heat. These units are exempt from the state law that requires landlords to provide heat (at least 68 degrees between September and June from 7 A.M. to 11 P.M.) and hot water. If you wilt in the summer, add another $30 to $50 a month for air conditioning (plus the cost of an air conditioner; once you leave luxury territory, most units don't come with one).

And on top of all that, make sure you have at least four times the amount you can spend on rent for all those up-front payments and fees. This is just in case you find your dream apartment in a building where the landlord and broker insist on the maximum fees (don't be afraid to try to bargain down the fees, though; as the economy softens, it becomes more likely you can get a reduction). If the amount starts to feel completely overwhelming, there is another option: a roommate (or roommates). More on that in a bit.

Once you've settled the money question, there are still more considerations and questions to ask the rental broker or superintendent:

- What sort of neighborhood would you prefer: something right in the middle of everything or something quieter?

- Do you want to live in a large building or a house? If you choose a small apartment building, does it have an elevator, and if not, how important is that to you? Picture yourself lugging your groceries or laundry up three or four flights of stairs.

- If you're looking at an apartment building, does it have a live-in super, or do you have to worry about getting an answering service when your pipes burst on a Sunday?

- How important is proximity to public transportation, and does it matter if that means the subway, commuter rail, or a bus line?

- How close is the apartment to your office? If you rely on public transportation, will you have to transfer between different types of transit? If so, that could add to your commute considerably.

- Does the building allow pets? If you find the dream apartment, but the landlord won't let you bring your yellow Lab, you've got a problem.

- If you have children, how happy would they be in the building you're looking at? What school district is the building in?

- What's nearby in the neighborhood? Is there a corner convenience store? How far away is the nearest supermarket? If eating out is important, what are the local restaurants like? Which banks have nearby branches or ATMs?

- How safe is the neighborhood?

- What about parking? Many buildings don't have parking, which means you'll have to figure out what to do with your car in a city where on-street parking is at a premium. Buildings that do have parking often charge extra for the privilege. Neighborhoods that are composed largely of single- and two-family homes often have enough on-street parking (for example, Jamaica Plain, Roslindale, and West Roxbury).

Before You Rent: Be Prepared

Try to open a local bank account as soon as possible. Chances are, you'll need a certified check to make that initial payment on your apartment. It would also be helpful to have:

- A picture ID
- A letter of employment, along with a contact who can verify your employment
- A listing of your bank accounts and credit-card numbers
- A listing of previous landlords, including contact information
- A tax return
- A pay stub

Once you do find an apartment you like, look it over for any problems (peeling paint, leaky faucets, and the like). Get the landlord or broker to put the problems in writing, along with a commitment to fix them. Otherwise, you might be unlucky and find yourself with a problem that doesn't get fixed for months, if at all.

To Look Alone or with a Broker

If you have the time, it's possible to find an apartment on your own in the Boston area. Get the early edition of the Sunday *Globe* on Saturday and start circling those ads. You might spend some more time looking, but you'll also save some money (no broker's fee in many cases). Plus, you'll get a much better feel for the neighborhoods you're interested in by driving around (just remember that parking is next to impossible for visitors in many Boston neighborhoods; most of the on-street spaces will be reserved for residents with local parking permits). If you're interested in a short-term sublet or roommate, be sure to check the bulletin boards at any supermarkets you happen to pass.

However, if your time is limited (say, for example, you're still living on the other side of the country and you can get to Boston for only a weekend before you're due to move here), a broker might make a lot more sense. A broker can arrange apartment viewings at your convenience and might have access to more apartments than are listed in the Sunday *Globe.* Plus, a broker will be very familiar with the neighborhoods he or she specializes in, so you'll be able to get detailed information you might not otherwise get if you're several thousand miles away.

When you do find a broker, make sure you have a basic idea of what you're looking for and how much you can afford. Brokers can be hard to get a hold of, especially in the late summer, when all those students start descending. Be careful: This will be your home for the next twelve months or so. Don't take everything the broker says as gospel, and don't let him or her pressure you into taking an apartment you're not completely sure about. Yes, the Boston market is tight, but not so tight that another apartment won't come on the market that's just what you're looking for.

Pros of Using a Broker

A good broker will:

- Save you time, especially if you're not already in the Boston area
- Have exclusives on apartments
- Have already done some of the research you would have done about specific buildings or neighborhoods
- Know a specific building's history and characteristics

Cons of Using a Broker

- A broker will charge between a half and a full month's rent.
- If you're looking for low-cost housing, don't expect a miracle worker.
- If you're really unlucky, your broker may have a kickback arrangement with some landlords.
- If you haven't decided on a neighborhood, it might be hard to find a broker familiar with more than one area.
- A broker provides information or listings that you might be able to find on your own.

After You Move In

You've made the move, you're settling in, and you notice problems that haven't been fixed, or you see something new that's wrong. Write them all down. Give a copy of your list to your landlord, and make sure you get some sort of acknowledgment. Otherwise, not only might the landlord not fix them, he might try to withhold part or all of your security deposit when you move out, even if the problems were there before you.

What if the problem is serious? Maybe the heat goes off and you can't find the super or landlord. Maybe the ceiling collapses and you can't get anybody to fix it. What to do? In Boston, several agencies can help resolve problems with landlords (see the listings that follow). Most suburban towns have equivalent departments; check with your town or city hall.

BOSTON FAIR HOUSING COMMISSION

(617) 635-4408

Investigates complaints of discrimination based on race, gender, marital status, or because of parental status.

BOSTON RENTAL HOUSING RESOURCE CENTER

(617) 635-3653

A general number to call with housing-related questions or problems.

INSPECTIONAL SERVICES DEPARTMENT

(617) 635-5306

This is the agency that enforces building and elevator codes; call them if you think your unit or building has code violations and you can't get the landlord to do anything about them.

MAYOR'S 24-HOUR HOTLINE

(617) 635-4500

Call this number in emergency situations when you can't reach your landlord; for example, the heat goes off or a pipe bursts at 2 A.M.

Moving Out

Moving out of an apartment can be simple or complex, depending in part on the type of lease you have and whether you're trying to move before your lease is up.

In general, landlords have thirty days after you move out to refund your security deposit, and they're not allowed to deduct money for reasonable wear and tear.

If you have a year lease, you can move once the lease is up. If you have a tenancy-at-will lease, you have to give your landlord at least thirty days' notice before you leave.

It gets more complex if you try to move out before your lease is up. Technically, you could be liable for the entire amount of the remaining lease. Many landlords will let you off the hook provided they can find another tenant to take the apartment; but even then, you might have to pay for the period of time the apartment is empty. Also be careful if you try to sublease your apartment or if you replace a roommate with somebody else whose name is not on the lease. Check your lease to see if you can do this. Even if it doesn't, check with your landlord to see if you can reach an arrangement—or be very, very careful!

When moving day comes, don't leave the apartment a mess—the landlord could deduct money from your security fee for cleaning it up. Remember to return your key if you had to pay a key deposit up front.

CITY FACT

Boston was originally named Tremontaine for the three hills early settlers saw from the harbor. Its name survives in Tremont Street. Only one of the hills remains: Beacon Hill.

Resources for Finding an Apartment

NEWSPAPERS

Boston Globe

The Sunday edition in particular is loaded with apartment ads. Get it on Saturday to get a head start. The ads are also available online at realestate.boston.com/renting.

Boston Phoenix

This free weekly also lists apartment rentals and roommate possibilities. The *Phoenix* comes out on Thursday (classifieds.boston-phoenix.com/ads.asp).

OTHER RESOURCES

Apartment Access
(617) 975-0003

www.apartmentaccess.com

Lists no-fee apartments, although you'll have to pay a $145 sign-up fee.

Apartment Depot
1246 Commonwealth Avenue
Brighton
(617) 232-1911

Allston/Brighton

Beantown Realty
166 Kelton Street
Brighton
(617) 719-4486

www.beantownrealty.com

Allston/Brighton, Cambridge

Benjamin Realty
1042 Beacon Street
Brookline
(617) 734-5050

www.bostonapartments.com/benjamin.htm

Boston and Brookline

Citylife Real Estate
218 Newbury Street
Back Bay
(617) 262-9500

www.ctlf.com

Back Bay and the South End

Comm. Ave. Associates

1101 Commonwealth Avenue
Allston
(617) 254-5712

www.commaveassociates.com

Allston/Brighton

Condos for Rent

www.bostoncondos.com/
rentalslink.htm

Links to agencies that rent condos in the Boston area

Craig's List

boston.craigslist.org/apa

A nonprofit Web site that lists no-fee apartments and sublets.

ERA Northeastern Metro Realty

58 Gainsborough Street
Back Bay
(617) 437-8801

www.realestateboston.com

Back Bay, Fenway, Jamaica Plain, South End

First Choice Realty

1310 Commonwealth Avenue
Allston
(617) 734-8200

www.bostonapartments.com/
firstchoice.htm

Allston/Brighton and Back Bay

Gibson DomainDomain

556 Tremont Street
South End
(617) 426-6900

www.gibsondomaindomain.com

Back Bay, South End, Dorchester, South Boston

Gibson Real Estate Charlestown

142 Main Street
Charlestown
(617) 242-3073

www.gibsonre.com

Charlestown

Greater Boston Properties

696 Tremont Street
South End
(617) 536-4900

www.gbproperties.com/
Rentals.htm

South End, Back Bay, Fenway, and South Boston

Greenline Realty

1956 Beacon Street
Brookline
(617) 731-5434

Allston/Brighton, Brookline

Hammond Residential
29 Commonwealth Avenue
Back Bay
(617) 536-8111

www.hammondresidential.com/
rental.html

Brighton, Brookline, Cambridge, Concord, Jamaica Plain, Newton, Somervillle, and West Roxbury

Jacob Realty
279 Newbury Street
Back Bay
(617) 236-4048

www.jacobrealty.com

Back Bay, Beacon Hill, Brighton, South End, and North End

Jamaica Plain Rentals
480 Centre Street
Jamaica Plain
(617) 524-APTS

www.jprentals.com

Jamaica Plain

Keliher Realty
251 Newbury Street
Back Bay
(617) 267-0100

www.bostonapartments.com/
keliher.htm

Back Bay and Beacon Hill

Maven Realty
402A Highland Avenue
Somerville
(617) 868-0100

www.mavenrealty.com

Cambridge and Somerville

Neighbors Realty
1284 Commonwealth Avenue
Allston
(617) 738-0295

www.neighborsrealty.com

Allston/Brighton

Phoenix Realty
231 Harvard Avenue
Allston
(617) 731-3311

www.phoenixrealty.org/
phoenix-apts.htm

Allston/Brighton

Prizma Associates
484 Commonwealth Avenue
Back Bay
(617) 236-8600

www.prizmaonline.com

Back Bay, Beacon Hill, Jamaica Plain, Cambridge, North End, and South End

Prudential Unlimited Realty
8 Alton Place, Suite 1
Brookline
(617) 264-7900

www.prudentialunlimited.com

Brookline and Brighton

Rooney Real Estate
700 East Broadway
South Boston
(617) 269-1000

www.rooney-re.com

South Boston

Skyline Realty
10 Magazine Street
Cambridge
(617) 547-8700

www.skylinerealty.com

Boston, Brookline, and
Cambridge

Toll and Isenberg Realty
1579 Commonwealth Avenue
Brighton
(617) 254-8117

www.bostonapartments.com/
toll.htm

Allston/Brighton and Brookline

Roommates

In an expensive place like Boston, roommates can be a way to enjoy everything the city has to offer without going bankrupt. So if you've come to the realization that you can't get the kind of apartment you want on the amount of money you have, it's time to look for one or more people to share a place.

Good roommates not only split the rent; especially in a new city, they can offer a sense of familiarity. When you go home, there's already somebody there you know.

Of course, you could get unlucky and wind up with the psycho roommate from hell.

Fortunately, there are steps you can take to make sure you wind up with a compatible roommate or roommates. Of course, there's no absolute guarantee, but taking a few steps could help reduce the odds of problems.

Probably the biggest issues are privacy and noise. So whether you find a prospective roommate on your own or through a referral service, get to know that person as well as possible. Go out for a heart-to-heart talk over coffee and see if you share similar feelings on such issues as:

- *Privacy.* What if you've had a rough day at work and just want to be left alone? What happens when one of you brings home a date? What happens if one of you brings home a date and he or she never leaves? How would you feel with a third person in the apartment? Would you want him or her to pay part of the rent?
- *Noise.* Are you both party animals? What if one of you is but the other isn't?
- *Hours.* If you're an early riser but your roommate is a night owl, you might have problems.
- *Responsibility.* Do you get the sense your potential roomie is responsible? If your name is on the lease, you're going to be responsible for your roommate's share of the rent if he or she suddenly decides to move to, oh, San Francisco.
- *Bills.* How will you split them? Do you share a phone or get separate numbers? Who pays for groceries? Is this person the kind who is going to force you to label your milk carton with your name?

CITY FACT

A giant steaming teakettle built in 1873 atop what is now a Starbucks next to City Hall would hold 227 gallons, 2 quarts, 1 pint, and 3 gills of tea.

The more you can talk out issues like these—and come to either an agreement or the realization you just won't work out together—the better off you'll be.

Often, the more roommates, the more problems can multiply. However, large groups can also bring a sense of stability. You'll often see flyers on Jamaica Plain or Allston/Brighton bulletin boards looking for a new roommate to join an established group of renters (typically of an entire house). These groups often mix both genders and age groups.

As with any situation, it's often best not to let problems fester. If a roommate does something that's starting to really bug you (like always drinking the milk and never replacing it), speak up early. Festering can lead to major problems later on.

Finding a Roommate

Boston has a number of referral services. They charge a fee, but it could be worth it if they help screen out crazed roommates. Even when you use a service, make sure you meet your prospective roommate first.

Easy Roommate

www.easyroommate.com

View listings for free; fee for posting a listing.

Matching Roommates

8 Alton Place
Brookline
(617) 232-2600

www.matchingroommates.com

Boston's oldest roommate matching service, started in 1966.

Roommate Access

(866) 823-2200

www.roommateaccess.com

Roommate Connection

316 Newbury Street, Suite 41
Back Bay
(617) 262-5712

www.roommateconnection.com

OTHER PLACES TO LOOK

Use your ears and eyes. If there's a neighborhood you're interested in, find out where the coffee shops or ice cream parlors are; many have bulletin boards where people post "roommate-wanted" flyers. The *Boston Phoenix* (see previous) also lists "roommate-wanted" ads.

Temporary Housing

You've just gotten a great job in Boston and you don't have time to find an apartment. What to do? There are a variety of options for short-term housing, from bed-and-breakfasts to furnished apartments to hostels. Hostels (and the Y) are cheap, but you can stay only for a few days. Furnished apartments can be quite expensive, as much as $4,000 a month for a two-bedroom apartment. Some require a minimum of one month's rent; others rent by the week. B&Bs are somewhere in between. If you do get a job that requires you to report immediately, try to get your new employer to pay for the costs of temporary housing.

AAA Corporate Rentals

120 Milk Street
(800) 487-5020

www.bostonapartments.com/aaa.htm

Short-term rentals.

Bed and Breakfast Agency of Boston

47 Commercial Wharf #3
(800) 248-9262

go.boston.com/sites/bnbagency11/bedbreakfast.html

Represents B&Bs across Boston.

Bobson Realty

29 Hancock Street
(617) 720-2282

www.bostonapartments.com/bobson

Furnished rooms by the week or month; from $150 a week.

Boston B&Bs

www.boston-online.com/Lodging/Inns

Listings for numerous B&Bs in the Boston area.

Boston Corporate Rentals

306 Newbury Street
(617) 262-3100

www.bostonshorttermrentals.com

Short-term rentals in the Back Bay, Beacon Hill, and the Waterfront.

Irish Embassy Hostel

232 Friend Street
(near North Station)
(617) 973-4841

www.angelfire.com/ma/IrishEmbassy

Rates start at $20 a night.

JVB Management, Ltd.
29 Commonwealth Avenue
Suite 105
(617) 424-8217

Short-term rentals.

Midtown Real Estate
151 Tremont Street
(800) 732-0151

Short-term rentals.

Short-term Solutions
247 Newbury Street
(617) 247-1199

www.short-term.com

YMCA
(617) 927-8040

The central branch, 316 Huntington Avenue, offers accommodations between June 26 and September 4, with rates starting at $42 a night for a single ($62 for a room with a bath).

Subletting

If you want to get a taste of a particular neighborhood for a couple of months, one option is subletting. Sublets are particularly available during the summer in areas such as Allston/Brighton, Brookline, and Cambridge, when students go back home and look for somebody to pay their rent for a couple of months. Look in the *Boston Phoenix* or take a trip over to the student unions at Boston University, Boston College, and MIT for a look at the bulletin boards.

CHAPTER 3

Advice on Finding a House

There's no getting around it: Boston is one of the most expensive places in the country to buy a house. Starter homes? What are those?

Why is Boston so expensive? A couple of reasons, both related to supply and demand. Boston is simply a popular place to live, thanks to its service-economy jobs and attractions from the natural (beaches, nearby skiing, and the like) to the cultural and recreational (major-leagues sports and world-class museums). Normally, the market responds to such a demand through increased production, which leads to more supply and reduced prices. The problem is that after 370 years, there's not much undeveloped land left inside Route 128 to build the sort of huge subdivisions you see in the rest of the country (you still see some large projects along and outside Route 495). Also, Greater Boston has long been at the forefront of zoning and conservation regulations (the first zoning codes in the country, in fact, were passed in the mid-1800s to oversee the development of the Back Bay neighborhood). This helps protect residents and communities from some of the worst effects of untrammeled development, but it also helps limit the number of new housing units that go up.

Types of Houses

Boston has a wide variety of housing types, although you might have to hunt around for that California-style house with the Spanish-tile roof (they're out there, but, sorry, no palm trees—at least not outdoors). Not surprisingly, there are tons of colonials and Capes. Neighborhoods close to downtown Boston, however, don't tend to have your basic single-family homes (there's only one colonial in all of the North End—Paul Revere's house, which isn't for sale). Instead, neighborhoods such as Beacon Hill and the Back Bay feature brownstones: exquisitely detailed three- or four-story houses pressing against the walls of their neighbors. A bit farther out, in areas such as South Boston and Somerville, you'll find row after row of triple-deckers, a type of house unique to eastern Massachusetts (see below for more information on them). Even farther out, you'll find your basic subdivision homes—everything from garrison colonials and Capes to split-levels.

MOVING TIP

Planning tip: Buying an older home? You'll love the charm. But older Massachusetts homes often have narrow, windy stairways to the second floor, so you might need to figure out in advance how to get that king-sized bed or large chest of drawers upstairs.

Old vs. New

Unlike in some parts of the country, "old" doesn't mean "second-rate" in the Boston area. In fact, many older homes are more desirable than newly constructed ones. They've stood the test of time, for one thing. They also often have details you just won't find in newer homes: gumwood moldings, built-in hutches, and large pantries. In the city of Boston, some 57 percent of all housing units were built before 1939, according to the Boston Redevelopment Authority. That figure includes most of the houses in some of the city's most desirable and pricey neighborhoods, such as Beacon Hill, the Back Bay, and the South End. There is an extensive, um, cottage industry in Massachusetts for renovating and restoring older homes (PBS's *This Old House* is shot in the Boston area for a reason). There are even stores where you can buy fixtures and wooden planks and beams stripped from old houses to add that authentic touch to your own old house. The state Home Improvement Contractor Program has tips on selecting a contractor and maintains a list of disciplinary actions against contractors at www.state.ma.us/homeimprovement.

CITY FACT

Most Greater-Boston communities now have recycling programs, but vary on which types of plastic they'll accept. Check with your local department of public works for acceptable types.

Still, there is new construction in the Boston area, and even within the Boston city limits, so if you do like the idea of a house built just for you, you can find one. In some of the older, wealthier suburbs, one recent trend has been to tear down older houses to put up newer, larger ones. The state Office of Consumer Affairs and Business Regulation has some tips on buying a new home at www.state.ma.us/consumer/Pubs/consttips.htm.

House or Condo?

One way to reduce your housing costs is to buy a condominium. Boston has a large number of condos, which typically cost less than a comparable house. However, many Boston condos are still far more expensive than much larger homes in the rest of the country. In some neighborhoods, the difference in price between a condo and a single-family home has shrunk in recent years. For both single-family homes and condos, location counts: A condo in the Back Bay could cost far more than a larger single-family home in Roslindale.

A condo is typically an apartment-like unit in a large building. You can also find large Victorians in Jamaica Plain and Brookline that have been carved into condos. In some suburbs, you'll even find townhouses that are sold as condos.

MOVING TIP

Take a tape measure and notebook with you when you've found *the* house or condo. Measure rooms; sketch your new home and write room measurements on your sketches. Before you move, you'll know whether your current furniture will fit and will have a good idea of how it should be arranged.

Condos are bought and sold just like houses, in the sense that you get a property deed, take on a mortgage, and so on. You own your unit outright and jointly own common land (hallways, parking areas, etc.) with the other owners. Unlike in an apartment, you can do pretty much whatever you want in terms of decorating (well, as long as you don't punch through the wall to the neighbor's unit). Usually, the condo association will hire a management company to run day-to-day affairs and maintenance.

As with buying a house, good legal advice is a must. You want somebody who can go over the condo association's finances and assets; if the association has just voted to buy a new roof, you'll be buying into the debt for it.

Here are some condo pros and cons:

PROS

- Condos typically cost less than a house, letting you get into a neighborhood you might not otherwise afford.
- You can decorate your unit any way you want.
- Somebody else does all the maintenance.

CONS

- Units are typically smaller than houses.
- Many condos are owned by investors, so your neighbors might be rowdy renters. The Boston condo market can be very volatile. In the early 1990s, the market crashed and many people found themselves unable to move, because the value of their units fell far below the balance on their mortgages.

Two-Families and Triple-Deckers

Buying a two-family home or a triple-decker is another way to save money. They typically cost more up front than a single-family home, but the idea is that you'll see dramatic savings on your mortgage payments because you'll have rent-paying tenants. Boston and some of its immediate neighbors, such as Cambridge and Somerville, have a huge supply of these homes. Tens of thousands of triple-deckers were built around the turn of the century (the twentieth century, that is).

In Boston, two-family homes often consist of two units stacked on top of each other; from the outside, they can look like a single-family home. Triple-deckers (also known as three-deckers) are a distinctive part of the Boston landscape. They have three units, one to a floor, each with a balcony. Triple-deckers are sociable buildings: You tend to see them in rows, in neighborhoods such as South Boston, Jamaica Plain, Hyde Park, and Roslindale.

PROS

- You earn income from tenants, which can reduce your monthly costs.
- They can be a good way to house an extended family.
- The city of Boston has a low-cost loan program for rehabbing two-families and triple-deckers.

CONS

- Do you really want to deal with tenants? Strong tenant-protection laws can make it difficult to evict a troublesome tenant. Check out world.std.com/~lawyer/landlord.html for tips on being a landlord in Massachusetts.

- Triple-deckers typically have very small yards.

Getting Ready to Buy

Buying a home can be a gut-wrenching experience, especially if you don't know the area at all. If at all possible, spend some time in the neighborhoods you're considering (see chapter 1). Do you want an urban environment, or do you prefer the rolling lawns of suburbia? What's the commute like? Where's the shopping? If you have kids, what are the schools like? See chapter 10 for information on the Massachusetts Comprehensive Assessment System tests, which many people now use as a rough guide to the quality of specific schools and districts.

CITY FACT

Writer Oliver Wendell Holmes was the first to call Boston "the Hub." Today the only people who use it are headline writers looking for a short synonym for "Boston," as in this *Globe* headline: "Mediocrity Fever Grips Hub."

And, of course, you'll have to keep price in mind. Identical houses in two different communities can have dramatically different price tags. The federal Department of Housing and Urban Development has a good guide to the basics of home buying at www.hud.gov/buying, which features a home-shopping checklist.

Look at world.std.com/~lawyer/buyer.html for tips on buying a house in Massachusetts. The state Office of Consumer Affairs and Business Regulation has more tips at www.state.ma.us/consumer/Info/homebuy.htm.

Things to Consider

THE HOUSE

- Price
- Size
- Room layout
- Yard
- General condition and maintenance
- Number of bathrooms and garage bays
- Amenities such as a fireplace and a finished basement
- Type of heating system: oil, gas, or electric

THE NEIGHBORHOOD

- Commute
- Kids (school, playgrounds, etc.)
- Safety
- Shopping, houses of worship, and other amenities
- Noise levels

Figuring Out the Money

Knowing how much you can afford to spend on a home is obviously a key consideration. First, you need to calculate just how much house you can buy (an alternate approach is determining how much you want to spend per month and then determining what sort of house you can get for that). Interest.com has online calculators that can help here: www.interest.com/calculators.

Once you do that, you need to shop for a mortgage. Bankrate.com has a database that lets you see what various lenders are charging for mortgages at www.bankrate.com/brm/rate/mtghome.asp. The site also has explanations of the different types of mortgages. Note that although you don't have to put down 20 percent anymore, if you don't, you'll likely face an extra monthly fee for mortgage insurance.

When figuring out how much house you can afford, make sure to incorporate such things as property taxes, water and sewer charges, and other utility costs. It would probably be a good idea to factor in some monthly savings for maintenance. Sooner or later, something's going to spring a leak or need replacing.

On Your Own or with a Broker?

If you're already in the Boston area, it's possible to find a house you fall in love with all by yourself. The Saturday *Globe* is filled with listings for open houses. However, if you're searching from afar, a broker is almost a requirement; you need somebody who can narrow down the field for you. Actually, even if you are local, a broker can save you considerable time, because he or she will get to know what you're looking for. Plus, the broker will have access to the Multiple Listing Service and other house listings.

In Massachusetts, buyer's brokers are rare. Most brokers work on commissions paid for by the seller (typically 6 percent). Of course, brokers are as honest as everybody else, but that might be something to keep in mind as you work with one. Ultimately, they are working for the seller, not for you, and they have a responsibility to get the highest possible price for the house.

The Home Inspector

Along with the broker and your lawyer, another person you'll get to know quite well is the home inspector. Home inspections are a must before you sign that final purchase and sales agreement. You want a trained professional looking over your prospective house from top to bottom to catch the things you might miss or that the seller might not point out. A good house inspector will look over visible parts of the house, such as the roof and the walls, as well as check out the plumbing and heating, air-conditioning, and electrical systems.

Finding a good inspector can be as simple as asking friends or your attorney for a recommendation. In general, experts advise against hiring inspectors recommended by brokers because they work for the seller, not you. State law requires professional home inspectors to carry $250,000 in insurance just in case they miss something.

You can get more home inspection tips at www.state.ma.us/reg/ Consumer/fspagehi.htm. You can find state-licensed home inspectors at license.reg.state.ma.us/loca/locaProf.asp.

Other Issues

State law requires homes to have functioning smoke detectors; the local fire department will provide a certificate of compliance. If you're buying a house built before 1978, you can take up to ten days to get a lead paint inspection.

Taxes

Once you buy a house or a condo, you (or your mortgage company) will get a property tax bill from your community every three months.

In general, Proposition 2½ , the Massachusetts equivalent of California's Proposition 13, limits how much your property tax bill will increase each year. The difference is that Proposition 2½ refers to a community's total tax revenue, not to taxes on a specific house. Here's how it works: Communities cannot increase their total tax revenue by more than 2.5 percent each year. Most of the time, this means that your tax bill won't go up by more than that. However, another state law requires communities to reassess the value of individual homes every three years. If the value of your house goes up faster than the value of other homes in your community, then your taxes could go up considerably more than 2.5 percent in a reassessment year (or go down if everybody else's houses go up in value more than yours).

But wait—there's more. Residents can vote to override Proposition 2½ limits to pay for specific projects (things like school roof repairs, new town buildings, and the like).

State law also lets towns set different tax rates for residential and commercial property. Many communities, including Boston, set a lower rate for residential property. In addition, the city of Boston offers partial exemptions for residents who live in a house in the city. In 2001, the amount of the exemption was $49,577, which works out to a tax savings of $524.53. Boston residents can get more information from the city Taxpayer Referral and Assistance Center at (617) 635-4287 or www.ci.boston.ma.us/trac/resexempt.asp.

Septic Systems

If you buy a house with a septic system, you'll become very familiar with Title V. This state regulation mandates a thorough inspection of septic systems before a house is sold (within a two-year period before the sale). If the system fails, you can't buy the house until the seller fixes whatever's wrong. If you do buy the house following the repairs, you'll have to get a similar inspection if you sell the house or add any sort of extension onto the house. Inspections cost about $400. You can read more on Title V and get listings of state-approved inspectors at www.state.ma.us/dep/brp/wwm/t5pubs.htm. You can also call the state's Title V hotline at (800) 266-1122.

Water and Sewer Rates

You can escape septic worries by moving to a community that has municipal sewers (not all houses will have sewage; there are even a few small parts of Boston that still rely on septic systems). Keep in mind, however, that Greater Boston has some of the highest water and sewer rates in the country. Communities served by the Massachusetts Water Resources Authority have to pay for the cleanup of Boston Harbor ($4 billion or so), and those costs will be reflected in your monthly bills. Each community decides how to pay its annual MWRA assessments; some communities, such as Boston, have managed to keep rates relatively stable in recent years through such work as plugging leaks in local sewer lines.

The way most communities figure sewage bills is to multiply the amount of water you consume by some rate, basing their equation on the assumption that what you consume ultimately goes down the drain. A problem arises if you use a lot of water outdoors, for example, filling a pool or watering a lawn the size of Rhode Island. If you expect to do that, you might want to check with your local board of public works. Some communities will let you install a separate water meter for outdoor use, so you get charged for using the water, but not for flushing it down the drain.

Homeowner Associations

Homeowner associations are rare in Massachusetts. Typically, when a developer is done with a subdivision, the city or town inspects it to ensure that it meets municipal requirements (for roads and the like) and any conditions set by the local planning and zoning boards. Once that's done, the community "accepts" the subdivision and the town takes over responsibility for such things as road repair and zoning requirements. One famous exception: Louisburg Square in the heart of Beacon Hill, which is run by an association of homeowners on the square. Once a year, the owners block off the square to traffic to assert their ownership. Many towns and parts of some Boston neighborhoods, such as the Back Bay, have quasi-associations in the form of historic districts. In these districts, deeds restrict what you can do to the exterior of your home; any modifications have to be approved by a city or town historic district commission. The joke in downtown Concord is that you can paint your house any color you want as long as it's white. The Back Bay was the last neighborhood in Boston to get cable TV because of a dispute between the cable company and the historic commission over wires in neighborhood alleys.

CITY FACT

Boston geography is summed up thusly:

"The geographical center of Boston is in Roxbury. Due north of the center we find the South End. This is not to be confused with South Boston, which lies directly east of the South End. North of the South End is East Boston and southwest of East Boston is the North End."

Condominium Associations

In contrast to the homeowners associations, condo associations are the norm in Massachusetts—after all, somebody has to figure out how to get things fixed and levy fees for maintenance. Typically, condo association boards function almost like city councils or boards of selectmen.

Swimming Pools

You might think there wouldn't be much call for outdoor swimming pools in the Boston area. After all, you can really only use them around here for three months a year (unless you want to spend a fortune heating them for use in the early spring and late fall). But truth be told, swimming pools are one of our vices, right up there with gourmet ice cream. If you look at a lot of houses, chances are you're going to see at least one with an in-ground or aboveground pool.

As much as they appeal to some, pools are considered something of a drag on the selling price of a house. Some people don't want the hassles of maintaining a pool (especially if, say, the previous owner put the thing right under oak trees, which means you'll be forever cleaning acorns out of it). Or maybe they don't want the risks and liability of one, especially if you have kids or are in a neighborhood filled with them. Removing a pool, especially an in-ground one, is no simple matter. Not only do you have to have all that cement removed, you have to make sure the resulting hole is carefully filled so that it doesn't collapse later on. Expect to pay several thousand dollars to have an in-ground pool removed.

Resources for Finding a House

BOSTON ASSESSING INFORMATION

www.ci.boston.ma.us/assessing/search.asp

Use this city database to look up the assessed value of Boston houses.

BOSTON CONDOS

www.bostoncondos.com

Connects you to the listings of numerous Boston condo brokers.

BOSTON GLOBE

(617) 929-2000

realestate.boston.com

The Sunday *Globe* has a large real-estate section. The Saturday paper is where you'll find listings of open houses. The Web site lets you search for a house based on location and price.

BOSTON HOME CENTER

(617) 635-HOME

www.ci.boston.ma.us/dnd/1_HomeCenter.asp

The city of Boston has numerous programs aimed at encouraging home ownership in the city, from low-cost rehab loans and grants to property-tax exemptions. The Boston Home Center provides information and applications for these programs, as well as listings of abandoned properties the city will sell at a low price to adventuresome homesteaders.

DOMANIA.COM

www.domania.com

This Web site can be very helpful when considering what sort of offer to make. You can type in an address on this site and see how much the property sold for, roughly how much it's appreciated in value since its last sale, and what its property taxes are like. The site also has tutorials on buying a home, getting a mortgage, and so on.

FSBO ONLINE

www.fsboonline.com/boston

Lists homes for sale by owner (i.e., without a broker).

HOMEFIND

www.homefind.com

Real-estate listings from the *Boston Herald* and its suburban newspapers.

JUST PROPERTY

www.justproperty.com

Free paper with property listings available in boxes around the Boston area. Listings are also available online.

MONSTERMOVING.COM

www.monstermoving.com

Tips on finding, buying, and maintaining a home, along with real-estate and broker listings.

Real-Estate Agencies in the Boston Area

Acton Real Estate Company
371 Massachusetts Avenue
Acton
(978) 263-1166

www.acton-realestate.com

Apple Country Realty
175 Sudbury Road
Concord
(978) 369-6850

www.applecountryrealty.com

Baron Associates
229 Berkeley Street
Back Bay
(617) 437-0337

www.gis.net/~baron

Barrett & Co.
33 Walden Street
Concord
(978) 369-6453

www.jmbarrett.com

Boston Realty Associates
1102 Commonwealth Avenue
Allston
(617) 277-5100

Bowes/Pennell & Thompson GMAC Real Estate
1010 Massachusetts Avenue
Arlington
(781) 648-3500

www.bowesrealtors.com

Bremis Real Estate
1173 Broadway
Somerville
(617) 623-2500
www.bremis.com

Cabot & Co.
213 Newbury Street
Back Bay
(617) 262-6200
www.cabotandcompany.com

Carlson GMAC Real Estate
(781) 937-8400
www.carsonre.com
Has offices across eastern
Massachusetts.

Castles Unlimited
837 Beacon Street
Newton Centre
(617) 964-3300
www.castlesunltd.com

Century 21 Avon
1675 Massachusetts Avenue
Cambridge
(800) 689-9910

Century 21 Carole White Associates
1766 Centre Street
West Roxbury
(800) 290-5281

Century 21 Cityside
655 Boylston Street
Back Bay
(617) 262-2600

Century 21 Dorchester Associates
906 Dorchester Avenue
Dorchester
(617) 265-1000

Century 21 Downing Associates
72 Hancock Street
Braintree
(800) 448-3410

Century 21 E. A. Hill
60 Great Road
Acton
(978) 263-5800
www.century21hill.com

CITY FACT

On January 15, 1919, a 58-foot-high tank of molasses in the North End burst, sending a gooey wave down Commercial Street that killed twenty-one people, a dozen horses, and at least one cat.

Century 21 Garden City Homes
324 Walnut Street
Newton
(617) 969-2121

Century 21 The Howard Group
1288 Beacon Street
Brookline
(617) 739-2111

Century 21 Marella Realty
367 Washington Street
Braintree
(800) 783-4740

Century 21 Pondside
619 Centre Street
Jamaica Plain
(617) 524-6900

Century 21 Shawmut Properties
134 Tremont Street
Brighton
(888) 230-2121

Century 21 Treon Realty
4456 Washington Street
Roslindale
(617) 327-2100

Century 21 Tullish & Clancy
457 Main Street
Weymouth
(800) 545-2162

Century 21 West Realty
161 Mt. Auburn Street
Watertown
(800) 244-5280

Century 21 Westward Homes
300 Franklin Village Drive
Franklin
(508) 528-7777

Chobee Hoy Associates
18 Harvard Street
Brookline
(617) 739-0067

www.chobeehoy.com

Christine White Realty Associates
300 Commercial Street, C-3
Boston
(617) 742-6290

world.std.com/~sisu

Waterfront units.

Citylife Real Estate
218 Newbury Street
Back Bay
(617) 262-9500

www.ctlf.com

CityState LLC
218 Cambridge Street
Beacon Hill
(617) 723-7797

www.citystatellc.com

Coastal Countryside Properties
231 Chief Justice Cushin
Cohasset
(781) 383-9922

www.coastalcountryside.com

Coldwell Banker Hunneman

70–80 Lincoln Street
Boston
(617) 426-4260

www.hunneman.com

Has offices across eastern
Massachusetts.

Cornerstone Properties

99B Charles Street
Beacon Hill
(617) 742-4453

www.conerstoneproperties.com

Condo sales.

Del Realty

104 High Street
Danvers
(800) 317-7272

www.delrealty.com

DeWolfe Companies

118 Newbury Street
Back Bay
(617) 536-4500

12 Clarendon Street
Back Bay
(617) 266-8000

171 Huron Avenue
Cambridge
(617) 864-8566

858 Walnut Street
Newton
(617) 965-7171

www.dewolfe.com

Dyer & Mullin ERA Realty

812A Route 3A
Cohasset
(781) 383-9100

ERA Maxwell Real Estate

843 Massachusetts Avenue
Cambridge
(617) 441-3939

ERA Mediate Real Estate

476 Columbus Avenue
South End
(617) 267-2666

www.mediaterealestate.com

ERA Northeastern Metro Realty

58 Gainsborough Street
Back Bay
(617) 437-8801

ERA The Norton Group

699 Broadway
Somerville
(617) 623-6600

Gallagher Real Estate

104 Spring Street
West Roxbury
(617) 325-7575

Gibson Domain

556 Tremont Street
South End
(617) 426-6900

227 Newbury Street
Back Bay
(617)375-6900

553 East Broadway
South Boston
(617) 268-2011

www.gibsondomaindomain.com

Hammond Residential
Real Estate
(617) 527-2500

www.hammondre.com

Offices in Belmont, Boston, Brookline, Cambridge, Newton, Wellesley, and Weston.

CITY
FACT

The colors of Boston's four subway lines have specific meanings. The Green Line goes through the leafy suburbs of Brookline and Newton. The Red Line used to terminate at Harvard, where the school color is crimson. The Blue Line runs along the ocean. The Orange Line used to run as an elevated above Washington Street, once known as Orange Street.

Innovative Moves
726 Centre Street
Jamaica Plain
(617) 522-0020

2A Corinth Street
Roslindale
(617) 325-8400

www.innovativemoves.com

Itzkan and Marchiel
160 Commonwealth Avenue
Back Bay
(617) 247-2909

www.itzkanmarchiel.com

Jack Conway Realtor
137 Washington Street
Norwell
(781) 871-0080

www.jackconway.com

Offices across eastern Massachusetts.

Karcher Family Realtors
128 Front Street
Scituate
(781) 545-6677

www.buyer1st.com

A buyer's broker firm.

Karp & Liberman Real Estate
93 Union Street Suite 322
Newton Centre
(716) 928-1212

www.karpliberman.com

Keller Williams Realty
665 Cochituate Road
Framingham
(508) 872-3113

LandVest
10 Post Office Square
Boston
(617) 723-1800
www.landvest.com

MassHomeSales.com
323 Boston Post Road
Sudbury
(978) 440-8686
www.masshomesales.com

Mohawk Real Estate
1594 Dorchester Avenue
Dorchester
(617) 436-1600

Nippon International Realty
93 Massachusetts Avenue
Back Bay
(617) 536-1792
www.nipponrealty.com
Specializes in finding homes for Japanese residents moving to Boston.

O'Kiley Real Estate
207 East Broadway
South Boston
(617) 269-3227
www.okiley.com

Premier Properties of Boston
142 Commercial Street
Boston
(617) 723-4240
www.homesboston.com
Waterfront condos.

Real Estate Affiliates of Massachusetts
(800) 471-4433
www.prudentialmass.com
Prudential real-estate offices across eastern Massachusetts.

Realtor.com
www.realtor.com
Web site of the National Association of Realtors. Lets you find a Realtor or home for sale.

Realty Executives
83 Great Road
Acton
(978) 266-0040

Realty Marketplace
1446 Dorchester Avenue
Dorchester
(617) 287-8715
www.realty-marketplace.com

realtyplan.com
(888) 877-8300
www.realtyplan.com
Web site that represents buyer's brokers in Massachusetts.

Re/Max Affiliates
2077 Centre Street
West Roxbury
(617) 323-5050

Re/Max Cosmopolitan Properties
165 Newbury Street
Back Bay
(617) 267-0003

Re/Max Old South Real Estate
579 Tremont Street
South End
(617) 536-3330

Re/Max Realty Associates
873 Concord Street
Framingham
(800) 542-5540

Re/Max Realty Plus
738 East Broadway
Dorchester
(888) 301-7005

Re/Max Select Realty
1211 Commonwealth Avenue
Allston
(617) 787-0700

A. E. Rondeau Real Estate
69 Appleton Street
South End
(617) 247-0300
www.aerondeau.com

Sea Coast Homes
679A Nantasket Avenue
Hull
(781) 925-1545
www.seacoasthome.com

South Boston Condos
(617) 268-5181
www.southbostoncondos.com

South End Realty Group
476 Columbus Avenue
South End
(617) 267-2666
www.southendrealty.com
Homes and condos.

Street & Co.
78 Charles Street
Beacon Hill
(617) 742-5235
www.streetandcompany.com

Success Real Estate
214 Quincy Avenue
Braintree
(781) 848-9064
www.successrealestate.com

Packing Up and Moving Out

By Monstermoving.com

CHAPTER 4

Getting Organized and Planning Your Move

Written for both the beginner and the veteran, this chapter contains information and resources that will help you get ready for your move. If money is foremost on your mind, you'll find a section on budgeting for the move and tips on how to save money throughout the move, as well as a move budget-planning guide. If time is also precious, you'll find timesaving tips and even suggestions for how to get out of town in a hurry. You'll find help with preliminary decisions, the planning process, and packing, as well as tips and advice on uprooting and resettling your family (and your animal companions). A budget worksheet, a set of helpful checklists, and a Moving Task Time Line complete the chapter.

Paying for Your Move

Moving can certainly tap your bank account. How much depends on a number of factors: whether your employer is helping with the cost, how much stuff you have, and how far you are moving.

To get an idea of how much your move will cost, start calling service providers for estimates and begin listing these expenses on the Move Budget-Planning Guide provided at the end of this chapter.

If you don't have the money saved, start saving as soon as you can. You should also check out other potential sources of money:

- Income from the sale of your spare car, furniture, or other belongings (hold a garage or yard sale).
- The cleaning and damage deposit on your current rental and any utility deposits. You probably won't be reimbursed until after your move, though, so you'll need to pay moving expenses up front in some other way.
- Your employer, who may owe you a payout for vacation time not taken.

Taxes and Your Move

Did you know that your move may affect your taxes? As you prepare to move, here are some things to consider:

- Next year's taxes. Some of your moving expenses may be tax-deductible. Save your receipts and contact your accountant and the IRS for more information. Visit www.irs.gov or call the IRS at (800) 829-3676 for information and to obtain the publication and forms you need.
- State income tax. If your new state collects income tax, you'll want to figure that into your salary and overall cost of living calculations. In 2000, the state income-tax rate in Massachusetts was 5.85 percent. That is scheduled to decrease to 5 percent by 2003. Of course, if your old state collects income tax, remember to find out how much if any of the current year's income will be taxable in the old state.
- Other income sources. You'll want to consider any other sources of income and whether your new state will tax you on this income. For example, if you are paying federal income tax on an IRA that you rolled over into a Roth IRA and if you move into a state that collects income tax, you may also have to pay state income tax on your rollover IRA.

- After you move or when filing time draws near, consider collecting your receipts and visiting an accountant.

The Budget Move (Money-Saving Tips)

Here you'll find some suggestions for saving money on your move.

SAVING ON MOVING SUPPLIES

- Obtain boxes in the cheapest way possible.

    Ask friends or colleagues who have recently moved to give or sell you their boxes.

    Check the classified ads; people sometimes sell all their moving boxes for a flat rate.

    Ask your local grocery or department store for their empty boxes.

- Borrow a tape dispenser instead of buying one.
- Instead of buying bubble wrap, crumple newspaper, plain unused newsprint, or tissue paper to pad breakables.
- Shop around for the cheapest deal on packing tape and other supplies.
- Instead of renting padding blankets from the truck rental company, use your own blankets, linens, and area rugs for padding. (But bear in mind that you may have to launder them when you arrive, which is an expense in itself.)

SAVING ON LABOR

- If you use professional movers, consider a "you pack, we drive" arrangement, in which you pack boxes, and the moving company loads, moves, and unloads your belongings.
- Call around and compare estimates.
- If you move yourself, round up volunteers to help you load and clean on moving day. It's still customary to reward them with moving-day food and beverages (and maybe a small cash gift). You may also have to volunteer to help them move someday. But you may still save some money compared to hiring professionals.

MOVING TIP

If you are renting a truck, you'll need to know what size to rent. The following are general guidelines of what size truck to rent. Because equipment varies, though, ask for advice from the company renting the truck to you.

10-foot truck: 1 to 2 furnished rooms

14- to 15-foot truck: 2 to 3 furnished rooms

18- to 20-foot truck: 4 to 5 furnished rooms

22- to 24-foot truck: 6 to 8 furnished rooms

- Save on child and pet care. Ask family or friends to watch your young children and pets on moving day.

SAVING ON TRIP EXPENSES

Overnight the Night Before You Depart

- Where will you stay the night before you depart? A hotel or motel might be most comfortable and convenient, but you could save a little money if you stay the night with a friend or relative.

- If you have the gear, maybe you'd enjoy unrolling your sleeping bag and "roughing it" on your own floor the night before you leave town. If you do this, try to get ahold of a camping sleeping pad or air mattress, which will help you get a good night's sleep and start your move rested and refreshed.

Overnight on the Road

- Look into hotel and motel discounts along your route. Your automobile club membership may qualify you for a better rate. Check out other possibilities, too. Associations such as AARP often line up discounts for their members, as do some credit cards.
- When you call about rates, ask if the hotel or motel includes a light breakfast with your stay.

MOVING TIP

As soon as you get here, get down to a local bookstore and invest in a good spiral-bound Boston-area map book. You'll need it!

- If your move travel involves an overnight stay and you're game for camping, check into campgrounds and RV parks along your route. Be sure to ask whether a moving truck is allowed. Some parks have size restrictions, some RV parks may not welcome moving trucks, and some limit the number of vehicles allowed in a campsite.

FOOD WHILE TRAVELING

Food is one of those comfort factors that can help make the upsetting aspects of moving and traveling more acceptable. Eating also gives you a reason to stop and rest, which may be exactly what you or your family needs if you're rushing to get there. Here are a few pointers to consider:

- Try to balance your need to save money with your (and your family's) health and comfort needs.
- Try to have at least one solid, nutritious sit-down meal each day.
- Breakfast can be a budget- and schedule-friendly meal purchased at a grocery or convenience store and eaten on the road: fruit, muffins, and juice, for example.
- Lunch prices at sit-down restaurants are typically cheaper than dinner prices. Consider having a hot lunch and then picnicking in your hotel or motel on supplies from a grocery store.

Scheduling Your Move

Try to allow yourself at least three months to plan and prepare. This long lead-time is especially important if you plan to sell or buy a home or if you are moving during peak moving season (May through September). If you plan to move during peak season, it's vital to reserve two to three months in advance with a professional moving company or truck rental company. The earlier you reserve, the more likely you are to get the dates you want. This is especially important if you're timing your move with a job start date or a house closing date or are moving yourself and want to load and move on a weekend when your volunteers are off work.

WHEN IS THE RIGHT TIME TO MOVE?

If your circumstances allow you to decide your move date, you'll want to make it as easy as possible on everyone who is moving:

- Children adjust better if they move between school terms (entering an established class in the middle of a school year can be very difficult).
- Elders have special needs you'll want to consider.
- Pets fare best when temperatures aren't too extreme, hot or cold.

THE "GET-OUT-OF-TOWN-IN-A-HURRY" PLAN

First the bad news: Very little about the move process can be shortened. Now the good news: The choices you make might make it possible to move in less time. The three primary resources in a successful move are time, money, and planning. If you're short on time, be prepared to spend more money or become more organized.

Immediately check into the availability of a rental truck or professional moving service. Next, give your landlord notice or arrange for an agent to sell your home. (If you own your home, you may find it harder to leave town in a hurry.) If your employer is paying for your move, ask if it offers corporate-sponsored financing options that will let you buy a new home before you sell your old one. Then consider the following potentially timesaving choices:

- Move less stuff. Of all the moving tasks, packing and unpacking consume the most time. The less you have to deal with, the quicker your move will go. Consider drastically lightening the load by selling or giving away most of your belongings and starting over in your new location. Although buying replacement stuff may drain your pocketbook, you can save some money by picking up some items secondhand at thrift stores and garage sales. (And after all, everything you have now is used, isn't it?)

- Make a quick-move plan. Quickly scan through chapters 4 and 5, highlighting helpful information. Use the checklists and the task time line at the end of this chapter to help you.

- Get someone else to do the cleaning. Before you vacate, you'll need to clean. You can be out the door sooner if you hire a professional cleaning company to clean everything, top to bottom, including the carpets. Again, the time you save will cost you money, but it may well be worth trading money for time.

Planning and Organizing

Start a move notebook. This could be as simple as a spiral-bound notepad or as elaborate as a categorized, tabbed binder. Keep track of this notebook. You'll find it invaluable later when chaos hits. In your notebook, write notes and tape receipts. Of course, keep this book with your notebook! You may find the checklists and the Moving Task Time Line at the end of this chapter helpful. You may also find it helpful to assign a "do-by" date to each task on the checklist. To help you gauge what you face in the coming weeks, perhaps you will find it useful at this point to scan through the task time lines before reading further.

The section of the Moving Task Time Line that will help you

MOVING TIP

Need boxes? Liquor stores are often good places to ask. But avoid boxes from supermarkets—you don't know what's been living in there.

the most at this point is "Decision Making: Weeks 12 to 9," which you'll find at the end of this chapter.

Preliminary Decisions

Before you even begin to plan your move, there are a number of decisions you'll need to make regarding your current residence, how you will move (do it yourself or hire a professional), and your new area.

LEAVING YOUR CURRENT HOME (RENTED PROPERTY)

Leaving a rental unit involves notifying your landlord and fulfilling your contractual obligations. This won't be a problem unless you have a lease agreement that lasts beyond your desired move date.

Your rights and options are dictated by state and local landlord/tenant laws and by your lease agreement. Exit fees can be expensive, depending on the terms of your lease. Here are some tips that may help you get out of a lease gracefully and save a few bucks at the same time.

- Know your rights. Laws governing landlord/tenant agreements and rights vary by state and municipality. Consult state and local laws, and obtain a pamphlet on renter's rights for your state and municipality. See chapter 2 for more information on renting in Massachusetts.

- Review your lease agreement. There's no point in worrying until you know whether you have anything to worry about—and no use in finding out too late that there were things you could have done.

- Look for a way out. Ask your landlord to consider letting you find a replacement tenant to fulfill your lease term (in some areas, this is a right dictated by law). If your move is due to a corporate relocation, your landlord or the property management company may be more willing to be flexible with exit fees—especially if you provide a letter from your employer. (And you may be able to get your employer to pick up the cost if you can't get the fees waived.)

- Adjust the timing. If you need to stay a month or two longer than your current lease allows and you don't want to sign for another six months or longer, ask your landlord for a month-to-month agreement lasting until your move date.

LEAVING YOUR CURRENT HOME (OWNED PROPERTY)

If you own your home, you'll either sell it or rent it out. If you sell, you'll either hire a real estate agent or sell it yourself. If you rent it out, you'll either serve as your own landlord or hire a property management agency to manage the property for you. Here are a few quick pros and cons to help you with the decisions you face.

Hiring a Selling Agent: Pros

- Your home gets exposure to a wide market audience, especially if the agent you choose participates in a multiple listing service.
- Homes listed with a real estate agent typically sell more quickly.
- Your agent will market your home (prepare and place ads and so on) and will also schedule and manage open houses and showings.
- Your agent will advise you and represent your interest in the business deal of selling including offers, negotiation, and closing, guiding you through the stacks of paperwork.

Hiring a Selling Agent: Cons

- Hiring an agent requires signing a contract. If, for whatever reason, you want out, you may find it difficult to break the contract (it's wise to read carefully and sign only a short-term contract. Typical real estate agent contracts are 90 to 120 days in length).
- You pay your agent a fee for the service, typically a percentage of the selling price.

Selling Your Home Yourself: Pros

- You don't pay an agent's fee.
- You retain more control over showings, open houses, walk-throughs, and so on.

Selling Your Home Yourself: Cons

- Selling a home takes time. You must arrange your own showings and schedule and conduct your own open houses. Combined with everything else that happens during move preparation (working, interviewing for jobs, finding a new home, planning your move, packing, and so on), you will probably be swamped already. Add home showings (which are based around the buyer's schedule, not yours), and you may find yourself looking for an agent to help you after all.

- You pay for marketing costs, which can add up. Consider the cost of flyers, newspaper ads, or listing your home on a "homes for sale by owner" Web site.

- Because you don't have a real estate agent to represent you in the sale, you may need to hire an attorney at that point, which could take up some of the savings.

MOVING TIP

Before buying anything for your new apartment or home, stop and consider what you'll need immediately and what you might be able to do without for a while. You'll spend a lot less if you can afford to wait and look for it on sale or secondhand.

RENTING OUT YOUR PROPERTY

If you prefer to rent out your home, you can turn it over to a property management agency or be your own landlord. The services an agency will perform depend on the agency and your agreement with it. The following table details some of the rental issues you'll need to consider. As you review these, ask yourself how far away you're moving and whether or not you can handle these issues from your new home. Remember that every piece of work you must hire out cuts into the money in your pocket at the end of the month.

Rental Issue	You As Landlord	Hired Property Manager
Vacancy	You interview candidates, show the property, and choose tenants	The agency finds and selects tenants
Cleaning	You clean or arrange for cleaning services between tenants	The agency arranges for cleaning services between tenants
Late Rent	You collect rent and pursue late rent	The agency collects rent and pursues late rent
Rental Income	The rent you collect is all yours	The agency charges a fee, usually a percentage of the monthly rent
Repairs	You handle repairs and emergencies or find and hire a contractor to do the work	The agency handles repairs and emergencies

Strategic Financial Issues Related to Renting Out Your Old Home

If your property is located in a desirable neighborhood that is appreciating in value 3 percent or more annually, keeping it may in the long run defray or overcome the management fees. However, if you have a mortgage and are near the beginning of your mortgage term, remember that most of your monthly mortgage payment is being applied to interest and not principal. Interest payments on the property will cease being deductible on your federal income taxes once you stop using it as your primary residence. The local property taxes may also go up; many counties give owner-occupied credits that reduce the actual tax total.

Deciding How to Move:
Hiring Professionals or Moving Yourself

At first, you may be inclined to handle your own move to save money. But there are other factors to consider, and depending on your situation, you may actually save money if you use professional services. Consider the range of service options some professional companies offer. The right combination could save you some of the headache but still compete with the cost of a do-it-yourself move. For example, some professional moving companies offer a "you pack, we drive" arrangement, in which you pack boxes, and the moving company loads, moves, and unloads your belongings. Call around and inquire about rates. Also consider the following list of pros and cons to help you decide what's best for you.

The section of the Moving Task Time Line that will help you the most at this point is "Decision Making: Weeks 12 to 9," which you'll find at the end of this chapter.

THE PROS OF USING PROS

- *Time.* You may not have the hours it will take to pack, move, and unpack, but professional movers do—that's their day job.
- *Materials.* The moving company provides boxes and packing materials.*
- *Packing.* The movers pack all boxes (unless your contract states that you will pack).*
- *Loading and unloading.* The movers load your belongings onto the moving van and unload your belongings at your destination.*
- *Unpacking.* The movers remove packed items from boxes and place items on flat surfaces.*
- *Debris.* The movers dispose of packing debris such as boxes, used tape, and padding.*
- *Experience.* The movers will know just what to do to transport your precious belongings in good condition.

- *Safety.* The movers do the lifting, which could save you a real injury.

Professional moving contracts typically include the services marked with an asterisk (*). Don't count on something unless you know for sure that the contract covers it, though. It's a good idea to ask your mover a lot of questions and read the contract carefully.

THE CONS OF USING PROS

- *Administrative chores.* Using professionals requires you to do some up-front work: obtaining estimates, comparing and nego-tiating prices and move dates, reviewing contracts, and compar-ing insurance options.
- *Loss of control.* The movers typically take charge of much of the packing and loading process, and you need to adapt to their schedule and procedures.

THE PROS OF A SELF-MOVE

- *Control.* You pack, so you decide which items get packed together, how they get packed, and in which box they reside.
- *Cost-cutting.* You may save some money. But as you compare costs, be sure to factor in all self-move-related moving and travel costs. These include fuel, tolls, mileage charge on the rented truck, food, and lodging. All these costs increase the longer your trip is.

MOVING TIP

Before you move, make sure to talk to the local utility and phone companies to make sure you have power, water, gas, phone, and so on, turned on the day of your move. And don't forget to have them shut off in your old place.

THE CONS OF A SELF-MOVE

- *Risk to your belongings.* Because of inexperience with packing, loading, and padding heavy and unwieldy boxes and furniture, you or your volunteers may inadvertently damage your property.
- *Risk to yourself and your friends.* You or your volunteers may injure yourselves or someone else.
- *Responsibility.* Loading and moving day are especially hectic, and you're in charge.
- *Reciprocal obligations.* If you use volunteers, you may be in debt to return the favor.

OTHER THINGS TO KNOW ABOUT PROFESSIONAL MOVING SERVICES

Your moving company may or may not provide the following services or may charge extra for performing them. Be sure to ask.

- Disassembling beds or other furniture
- Removing window covering hardware (drapery rods, mini-blinds) or other items from the walls or ceiling
- Disconnecting and installing appliances (dryer, washer, automatic ice maker)
- Disconnecting and installing outside fixtures such as a satellite dish, a hose reel, and so on
- Moving furniture or boxes from one room to another

MOVING INSURANCE IN A PROFESSIONAL MOVE

By U.S. law, the mover must cover your possessions at $0.60 per pound. This coverage is free. Consider taking out additional coverage, though, because under this minimal coverage, your three-pound antique Tiffany lamp worth thousands of dollars at auction fetches exactly $1.80 if the moving company breaks it.

Your homeowner's or renter's insurance provider may be willing to advise you on moving insurance options, and the moving company will offer you a number of insurance options. Be sure you understand each option—what it covers and what it costs you. Ask a lot of questions and read everything carefully. It's best to be prepared and well informed should something break or show up missing.

STORAGE

If you want your moving company to store some or all of your possessions temporarily, inquire about the cost and the quality of their facilities.

*   Are the facilities heated (or air-conditioned, depending on the time of year you'll be using storage)?
*   Does the moving company own the storage facility or subcontract storage to another company? If your movers subcontract, does your contract with them extend to the storage facility company?

MOVING TIP

Have a gun? Check with your new community's police department before you move. Massachusetts has more stringent gun ownership regulations than most other states—you'll need to get a permit from your local police.

Storage Companies in the Boston Area

Benny's Moving and Storage
60 Coolidge Avenue
Watertown
(888) 668-4649

www.bennysmoving.com

Brookline Moving
123 Kent Street
Brookline
(617) 566-6922

www.brooklinemoving.com

Brookline Transportation
65 Sprague Street
Boston
(800) 766-7724

www.usamover.com

Casey & Hayes
Storage & Moving
430 East First Street
South Boston
(617) 269-5900

Daley & Wanzer
Moving & Storage
821 Nantasket Avenue
Hull
(781) 925-0015

Door to Door Storage
(888) 366-7222

www.doortodoor.com

Fortress
99 Boston Street
Boston
(617) 288-3636

Gentle Giant Moving
29 Harding Street
Somerville
(800) 466-8844

www.gentlegiant.com

Humboldt Storage and Moving
100 New Boston Drive
Canton
(800) 225-9845

www.humboldt.com

John Palmer Moving & Storage
7 Craig Road
Acton
(800) 442-6683

Larkin Moving and Storage
3175 Washington Street
Jamaica Plain
(617) 522-3300

Lipsky Moving and Storage
36R Jefferson Avenue
Salem
(877) 473-2468

www.lipsky-moving.com

MacDonald Moving & Storage
31 Court Street
Newtonville
(617) 782-9897

Mal Farrell Storage
15 Rocsam Park Road
Braintree
(781) 849-0666

Mark's Moving & Storage
1455 Concord Street
Framingham
(800) 966-6275

www.marksmoving.com

**Metropolitan
Moving & Storage**
134 Massachusetts Avenue
Cambridge
(617) 547-8180

www.metmoving.com

**Michael's
Moving & Storage**
76 Rosedale Road
Watertown
(888) MOVE-761

www.michaelsmovers.com

Olympic Moving & Storage
17 Bridge Street
Watertown
(617) 926-5555

**Road Warrior Moving
and Storage**
86 Rear Lincoln Street
Brighton
(617) 782-5400

www.roadwarrior.baweb.com

Titan Moving & Storage
32 Rugg Road
Brighton
(617) 782-0383

Viking Moving and Storage
43 Braintree Street
Boston
(800) 239-6683

www.vikingmoving.com

Whitehouse
Moving & Storage
361A Somerville Avenue
Somerville
(617) 354-2751

MOVING TIP

Start packing as soon as you get boxes. Some things you can pack long before the move. For example, off-season holiday decorations and off-season clothes can be boxed right away. The more you do early on, the less there is to do closer to move day, when things are hectic anyway.

CHOOSING A MOVER

- Start by asking around. Chances are your friends, family, or colleagues will have a personal recommendation.
- Take their recommendations and list them in a notebook, each on a separate sheet. Call these companies to request a no-obligation, free written estimate, and take notes on your conversation.
- Find out if the company you're talking to offers the services you need. For example, if you want to ship your car, boat, or powered recreational craft in the van along with your household goods, ask if this service is available.
- Do a little investigating. Ask the company to show you its operating license, and call the Better Business Bureau to ask about complaints and outstanding claims.

GETTING AN ESTIMATE

You need to know what kind of estimate the moving company is giving you. The two most common are "non-binding" and "binding." A non-binding estimate (usually free, but potentially less accurate) is one in which the moving company charges you by the hour per man per truck and quotes you an approximate figure to use in your planning. Depending on the circumstances, your final cost could be significantly greater than what shows up in the estimate.

The second type is a binding estimate, which you typically pay for. In this type, the professional mover performs a detailed on-site inspection of your belongings and quotes a flat price based on the following:

- The amount of stuff you're moving, whether it is fragile or bulky, and how complicated it is to pack
- Final weight
- Services provided
- Total length of travel

Once you choose a mover, it's a good idea to have a representative visit your home, look at your belongings, and give you a written (binding) estimate. Getting a written estimate may cost you money, but it helps prevent surprises when it comes to pay the final bill.

You play a big role in making sure that the estimate you receive is accurate. Be sure you show the moving company representative everything you plan to move.

- Remember to take the representative through every closet, out to the garage, into the shed, down to the basement, up into the attic, and to your rented storage facility if you have one.
- Tell the representative about any item you don't plan to move (because you plan to get rid of it before you move). Then be sure to follow through and get rid of it so there are no surprises on moving day.
- Point out any vehicles you want to ship in the van along with your household goods and ask your representative to include the cost in your estimate.

WHAT MIGHT INCREASE YOUR FINAL BILL

It is reasonable to expect that certain circumstances will unexpectedly increase your final bill, including:

- You do the packing and it's incomplete or done improperly.
- Circumstances unexpectedly increase the time and labor involved in your move. For example:

  You're moving out of or into a high-rise and movers don't have access to an elevator (perhaps it's broken).

  Access at either location is restricted (for example, there is no truck parking close by or the movers have to wait for someone to unlock).

- You change your move destination after you receive your written estimate.
- You require delivery of your belongings to more than one destination.

Researching Your New Area

The section of the Moving Task Time Line that will help you the most at this point is "Decision Making: Weeks 12 to 9," which you'll find at the end of this chapter. Other chapters of this book discuss the details of your destination city. Here are some additional move-related tips and resources.

GENERAL CITY INFORMATION

- Visit your local library and read up on your new area.
- Go online and look for the local newspaper (for the Boston area, see www.boston.com, www.bostonherald.com, and www.townonline.com).
- Have a friend or family member mail you a week's worth of newspapers from your destination city or have a subscription delivered via postal mail.
- Visit www.monstermoving.com for easy-to-find city information and links to local services, information, and Web sites.

JOBS, HOUSING, AND COST OF LIVING

Visit www.monstermoving.com for job information, links to apartments for rent, and real estate and other services, as well as free cost-of-living information.

CHOOSING SCHOOLS

Selecting schools is of supreme importance for family members who will attend public or private schools.

Do Your Homework

- Ask your real estate agent to help you find school information and statistics or a list of contacts for home school associations.
- Search the Web.

   Visit www.2001beyond.com. There you can compare up to four districts at once. Information on both public and private schools is provided. The extensive twelve-page report provides information on class size, curriculum, interscholastic sports, extracurricular activities, awards, merits, and SAT scores. It also provides the principal's name and phone number for each school in the district. You may need to pay a nominal fee for the twelve-page report (or the cost may be covered by a sponsoring real estate professional, if you don't mind receiving a phone call from an agent).

   Visit www.monstermoving.com, which provides links to school information. Also see chapter 10 for more information on Massachusetts schools.

Visit Schools

Arrange to visit schools your children might attend, and bring them along. Your children will pick up on subtleties that you will miss. As you talk with your children about changing schools, try to help them differentiate between their feelings about moving to a new school and area and their feelings about that particular school by asking direct but open-ended questions (questions that invite dialogue because they can't be answered with a simple "yes" or "no": "What was the best or worst thing you saw there?" for example, or "Which electives looked the most interesting?").

PLANNING AND TAKING A HOUSE- OR APARTMENT-HUNTING TRIP

Preparing and planning in advance will help you make the most of your trip. Ideally, by this point, you will have narrowed your search to two or three neighborhoods or areas.

- Gather documents and information required for completing a rental application:

   Rental history. Landlord name, contact information, dates occupied.

   Personal references. Name and contact information for one or two personal references.

   Employment information. Current or anticipated employer name and contact information.

   Bank account number.

- Consider compiling all this information onto a "rental resume." Even though most landlords won't accept a rental resume in lieu of a completed application, spending the time up front could be helpful in a market where rentals are scarce. Handing landlords a rental resume lets them know you're serious about finding the right place and are professional and organized in how you conduct your affairs.

- Be prepared to pay an application fee and deposits. Deposit the funds in your account and bring your checkbook. Typically, landlords require first and last months' rent and a flat damage and cleaning deposit.

- Take your move planning notebook. List properties you want to visit, one per notebook page. Clip the classified ad and tape it onto the page. Write notes about the property, rent rate, deposit amount, and terms you discuss with the landlord or property manager.

Planning

Now that you've made pre-move decisions, it's time to plan for the physical move. First, you'll need to organize your moving day. Next, you'll need to prepare to pack.

These are the sections of the Moving Task Time Line that will help you the most at this point:

- "Organizing, Sorting, and Notifying: Weeks 9 to 8"
- "Finalizing Housing Arrangements and Establishing Yourself in Your New Community: Weeks 8 to 6"
- "Making and Confirming Transportation and Travel Plans: Week 6"
- "Uprooting: Weeks 5 to 4"
- "Making and Confirming Moving-Day Plans: Week 3"

You'll find the Moving Task Time Line at the end of this chapter.

PLANNING FOR MOVING DAY

The Professional Move: Some Planning Considerations

- Confirm your move dates and finalize any last contract issues.
- Ask what form of payment movers will accept (check, money order, certified check, traveler's checks), and make necessary arrangements.

The Self-Move: Organizing Volunteers

- Ask friends and relatives to "volunteer" to help you load the truck on moving day.
- Set up shifts, and tactfully let your volunteers know that you are counting on them to arrive on time and stay through their shift.
- A week or two before moving day, call everyone to remind them.
- Plan on supplying soft drinks and munchies to keep your crew going.

PLANNING CARE FOR YOUR CHILDREN AND PETS

Moving day will be hectic for you and everyone, and possibly dangerous for your young children. Make plans to take younger children and pets to someone's home or to a care facility.

PLANNING YOUR MOVING-DAY TRAVEL

Driving

- If you will be renting a truck, be prepared to put down a sizable deposit the day you pick up the truck. Some truck rental companies accept only a credit card for this deposit, so go prepared.
- If you belong to an automobile club such as AAA, contact the organization to obtain maps, suggested routes, alternate routes, rest-stop information, and a trip packet if it provides these services.
- Visit an online map site such as www.mapblast.com, where you'll find not only a map but also door-to-door driving directions and estimated travel times.
- Find out in advance where you should turn in the truck in your new hometown.

MOVING TIP

Bring some towels, soap, and a shower curtain with you in the car—after a long, hard day of moving, you'll want a shower!

Traveling by Air, Train, or Bus

- Arrange for tickets and boarding passes.
- Speak with the airline to request meals that match dietary restrictions.
- Speak with the airline or the train or bus company to make any special arrangements such as wheelchair accessibility and assistance.
- Plan to dress comfortably.
- If you will be traveling with young children, plan to dress them in bright, distinctive clothing so you can easily identify them in a crowded airport, train station, or bus terminal.

PREPARING TO PACK: WHAT TO DO WITH THE STUFF YOU HAVE

Moves are complicated, time-consuming, and exhausting. But the process has at least one benefit: A move forces us to consider simplifying our lives by reducing the amount of our personal belongings. If we plan to keep it, we also must pack it, load it, move it, unload it, and unpack it. Here are some suggestions for sifting through your belongings as you prepare for packing.

- Start in one area of your home and go through everything before moving to the next area.
- Ask yourself three questions about each item (sentimental value aside):

    Have we used this in the last year?

    Will we use it in the coming year? For example, if you're moving to a more temperate climate, you might not need all your wool socks and sweaters.

    Is there a place for it in the new home? For instance, if your new home has a smaller living room, you might not have room for your big couch or need all your wall decorations.

If you answer "no" to any of these questions, you might want to consider selling the item, giving it away, or throwing it out.

Packing

Here are some tips to help you with one of the most difficult stages of your move—packing.

- Follow a plan. Pack one room at a time. You may find yourself leaving one or two boxes in each room open to receive those items you use right up until the last minute.
- On the outside of each box, describe the contents and room destination. Be as specific as you can, to make unpacking easier. If you are using a professional moving service but doing the packing yourself, consider numbering boxes and creating a separate list of box contents and destinations.

- Put heavy items such as books in small boxes to make them easier to carry.
- Don't put tape on furniture because it may pull off some finish when you remove it.
- As you pack, mark and set aside the items that should go in the truck last (see checklist at the end of this chapter). Mark and set aside your "necessary box" (for a list of items to include in this box, see the checklist at the end of this chapter).

PACKING FRAGILE ITEMS

- When packing breakable dishes and glasses, use boxes and padding made for these items. You may have to pay a little to buy these boxes, but you're apt to save money in the long run because your dishes are more likely to arrive unbroken. Dishes and plates are best packed standing on edge (not stacked flat on top of each other).
- Pad mirrors, pictures, and larger delicate pieces with sheets and blankets.
- Computers fare best if they are packed in their original boxes. If you don't have these, pack your hardware in a large, sturdy box and surround it with plenty of padding, such as plastic bubble pack.
- Use plenty of padding around fragile items.
- Mark "FRAGILE" on the top and all sides of boxes of breakables so that your labeling is easily seen no matter how a box is stacked.

MOVING TIP

Take a tape measure and your notebook with you. Measure rooms; sketch your new home and write room measurements on your sketch. Before you move, you'll know whether your current furniture will fit and have a good idea of how it should be arranged.

WHAT NOT TO PACK

- Don't pack hazardous, flammable, combustible, or explosive materials. Empty your gas grill tank and any kerosene heater fuel as well as gasoline in your power yard tools. These materials are not safe in transit.
- Don't pack valuables such as jewelry, collections, important financial and legal documents, and records in the moving van. Keep these with you in the trunk of your car or in your suitcase.

PACKING AND UNPACKING
SAFELY WITH YOUNG CHILDREN

No matter how well you've kid-proofed your home, that lasts only until the moment you start packing. Then things are in disarray and within reach of youngsters. Here are some tips to keep your toddlers and children safe.

- Items your youngsters have seldom or never seen will pique their curiosity, presenting a potential hazard, so consider what you are packing or unpacking. If you stop packing or unpacking and leave the room even for a moment, take your youngsters with you and close the door or put up a child gate.
- Keep box knives and other tools out of a child's reach.
- As you disassemble or reassemble furniture, keep track of screws, bolts, nuts, and small parts.
- Be aware of how and where you temporarily place furniture and other items. (That heavy mirror you just took down off the wall—do you lean it up against the wall until you go get the padding material, inviting a curious youngster to pull or climb on it?) For the same reason, consider how high you stack boxes.
- Upon arriving at your destination, if you can't find someone to baby-sit, set aside a room in your home where your young children can safely play. Set up the TV and VCR and unpack the kids' videos, books, coloring books and crayons or markers, and some toys and snacks.
- Walk through your new home with children and talk about any potential dangers such as a swimming pool or stairs, establishing your safety rules and boundaries.

- If you have young children who are unaccustomed to having stairs in the home, place a gate at the top and one at the bottom. If your child is walking and over toddler age, walk up and down the stairs together a few times holding the railing until he or she becomes accustomed to using the stairs.

Handle with Special Care: Uprooting and Settling the People and Pets in Your Life

The most important advice you can take is this: Involving children as much as possible will help transform this anxiety-causing, uncertain experience into an exciting adventure. It would take a book to cover this topic comprehensively, but here are some suggestions for making the transition easier:

- Involve children early. Ask for their input on decisions and give them age-appropriate tasks such as packing their own belongings and assembling an activity bag to keep them busy while traveling.
- Don't make empty promises. Kids can hear the hollow ring when you say, "It'll be just like here. Just give it time" or "You can stay friends with your friends here." These things are true, but you know they're not true in the same way if you're moving long distance.
- Deal with fear of the unknown. If possible, take children with you to look at potential neighborhoods, homes or apartments, and schools. It may be more expensive and require extra effort, but it will ease the transition and help children begin to make the adjustment.

MOVING TIP

A few weeks before you move, start eating the food in your freezer. Also use up canned food, which is bulky and heavy to move.

- Provide as much information as you can. If it's not possible to take children with you when you visit new neighborhoods, homes or apartments, and schools, take a camera or video recorder. Your children will appreciate the pictures, and the preview will help them begin the transition. You can also use a map to help them understand the new area and the route you will take to get there.

- Make time to talk with your children about the move. Especially listen for—and talk about—the anxieties your children feel. By doing so, you will help them through the move (your primary goal), and you'll deepen your relationship at the same time, which may be more important in the long run.

- Share your own anxieties with your children, but be sure to keep an overall positive outlook about the move. Because most aspects of a move are downers, a negative outlook on your part may shed gloom over the whole experience, including its good aspects. On the other hand, a positive outlook on your part may counteract some of your child's emotional turmoil, uncertainty, and fear.

- Make it fun. Give older children a disposable camera and ask them to photograph your move. Once you arrive and are settled in, make time together to create the "moving" chapter of your family photo album.

HELPING FAMILY MEMBERS MAINTAIN FRIENDSHIPS

Moving doesn't have to end a friendship.

- Give each child a personal address book to record the e-mail address, phone number, and postal mail address for each of his or her friends.

- Stay in touch. E-mail is an easy way. Establish an e-mail address for every family member (if they don't already have one) before you move so he or she can give it out to friends. Many Web mail services are free and can be accessed from anywhere you can access the Internet. Examples include www.msn.com, www.usa.net, and www.yahoo.com.

- Make (and follow through with) plans to visit your old hometown within the first year of your move. Visit friends and drive by your old home, through neighborhoods, and past landmarks.

This reconnection with dear friends and fond memories will help your family bring finality to the move.

TRAVELING WITH YOUR PET

- Keep a picture of your pet on your person or in your wallet just in case you get separated from Fido or Fluffy during the move.
- Place identification tags on your pet's collar and pet carrier.
- Take your pet to the vet for an examination just before you move. Ask for advice on moving your particular pet. Specifically ask for advice on how you can help your pet through the move: what you can do before, during, and after the move to help your pet make the transition smoothly.
- Find out if you will need any health certificates for your pet to comply with local regulations in your new home and obtain them when you visit the vet.
- If your pet is prone to motion sickness or tends to become nervous in reaction to excitement and unfamiliar surroundings, tell your veterinarian, who may prescribe medication for your pet.
- Ask for your pet's health records so you can take them to your new vet.
- If your pet is unusual—say, a ferret or a snake or other reptile—there might be laws in your new city or state regarding the transportation or housing of such an animal. Contact the department of agriculture or a local veterinarian to find out.
- Cats: It's wise to keep your cat indoors for the first two weeks until it recognizes its new surroundings as home.
- Dogs: If appropriate, walk your dog on a leash around your neighborhood to help it become familiar with its new surroundings and learn its way back home.
- If your pet will travel by plane, check with your airline regarding fees and any specific rules and regulations regarding pet transport.
- Your pet will need to travel in an approved carrier (check with your airline regarding acceptable types and sizes).
- Your airline may require a signed certificate of health dated within a certain number of days of the flight. Only your vet can produce this document.

Move Budget-Planning Guide

Housing

Home repairs	$ _____
Cleaning supplies and services	$ _____

Rental expenses in new city

Application fees (varies—figure $15 to $35 per application)	$ _____
First and last month's rent	$ _____
Damage and security deposit	$ _____
Pet deposit	$ _____
Utility deposits	$ _____
Storage unit rental	$ _____

Total . . . . **$** _____

Moving

Professional moving services or truck rental	$ _____
Moving supplies	$ _____
Food and beverage for volunteers	$ _____
Tips for professional movers; gifts for volunteers	$ _____

Moving travel:

Airline tickets	$ _____
Fuel	$ _____
Tolls	$ _____
Meals: per meal $ _____ × _____ meals	$ _____
Hotels: per night $ _____ × _____ nights	$ _____

Total . . . . **$** _____

(continues on next page)

Other Expenses

$ _____

$ _____

$ _____

$ _____

$ _____

$ _____

$ _____

Total . . . . $ _____

GRAND TOTAL . . . . $ _____

Utilities to Cancel

Utility	Provider name and phone	Cancel date[1]
Water and sewer		
Electricity		
Gas		
Phone		
Garbage		
Cable		
Alarm service		

[1] If you are selling your home, the shutoff of essential services (water, electricity, gas) will depend on the final closing and walk-through. Coordinate with your real estate agent.

Utilities to Connect

Utility	Provider name and phone	Service start date	Deposit amount required
Water and sewer			
Electricity			
Gas			
Phone			
Garbage			
Cable			
Alarm service			

Other Services to Cancel, Transfer, or Restart

Service	Provider name and phone	Service end date[1]	Service start date[1]
Subscriptions and Memberships			
Newspaper			
Memberships (health club and so on)			
Internet Service Provider			

[1] If applicable

(continues on next page)

Other Services to Cancel, Transfer, or Restart (continued)

Service	Provider name and phone	Service end date[1]	Service start date[1]
Government and School			
Postal mail change of address			
School records			
Voter registration			
Vehicle registration			
Financial			
Bank account[2]			
Direct deposits and withdrawals			
Safe deposit box			
Professional			
Health care (transfer doctors' and dentists' records for each family member)			
Veterinarian (transfer records)			
Cleaners (pick up your clothes)			

[1] If applicable; [2] Open an account in your new town before closing your existing account.

Checklists

MOVING SUPPLIES

Packing and Unpacking

_____ Tape and tape dispenser. (The slightly more expensive gun-style dispenser is a worthwhile investment because its one-handed operation means you don't need a second person to help you hold the box closed while you do the taping.)

_____ Boxes. (It's worth it to obtain specialty boxes for your dinnerware, china set, and glasses. Specialty wardrobe boxes that allow your hanging clothes to hang during transport are another big help.)

_____ Padding such as bubble wrap.

_____ Markers.

_____ Scissors or a knife.

_____ Big plastic bags.

_____ Inventory list and clipboard.

_____ Box knife with retractable blade. (Get one for each adult.)

Loading and Moving

_____ Rope. (If nothing else, you'll need it to secure heavy items to the inside wall of the truck.)

_____ Padding blankets. (If you use your own, they may get dirty and you'll need bedding when you arrive. Padding is available for rent at most truck rental agencies.)

_____ Hand truck or appliance dolly. (Most truck rental agencies have them available for rent.)

_____ Padlock for the cargo door.

THE "NECESSARY BOX"

Eating

____ Snacks or food. (Pack enough durable items for right before you depart, your travel, and the first day in your new home— as well as disposable utensils, plates, and cups.)

____ Instant coffee, tea bags, and so on.

____ Roll of paper towels and moistened towelettes.

____ Garbage bags.

Bathing

____ A towel for each person.

____ Soap, shampoo, toothpaste, and any other toiletries.

____ Toilet paper.

Health Items

____ First aid kit including pain relievers.

____ Prescription medicines.

Handy to Have

____ List of contact information. (Make sure you can reach relatives, the moving company, the truck driver's cell phone, and so on.)

____ Small tool kit. (You need to be able to take apart and reassemble items that can't be moved whole.)

____ Reclosable plastic bags to hold small parts, screws, and bolts.

____ Spare lightbulbs. (Some bulbs in your new home might be burned out or missing.)

____ Nightlight and flashlight.

OVERNIGHT BAG

____ Enough clothes for the journey plus the first day or two in your new home.

____ Personal toiletries.

ITEMS FOR KIDS

____ Activities for the trip.

____ Favorite toys and anything else that will help children feel immediately at home in their new room.

Pet Checklist

____ Food.

____ A bottle of the water your pet is used to drinking.

____ Dishes for food and water.

____ Leash, collar, and identification tags.

____ Favorite toy.

____ Medicines.

____ Bed or blanket.

____ Carrier.

____ Paper towels in case of accidents.

____ Plastic bags and a scooper.

____ Litter and litter box for your cat or rabbit.

Last Items on the Truck

CLEANING

____   Vacuum cleaner.

____   Cleaning supplies.

GENERAL

____   Necessary box.

____   Setup for kids' temporary playroom.

____   Other items you'll need the moment you arrive.

New Home Safety Checklist

GENERAL

____   Watch out for tripping hazards. They will be plentiful until you get everything unpacked and put away, so be careful and keep a path clear at all times.

HEAT, FIRE, ELECTRICAL

____   Be sure nothing gets placed too close to heaters.

____   Test smoke, heat, and carbon monoxide detectors. Find out your fire department's recommendations regarding how many of these devices you should have and where you should place them. If you need more, go buy them (remember to buy batteries) and install them.

____   Find the fuse or breaker box before you need to shut off or reset a circuit.

WATER

_____ Check the temperature setting on your water heater. For child safety and fuel conservation, experts recommend 120 degrees Fahrenheit.

_____ Locate the water shutoff valve in case of a plumbing problem.

Moving Task Time Line

DECISION MAKING: WEEKS 12 TO 9

_____ Consider your moving options (professional versus self-move) and get quotes.

_____ If you are being relocated by your company, find out what your company covers and what you will be responsible for doing and paying.

_____ Set a move date.

_____ Choose your moving company or truck rental agency and reserve the dates.

If You Own Your Home

_____ Decide whether you want to sell or rent it out.

_____ If you decide to sell, choose a real estate agent and put your home on the market or look into, and begin planning for, selling it yourself.

_____ If you decide to rent out your home, decide whether you want to hire a property management agency or manage the property yourself.

_____ Perform (or hire contractors to perform) home repairs.

If You Currently Rent

_____ Notify your landlord of your plans to vacate.

_____ Check into cleaning obligations and options.

Tour Your New City or Town

_____ Research your new area at the library or online at www.monstermoving.com.

_____ Contact a real estate agent or property management agency to help you in your search for new lodgings.

_____ Go on a school-hunting and house- or apartment-hunting trip to your new town or city.

Additional items:

ORGANIZING, SORTING, AND NOTIFYING: WEEKS 9 TO 8

_____ Obtain the post office's change of address kit by calling 1-800-ASK-USPS or visiting your local post office or www.usps.gov/moversnet/ (where you'll find the form and helpful lists of questions and answers).

_____ Complete and send the form.

_____ List and notify people, businesses, and organizations who need to know about your move. You may not think of everyone at once, but keep a running list and add people to your list and notify them as you remember them. As you notify them, check them off your list.

_____ Start sorting through your belongings to decide what to keep. Make plans to rid yourself of what you don't want: Pick a date for a garage sale; call your favorite charity and set a date for them to come pick up donations; call your recycling company to find out what they will accept.

_____ For moving insurance purposes, make an inventory of your possessions with their estimated replacement value.

_____ If you have high-value items (such as antiques) that you expect to send with the moving company or ship separately, obtain an appraisal.

Additional items:

_____

_____

_____

_____

_____

_____

_____

FINALIZING HOUSING ARRANGEMENTS
AND ESTABLISHING YOURSELF
IN YOUR NEW COMMUNITY: WEEKS 8 TO 6

_____ **Home.** Select your new home and arrange financing; establish a tentative closing date or finalize rental housing arrangements.

_____ **Schools.** Find out school calendars and enrollment and immunization requirements.

_____ **Insurance.** Contact an agent regarding coverage on your new home and its contents as well as on your automobile.

_____ **Finances.** Select a bank, open accounts, and obtain a safe deposit box.

_____ **New Home Layout.** Sketch a floor plan of your new home and include room measurements. Determine how your present furniture, appliances, and decor will fit.

_____ **Mail.** If you haven't found a new home, rent a post office box for mail forwarding.

_____ **Services.** Find out the names and phone numbers of utility providers and what they require from you before they will start service (for example, a deposit, a local reference). (You can list your providers and service start dates on the checklist provided in this chapter.) Schedule service to start a few days before you arrive.

Additional items:

_____

_____

_____

_____

_____

_____

MAKING AND CONFIRMING TRANSPORTATION AND TRAVEL PLANS: WEEK 6

_____ Schedule pick-up and delivery dates with your mover.

_____ Make arrangements with your professional car mover.

_____ If you need storage, make the arrangements.

_____ Confirm your departure date with your real estate agent or landlord.

_____ Make your travel arrangements. If you will be flying, book early for cheaper fares.

_____ Map your driving trip using www.mapblast.com or ask your automobile club for assistance with route and accommodation information.

Additional items:

_____

_____

_____

_____

_____

_____

_____

_____

_____

_____

_____

_____

_____

_____

_____

UPROOTING: WEEKS 5 TO 4

_____ Hold a garage sale or donate items to charity.

_____ Gather personal records from all health care providers, your veterinarian, lawyers, accountants, and schools.

_____ Notify current utility providers of your disconnect dates and your forwarding address. (You can list your providers and service end dates on the checklist provided in this chapter.)

Additional items:

MAKING AND CONFIRMING
MOVING-DAY PLANS: WEEK 3

____ Make arrangements for a sitter for kids and pets on moving day.

____ Call moving-day volunteers to confirm move date and their arrival time.

____ Obtain traveler's checks for trip expenses and cashier's or certified check for payment to mover.

____ Have your car serviced if you are driving a long distance.

Additional items:

WEEK 2

_____ If you have a pet, take it to the vet for a checkup. For more pet-moving tips, see the section earlier in this chapter on moving with pets.

_____ Arrange for transportation of your pet.

_____ If you are moving into or out of a high-rise building, contact the property manager and reserve the elevator for moving day.

_____ Reserve parking space for the professional moving van or your rental truck. You may need to obtain permission from your rental property manager or from the city.

_____ Drain oil and gas from all your power equipment and kerosene from portable heaters.

Additional items:

MOVING WEEK

_____ Defrost the freezer.

_____ Give away any plants you can't take with you.

_____ Pack your luggage and your necessary box for the trip (see the list provided in this chapter).

_____ Get everything but the day-to-day essentials packed and ready to go.

Additional items:

_____

_____

_____

_____

_____

_____

_____

_____

_____

_____

_____

_____

MOVING DAY

_____ Mark off parking space for the moving van using cones or chairs.

_____ See "Moving Day" section of chapter 5 for further to-do items.

Getting from Here to There: Moving Day and Beyond

This chapter guides you through the next stage in your move: moving day, arriving, unpacking, and settling in. Here you'll find important travel tips for both the self-move and the professional move, information related to a professional car move, and pointers for your first days and weeks in your new home.

The Professional Move

Early on moving day, reserve a large place for the moving truck to park. Mark off an area with cones or chairs. If you need to obtain parking permission from your apartment complex manager or the local government, do so in advance.

GUIDE THE MOVERS

Before work starts, walk through the house with the movers and describe the loading order. Show them the items you plan to transport yourself. (It's best if these are piled in one area and clearly marked, maybe even covered with a sheet or blanket until you're ready to pack them in your car.)

Remain on site to answer the movers' questions and to provide special instructions.

BEFORE YOU DEPART

Before you hit the road, you will need to take care of some last-minute details:

- Walk through your home to make sure everything was loaded.
- Sign the bill of lading. But first, read it carefully and ask any questions. The bill of lading is a document the government requires movers to complete for the transportation of supplies, materials, and personal property. The mover is required to have a signed copy on hand, and you should keep your copy until the move is complete and any claims are settled.
- Follow the movers to the weigh station. Your bill will be partly based on the weight of your property moved.

UNLOADING AND MOVING IN

Be sure to follow each of these details once the movers arrive at your new home:

- Have your money ready. (Professional movers expect payment in full before your goods are unloaded.)
- Check for damage as items are unpacked and report it right away.
- Unless the company's policy prohibits the acceptance of gratuities, it is customary to tip each mover. Twenty dollars is a good amount; you may want to tip more or less based on the service you receive.

The Self-Move

The following tips should help you organize and guide your help, as well as make the moving day run considerably smoother:

- The day before your move, create a task list. Besides the obvious (loading the truck), this list will include tasks such as disconnecting the washer and dryer and taking apart furniture that can't be moved whole.

- Plan to provide beverages and food for your volunteers. Make it easy on yourself and provide popular options such as pizza or sub sandwiches (delivered), chilled soda pop, and bottled water (in an ice chest, especially if you're defrosting and cleaning the refrigerator).

- On moving day, remember that you are only one person. If you need to defrost the freezer or pack last-minute items, appoint someone who knows your plan to oversee the volunteers and answer questions.

- Be sure you have almost everything packed before your help arrives. Last-minute packing creates even more chaos and it's likely that hastily packed items will be damaged during loading or transit.

MOVING TIP

Before you leave, measure your current home and sketch a plan, showing room measurements and furniture placement. Take the plan with you, along with a tape measure and notebook, and draw up similar plans for the house or rental unit you're thinking of choosing. Sketches needn't be very detailed at this stage to help you avoid unpleasant surprises—no point in dragging that California king bed across country if it won't fit in the bedroom.

- If you end up with an even number of people, it's natural for people to work in pairs because they can carry the items that require two people. If you have an odd number of people, the extra person can rotate in to provide for breaks, carry light items alone, or work on tasks you assign.

- Be sure to match a person's physical ability and health with the tasks you assign.

- Appoint the early shift to start on tasks such as disconnecting the washer and dryer and taking apart furniture (such as bed frames) that can't be moved whole.

- Before work starts, walk through the house with your volunteers and describe your loading plan.

- Know the moving truck and how it should be packed for safe handling on the road (ask the truck rental company for directions).

- Load the truck according to the directions the truck rental agency gave you. Tie furniture items (especially tall ones) to the inside wall of the truck. Pack everything together as tightly as possible, realizing that items will still shift somewhat as you travel.

MOVING TIP

Bring a box of light bulbs with you—especially if you're arriving after dark. And don't forget a roll or two of toilet paper and paper towels.

Move Travel

Boston is easily reached by car, plane, train, and bus.

BY CAR

From the west, the Massachusetts Turnpike (I-90) provides quick access into Boston. From the south and north, I-93 heads right into the city; expect serious delays at rush hour, however. I-95 heads toward the city from the north and southwest. Both ends terminate at what the locals call Route 128, which circles the city roughly twelve miles out.

This could be your first introduction to the vagaries of Boston roads. Route 128 is also known as I-95 for a long stretch, but south of the city, parts of it are known as I-93 and Route 1. To the north of the city, I-95 splits off from Route 128 and heads toward Maine (while Route 128 goes on to Cape Ann).

Massachusetts Turnpike Authority

www.masspike.com

MOVING TIP

If you can, avoid moving to Boston on Labor Day weekend. That's when tens of thousands of college students arrive for the fall semester.

BY PLANE

Major U.S. airlines and many foreign airlines provide regular service to Boston's Logan International Airport, which is located just across Boston Harbor from the main part of the city. If you drive, just follow the exit signs and then the signs for the tunnel. And get ready for another serious introduction to Boston driving. The tunnel dumps you out into a tiny intersection that gives you roughly fifteen seconds to decide whether to get onto Route 93 north or swing around under the elevated highway for Route 93 south (which will also get you to the Massachusetts Turnpike for points west). Logan is serviced by Logan Express buses, which will get you to depots in Framingham (west), Braintree (south), and Woburn (north), and by Logan Dart, a bus that will get you to South Station (where you can pick up commuter rail and the Red Line subway). If you want to take the subway directly from the airport, hop on one of the free shuttles from your terminal to the airport stop on the Blue Line.

Heading to downtown Boston? A quick way is the water shuttle to Rowes Wharf.

Massachusetts Port Authority

(800) 23-LOGAN

www.massport.com

MassPort runs the airport, the Logan Express and Logan Dart buses, and the water shuttle. The Web site provides real-time updates of arrivals and airport traffic and parking conditions.

BY TRAIN

Amtrak provides frequent service to Boston from Washington, Philadelphia, and New York. Acela express trains have reduced the trip from New York to three and a half hours. Boston has three stops: Route 128 (handy for getting to western and southern suburbs), Back Bay, and South Station. You can transfer to a number of commuter-rail lines at Back Bay and South Station, or the Orange Line subway at Back Bay and the Red Line at South Station. There is also Amtrak service from Chicago and points west with stops at Back Bay and South Station.

MOVING TIP

If you plan to drive your own rental van or truck, try to make the trip in a car first—the Boston area has lots of narrow and height-restricted roads that will leave you cursing as you're forced to detour. Moving trucks are prohibited on all parkways.

Amtrak
(800) USA-RAIL
www.amtrak.com

Massachusetts Bay Transportation Authority
(617) 222-5000
www.mbta.com

BY BUS

Bonanza, Concord Trailways, and Greyhound provide scheduled service to Boston. All terminate at the South Station terminal, across the street from the train station. Expect a four-and-a-half-hour ride from New York.

Bonanza
(888) 751-8800
www.bonanzabus.com

Concord Trailways

(800) 639-3317

www.concordtrailways.com

Greyhound

(800) 229-9424

www.greyhound.com

SELF-MOVE—DRIVING A TRUCK

- A loaded moving truck handles far differently from the typical car. Allow extra space between you and the vehicle you're following. Drive more slowly and decelerate and brake sooner; there's a lot of weight sitting behind you.

- Realize that no one likes to follow a truck. Other drivers may make risky moves to get ahead of you, so watch out for people passing when it's not safe.

MOVING TIP

Draw up a detailed plan of your new home, including scale drawings of each room that show each piece of furniture you plan to take with you. Label furniture and boxes as to where they go in the new home and have copies of the plan to put in each room there. This will give you at least a chance that most of the work of moving in will need to be done only once.

- Know your truck's height and look out for low overhangs and tree branches. Especially be aware of filling station overhang heights.

- Most accidents in large vehicles occur when the driver is backing up. Before you back up, get out, walk around, and check for obstacles. Allow plenty of maneuvering room and ask someone to help you. Ask that person to stay within sight of your side-view mirror, and talk over the hand signals to be used as he or she guides you.

- Stop and rest at least every two hours.

- At every stop, do a walk-around inspection of the truck. Check tires, lights, and the cargo door. (If you're towing a trailer, check trailer tires, door, hitch, and hitch security chain.) Ask your truck rental representative how often you should check the engine oil level.

- At overnight stops, park in a well-lighted area and lock the truck cab. Lock the cargo door with a padlock.

IF YOU'RE FLYING OR TRAVELING BY TRAIN OR BUS

- Coordinate with the moving van driver so that you arrive at your destination about the same time.
- Plan for the unexpected, such as delays, cancellations, or missed connections.
- Keep in touch with the truck driver (by cell phone, if possible), who may also experience delays for any number of reasons: mechanical problems, road construction, storms, or illness.
- Dress comfortably.
- If you are traveling with young children, dress them in bright, distinctive clothing so you can easily identify them in a crowded airport, train station, or bus terminal.

PROFESSIONAL MOVERS MAY NEED HELP, TOO

Make sure the movers have directions to your new home. Plan your travel so that you will be there to greet them and unlock the doors to your house or apartment. Have a backup plan in case one of you gets delayed. It is a good idea to exchange cell phone numbers with the driver so you can stay in touch in case one of you is delayed.

TIPS FOR A PROFESSIONAL CAR MOVE

A professional car carrier company can ship your car. Alternatively, your moving company may be able to ship it in the van along with your household goods. Ask around and compare prices.

- Be sure that the gas tanks are no more than one-quarter full.
- It's not wise to pack personal belongings in your transported auto because insurance typically won't cover those items.
- If your car is damaged in transport, report the damage to the driver or move manager and note it on the inventory sheet. If you don't, the damage won't be eligible for insurance coverage.

Unpacking and Getting Settled

You made it. Welcome home! With all the boxes and bare walls, it may not feel like home just yet, but it soon will. You're well on your way to getting settled and having life return to normal. As you unpack boxes, arrange the furniture, and hang the pictures, here are a few things to keep in mind:

- Approach unpacking realistically. It's not necessary (and probably not possible) to unpack and arrange everything on the first day.
- Find your cleaning supplies and do any necessary cleaning.
- Consider your family's basic needs (food, rest, bathing) and unpack accordingly:

    Kitchen. Start with the basics; keep less frequently used items in boxes until you decide your room and storage arrangements.

    Bedrooms. Unpack bedding and set up and make beds.

    Bathroom. Because this tends to be a small room with little space for boxes, unpack the basics early and find a place to store the still-packed boxes until you have a chance to finish.

MOVING TIP

If you have children and you're moving during the school year, make sure you have their birth certificates handy and that they have all the shots they'll need to enroll in their new schools. You can get Massachusetts school immunization info at www.state.ma.us/dph/cdc/epiimm2.htm.

MAINTAINING NORMALCY . . . STARTING FRESH

During the move and the days following, it's good to keep things feeling as normal as possible. But this can also be a fresh starting point:

a time to establish (or reestablish) family rituals and traditions. Beyond the family, this is a time to meet and connect with new neighbors, schoolmates, and your religious or other community.

- Keep regular bedtimes and wake-up times (naps for kids if appropriate).
- If you typically eat dinner together, continue to do this, despite the chaos.
- If you typically have a regular family time—an activity or outing—don't feel bad if you must skip it one week because of move-related chores, but restart this ritual as soon as you can. In fact, your family may appreciate this special time even more in the midst of the upheaval and change.

Rome wasn't built in a day, and neither are friendships. If your move means you have to start over, take heart: Persistence and work will pay off over time. Here are a few suggestions for making your first connections with people—individuals and communities of people—in your new area.

- Encourage family members who need encouragement in making new friends.

MOVING TIP

Reserve a large place for the moving truck to park on the day you move out. Mark off an area with cones or chairs. If you need to obtain parking permission from your apartment complex manager or the city, do so in advance.

- Provide opportunities for building friendships from day one. Take a break from unpacking and knock on doors to meet neighbors. (It's not a good idea to start a friendship by asking for help unloading, though!)
- Get involved in activities your family enjoys and make time in your schedule for people, even though moving and resettling is a hectic and busy time.
- Meet and connect with your religious or other community.

DISCOVERING YOUR COMMUNITY

Here you'll find suggestions for getting settled in your new surroundings.

MOVING TIP

If you're driving some distance, get your car checked out by a mechanic before moving day—the last thing you want on your big day is to get stuck in some rest stop in Connecticut.

- Be sure every family member gets a feel for the neighborhood and main streets; memorizes your new address; learns (or carries) new home, office, and cell phone numbers; and knows how to contact local emergency personnel, including police, fire, and ambulance.
- Go exploring on foot, bike, mass transit, or by car (turn it into a fun outing), and start learning your way around.
- Locate your local post office and police and fire stations, as well as hospitals and gas stations near your home.
- Scout your new neighborhood for shopping areas.
- Register to vote.
- If you are moving from outside Massachusetts, visit the Registry of Motor Vehicles to obtain your driver's license and register your vehicle (see below).
- If you haven't already done so, transfer insurance policies to an agent in your new community.

Public Utilities

Boston Department of Public Works
(617) 635-4900

www.cityofboston.com/publicworks

Responsible for street and sidewalk repairs, snow removal, sanitation, recycling, and spring and fall yard-waste pickups in Boston.

Boston Water and Sewer Commission

(617) 989-7000

www.bwsc.org

Note: In other communities, water and sewer services are provided by the city or town department of public works. Check with your town or city hall for contact information.

Department of Telecommunications and Energy

Complaint line: (800) 392-6066

www.state.ma.us/dte

Oversees telephone, electric, and natural-gas utilities in Massachusetts.

Keyspan Energy Services (formerly Boston Gas)

(800) 233-5325

www.bostongas.com

Massachusetts Electric

(800) 322-3223

www.masselectric.com

Serves most of the towns not served by Nstar.

Nstar (formerly Boston Edison)

(617) 424-2000

www.nstaronline.com

Provides electric service to Boston and many surrounding communities. Also provides natural-gas service to several suburban communities.

Cable Television

AT&T Broadband

(617) 787-8888

www.attbroadband-ne.com

Covers Boston, Brookline, and many other communities in eastern Massachusetts.

RCN

(800) 746-4726

www.rcn.com

Competes with AT&T Broadband in a growing number of neighborhoods in Boston and surrounding towns.

High Speed Internet Access

AT&T Broadband

(617) 787-8888

www.attbroadband-ne.com

Covers Boston, Brookline, and many other communities in eastern Massachusetts with cable-modem access.

DSL Reports

www.dslreports.com

Type in your address on this site, see which companies offer high-speed DSL in your neighborhood, then read comments from users of those companies.

RCN

(800) 746-4726

www.rcn.com

Competes with AT&T Broadband in a growing number of neighborhoods in Boston and surrounding towns with cable-modem access.

Speakeasy.net

(800) 556-5829

www.speakeasy.net

Verizon Online DSL

(877) 525-2DSL

www.bell-atl.com/infospeed

The World

(617) 739-0202

www.theworld.com

Does not provide high-speed access by itself. However, it is the oldest Internet service provider in the nation, has local dial-up numbers across eastern Massachusetts, and provides low-cost hourly access in cities across the country, which makes it handy for when you travel.

Telephone

AT&T

(800) 222-0300

www.att.com/home

MOVING TIP

Unless company policy prohibits acceptance of gratuities, it is customary to tip each professional mover. Twenty dollars is a good amount; you may want to tip more or less based on the service you receive. If you move yourself, you might also want to give each of your volunteers a gift. Cash or a gift certificate is a nice gesture. Perhaps one of your volunteers is a plant lover and will cheerfully accept your houseplants as a thank-you gift. It's also a good idea to supply plenty of soft drinks or water and snacks for them.

Cingular

(866) CINGULAR

www.cingular.com

MCI

(800) 444-3333

www.mci.com

RCN
(800) 746-4726

www.rcn.com

Sprint
(800) 877-4646

csg.sprint.com/longdistance

Verizon
(800) 870-9999

www.bellatlantic.com/
foryourhome/MA/

Police, Fire, and EMTs

Police, fire, and emergency medical coverage are generally provided by each local community. Wherever you are in the state, dialing 911 on a wired phone will get you to the nearest emergency dispatch center (wireless 911 calls are routed to the state police). The state police patrols interstate highways, including the Massachusetts Turnpike and parkways in the Boston area. State parks are patrolled by state environmental police. In Massachusetts, unlike in other states, county sheriff's offices have few law-enforcement duties; they are chiefly responsible for running county jails.

Massachusetts State Police
(508) 820-2300

www.state.ma.us/msp

Other Emergency Services

Bureau of Communicable Disease, West Nile Virus Information
(866) MASS-WNV

www.state.ma.us/dph/wnv/
wnv1.htm

Provides daily updates on mosquito and bird statistics related to the disease.

FBI (Boston)
(617) 742-5533

Massachusetts Poison Control System
(617) 232-2120 (Boston, 24 hours)
(800) 682-9211
(Outside Boston, 24 hours)

www.mapoison.org

Samaritans of Boston (crisis counseling)
(617) 247-0220 (24 hours)

www.samaritansofboston.org

U.S. Coast Guard
(888) 708-3879

Pest Control

Best Pest Control Services
Somerville
(617) 625-4850
www.bestpest.com

**Dennis the Mennis
Pest Control**
29 Locust Street
Lynn
(781) 592-0023
www.dennisthemennis.com

Orkin Exterminating
Brighton
(617) 254-3560
www.orkin.com

Pest Control Services
263 Washington Street
Dedham
(888) PESTMGMT
www.pest-mgmt.com

Preferred Pest Control
Park Street
West Roxbury
(617) 323-5590

Reasonable Pest Control
Quincy
(866) 228-7378
www.reasonablepestcontrol.
webatonce.com

MOVING TIP

Don't pack hazardous, flammable, combustible, or explosive materials. Empty your gas grill tank and any kerosene heater fuel as well as gasoline in your power yard tools. These materials are not safe in transit.

Don't pack valuables such as jewelry, collections, important financial and legal documents, and records in the moving van. Keep these with you in the trunk of your car or in your suitcase.

Terminix
(800) 837-6464
www.terminix.com

VEHICLE REGISTRATION

The Massachusetts Registry of Motor Vehicles charges $87.50 to convert a typical out-of-state registration. You'll also have to pay $50 for a title fee and 5 percent sales tax based on the value of your car. Nineteen ninety-five and later model cars with 7,500 miles or fewer on the odometer must meet California emissions standards. You'll also have to show proof of Massachusetts insurance (so you need to buy insurance coverage before applying for registration).

The registry charges $87.50 to convert a license from another state or territory, Canada, or Mexico (and another $15 for a motorcycle license). Residents of countries other than Canada and Mexico must pass written, road, and eye tests.

Disabled drivers can obtain a placard for temporary use or permanent license plates for the same cost as regular registration. The required forms are available at RMV offices across the state or online in the "Forms and Files" section at www.massrmv.com.

In addition, a number of Boston-area cities and towns, including Boston, Cambridge, and Somerville, require residential parking permits if you want to park your car on the street. See chapter 1 for more information on requirements in specific communities.

Auto insurance is mandatory in Massachusetts. At a minimum, you have to buy insurance that covers personal injury to others, injury caused by uninsured drivers, and damage to another's property. Unlike in most other states, in Massachusetts insurance rates are set each year by the state. Exactly how much you pay will depend on

MOVING TIP

Save the TV, VCR, kids' videos, and a box of toys to be loaded on the truck last. Upon arriving at your destination, if you can't find someone to baby-sit, set aside a room in your home where your young children can safely play. Set up the TV and VCR and unpack the kids' videos along with some toys and snacks.

where you garage your car (expect to pay a lot more in Boston than in the suburbs) and your driving experience (drivers with a clean record for at least six years get a fairly hefty discount). In recent years, some insurers have offered additional good-driver discounts of up to 12 percent. For more information, see the state Division of Insurance's auto-insurance site at www.state.ma.us/doi/Consumer/CSS_auto.html.

MOVING TIP

When figuring out how to get to your new home, don't rely on an online mapping service. Boston-area road oddities such as rotaries often give them conniptions and can result in wildly inaccurate or out-of-the-way directions.

After you've registered your car, you have seven days to get an emissions and safety inspection at a state-licensed garage. The inspection costs $29 and is good for one year. Once a year, you'll get an auto-excise bill from your city or town. It'll be for 2.5 percent of the depreciated value of your car.

TAKING CARE OF THE FINANCIAL IMPLICATIONS OF YOUR MOVE

Now that you have arrived, you can take care of some of the financial and tax implications of your move. Here are some things to think about (it's also wise to consult an accountant):

- Some of your moving expenses may be tax-deductible. Prepare for tax filing by collecting receipts from your move. Also contact the Internal Revenue Service to obtain the publication and form you need. Visit www.irs.gov or call (800) 829-3676.

- State income tax. Massachusetts charged a tax rate of 5.85 percent in 2000. The rate is due to decrease to 5 percent by 2003. For help with your relocation-related taxes, visit www.virtualrelocation.com and click on "Tax Advice."

MOVING TIP

Start eating those canned foods a few weeks before you move—or donate them to a local food pantry. They're bulky and heavy.

• Other income sources may have tax implications. As you prepare to file, you'll want to consider any other sources of income and whether Massachusetts will tax you on this income. For example, Massachusetts has a capital-gains tax rate of 12 pecent.

Home at Last

Once the truck is unloaded, the boxes are unpacked, and the pictures are hung, once you're sleeping in a *bed*—instead of on a loose mattress—you'll dream sweet dreams. Tomorrow, with the stress of this move slipping away behind you and the next move not even a faint glimmer on the horizon of your mind, you'll begin to discover the opportunities and savor the possibilities of your new city, new job, new school—your new home.

Getting to Know Your Town

CHAPTER 6

What's Around Town

In 1858 Oliver Wendell Holmes called Boston "the Hub" for the first time (he modestly said Boston was just the hub of the solar system; later generations extended the definition to the entire universe). Okay, so maybe he was exaggerating a bit, but Boston offers a wealth of things to do and see. If not the hub of the universe, Boston is at least the hub of New England, with world-class museums, dining that spans all cuisines and price ranges, major league sports, and stimulating intellectual activities—all in a compact size that's easy to navigate by public transit or even by foot.

Unlike some cities that regularly plow their past under, Boston is defined and guided by its history. Boston's early, almost random, street layout may cause drivers no end of grief, but it makes the city a walker's paradise and gives some neighborhoods, such as the North End, a unique European feel. There are so many charming areas and scenes, many immortalized on post cards: sailboats serenely gliding across the Charles River under Beacon Hill, the Swan Boats in the Public Garden, gaslights along cobblestone streets on Beacon Hill. But all of Boston's neighborhoods have their hidden charms, from the Stony Brook forest in West Roxbury and Hyde Park to the Victorian houses of Jamaica Plain and Dorchester.

A key to understanding and enjoying Boston, of course, is history. Boston occupies a storied place in American history, from the Revolution to the discovery of the telephone. Today Bostonians take pride in that history (in the 1800s, Boston almost let the Old State

House, the seat of colonial government and scene of the Boston Massacre, be shipped off to Chicago), and it sometimes permeates life here. Before contractors began excavating for the massive Big Dig tunnel project, archaeologists went to the sites to uncover relics from Boston's colonial past. New buildings are scrutinized for their impact on surrounding buildings; the *Boston Globe*'s architecture critic, Robert Campbell, won a Pulitzer Prize for his columns on the importance of maintaining Boston's unique feel.

But don't think that Boston is stuck in the past. All those colleges, research centers, and high-tech and financial-services companies help ensure that Boston doesn't become ossified. You'll see this in architecture (the all-glass Hancock Building is a modern classic), music (you'll be able to satisfy your musical tastes, no matter what they are, in Boston), and stimulating discussions and lecture series. Food used to be a holdout, but recent years have seen an explosion of restaurants that offer daring new dishes (but don't worry, you can still easily find such classics as New England clam chowder).

In recent years, Boston has rediscovered its waterfront and Boston Harbor, once regarded mainly as a place to put factories and sewage. With an expensive harbor cleanup nearing completion, seals and even dolphins have returned to the harbor. Many of the islands are now part of a nascent national recreational area.

Note: Two valuable resources will be the Thursday *Boston Globe*, which has a comprehensive Calendar section, and the *Boston Phoenix*, a free alternative weekly available in boxes throughout downtown and nearby areas.

Libraries

The Boston Public Library (BPL) is one of the oldest and largest public library systems in the country. The main branch in Copley Square serves as a research library (its telephone reference desk is excellent at answering the most obscure questions) and doubles as a museum, with murals by John Singer Sargent and a sculpture courtyard. Neighborhood branches offer many services, including children's story hours and museum passes. Most libraries in Greater Boston are members of regional systems that let patrons obtain books from neighboring communities. Under state law, any Massachusetts resident can obtain a BPL card (Boston residents in turn can get a card at the libraries in neighboring communities).

BPL Main Branch
700 Boylston Street
Copley Square
Back Bay
(617) 536-5400

www.bpl.org

www.bpl.org/WWW/directions.html

Neighborhood branch information.

Museums and Zoos

One thing the Boston area doesn't lack is museums. From big-name museums like the Museum of Fine Arts and the Museum of Science to smaller, college-based facilities, you could spend months in galleries and exhibits and still not see them all. CityPass ($30.25 for adults; $14 for teens 12–17) is a discount ticket that gets you into six museums and attractions (New England Aquarium, JFK Library, Museum of Fine Arts, the Isabella Stewart Gardner Museum, and the Museum of Science): www.citypass.net/boston.html. You can find directions to local museums via public transportation at www.mbta.com/newsinfo/geninfo/museums. Some museums have limited hours; call ahead (or check out the Web site) first.

Adams National Historic Site
135 Adams Street
Quincy
(617) 770-1175

www.nps.gov/adam

See where two U.S. presidents were born.

Larz Anderson Auto Museum
Larz Anderson Park
15 Newton Street
Brookline
(617) 522-6547

www.mot.org

Lots and lots of old cars.

Armenian Library and
Museum of America
65 Main Street
Watertown
(617) 926-2562

Large collection of Armenian textiles and a permanent exhibit on the Armenian genocide.

Boston African-American
National Historic Site
14 Beacon Street
Beacon Hill
(617) 742-5415

www.nps.gov/boaf

Fifteen pre–Civil War buildings related to Boston's nineteenth-century African-American community.

Boston Children's Museum
300 Congress Street
Waterfront
(617) 426-8855

www.bostonkids.org

Bostonian Historical Society
and Museum
206 Washington Street
Downtown Crossing
(617) 720-1713

www.bostonhistory.org

Located in the Old State House, the seat of colonial government. Right next to the Boston National Historic Park visitor center.

Boston Tea Party Ship
and Museum
Congress Street Bridge
Waterfront
(617) 338-1773

www.bostonteapartyship.com

Throw some tea in the harbor.

Boston University Art Gallery
855 Commonwealth Avenue
Allston
(617) 353-3329

www.bu.edu/art

Free exhibits September–May, mainly of twentieth-century art.

Charles River Museum
of Industry
154 Moody Street
Waltham
(781) 893-5410

www.ultranet.com/~crmi

Explores the history of American industry and technology.

Commonwealth Museum

220 Morrissey Boulevard
Columbia Point, Dorchester
(617) 727-9268

www.state.ma.us/sec/mus/
musidx.htm

Exhibits on Massachusetts history, from colonial days to the Big Dig, many based on materials in the official state archive, located at the same site. Free.

Davis Museum and Cultural Center Wellesley College

Wellesley
(781) 283-3382

www.wellesley.edu/
DavisMuseum/davismenu.html

Art exhibits. Free.

DeCordova Museum

51 Sandy Pond Road
Lincoln
(781) 259-8355

www.decordova.org

Contemporary art museum and statue garden, not far from Walden Pond.

Dreams of Freedom

1 Milk Street
Boston
(617) 695-9990

www.dreamsoffreedom.org

Devoted to the immigrant experience in Boston.

Franklin Park Zoo

1 Franklin Park Road
(617) 541-LION

www.zoonewengland.com

If you've been to the zoos in the Bronx, Atlanta, or San Diego, you might be disappointed by this zoo, which largely feels like a holdover from the 1950s. However, the Tropical Forest building is well worth a visit for its tropical birds and other animals—especially the gorilla exhibit, which features a realistic-looking home for these primates. Kids love to sit in the front of the old Jeep that has been partially placed inside the lion exhibit (don't worry, the windshield has been replaced with unbreakable glass).

Isabella Stewart Gardner Museum

280 The Fenway
(617) 566-1401

www.gardnermuseum.org

Unique art museum, featuring European masterpieces and reflecting the taste of a woman who left her home as a museum on the condition it be left exactly as it was when she died.

Harvard Museum of Natural History
26 Oxford Street
Cambridge
(617) 495-3045

www.hmnh.harvard.edu

Specializing in rocks, gems, birds, and bugs. Home of the famous, if somewhat overrated, glass flowers.

Harvard University Art Museums
32 Quincy Street and Broadway
Cambridge
(617) 495-9400

www.artmuseums.harvard.edu

Three museums housing more than 150,000 objects from ancient times to the modern era from around the world.

Institute of Contemporary Art
955 Boylston Street
Back Bay
(617) 266-5152

www.icaboston.org

John F. Kennedy Birthplace
83 Beals Street
Brookline
(617) 566-1689

www.nps.gov/jofi

John F. Kennedy Library and Museum
Columbia Point
Dorchester
(877) 616-4599

www.cs.umb.edu/jfklibrary

Changing exhibits on the life and times of both John and Jacqueline Kennedy.

Longfellow National Historic Site
105 Brattle Street
Cambridge
(617) 876-4491

www.nps.gov/long

Home of the author of "The Midnight Ride of Paul Revere."

Longyear Museum
120 Seaver Street
Brookline
(617) 278-9000

MOVING TIP

Moving from New York State? Keep your E-ZPass transponder on your car windshield—it works on the Massachusetts Turnpike, which'll save you some time at toll plazas.

www.longyear.org

Dedicated to the life of Mary Baker Eddy, the founder of Christian Science.

McMullen Museum of Art Boston College

Newton
(617) 552-8100

www.bc.edu/bc_org/avp/cas/artmuseum

Permanent exhibits include Flemish tapestries, Italian paintings from the sixteenth to nineteenth centuries and nineteenth-century European and American paintings.

MIT List Visual Arts Center

20 Ames Street, E15
Cambridge
(617) 253-4680

web.mit.edu/lvac

Contemporary art exhibits at MIT.

MIT Museum

265 Massachusetts Avenue
Cambridge
(617) 253-4444

web.mit.edu/museum

Highlighting the intersection of art and technology—and the Hall of Hacks (unusual tricks pulled by MIT students).

Museum of Afro American History

Joy Street and Smith Court
Beacon Hill
(617) 725-0022

www.afroammuseum.org

Museum of Bad Art

Basement, Dedham Community Theater
580 High Street
Dedham
(617) 325-8224

www.glyphs.com/moba

Only the very worst art goes on display in this museum. Free.

Museum of Fine Arts

465 Huntington Avenue
(617) 267-9300

www.mfa.org/home.htm

Boston's largest art museum, where you'll find the big-name traveling exhibits. Collections range from prehistoric to modern. It's especially strong in Egyptian and early American art.

Museum of the National Center of Afro-American Artists

300 Walnut Avenue
Roxbury
(617) 442-8614

www.afamnet.com/ncaaamuseum

Museum of Science

On the Charles River Bridge
between Boston and Cambridge
(617) 723-2500

www.mos.org

Lots of exhibits with buttons to press, plus a planetarium and OmniMax theater.

New England Aquarium

Central Wharf
Waterfront
(617) 973-5200

www.neaq.org

Features a spiral ramp around a giant ocean tank. Also has a large penguin exhibit and runs whale-watch tours.

Frederick Law Olmsted National Historic Site

99 Warren Street
Brookline
(617) 566-1689

www.nps.gov/frla

Home of the designer of Boston's Emerald Necklace park system (and New York's Central Park).

Peabody Essex Museum

East India Square
Salem
(800) 745-4054

www.pem.org

Art and cultural artifacts, with a special emphasis on maritime art and history.

Peabody Museum of Archaeology and Ethnology

11 Divinity Avenue
Cambridge
(617) 496-1027

www.peabody.harvard.edu

Yet another Harvard museum!

Plimouth Plantation

Off Route 3 in Plymouth
(508) 746-1622

www.plimoth.org

See how the Pilgrims lived; guides dress and talk like Pilgrims. Open April through November.

Paul Revere House

19 North Square
North End
(617) 523-2338

www.paulreverehouse.org

Oldest house in Boston, once owned by you know who.

Rose Art Museum Brandeis University

415 South Street
Waltham
(781) 736-3434

www.brandeis.edu/rose

Contemporary art. Free.

**Spellman Museum of
Stamps and Postal History
Regis College**
235 Wellesley Street
Weston
(781) 768-8367

www.spellman.org

U.S.S. *Constitution* Museum
Charlestown Navy Yard
(617) 426-1812

www.ussconstitutionmuseum.org

Old Ironsides.

Art Galleries

Newbury Street is home to Boston's chi-chi galleries, but you'll also
find a number of galleries in other neighborhoods, in particular the
South End.

NEWBURY STREET

Alpha Gallery
14 Newbury Street
(617) 536-4465

Contemporary American and
European art.

Arden Gallery
129 Newbury Street
(617) 247-0610

www.ardengallery.com

Contemporary paintings and
sculpture.

Kelly Barrette Fine Art
129 Newbury Street
(617) 266-2475

www.kellybarrettefineart.com

Contemporary work by Boston
and New York artists.

CITY FACT

Eben Horsford, who discovered baking
powder in the nineteenth century, paid for
a statue of Leif Ericsson on the Commonwealth Avenue Mall at Charlesgate to
commemorate his belief that the Vikings
sailed up the Charles River.

Barton-Ryan Gallery
38 Newbury Street, 4th floor
(617) 867-0662

www.bartonryan.com

Chase Gallery
129 Newbury Street
(617) 859-7222

www.chasegallery.com

Gallery NAGA
67 Newbury Street
(617) 267-9060

www.gallerynaga.com

Judy Ann Goldman Fine Art
14 Newbury Street
(617) 424-8468

Robert Klein Gallery
38 Newbury Street
(617) 267-7997

Photographs.

Barbara Krakow Gallery
10 Newbury Street
(617) 262-4490

www.barbarakrakowgallery.com

Mercury Gallery
8 Newbury Street, 2nd floor
(617) 859-0054

www.mercurygallery.com

Miller Block Gallery
14 Newbury Street, 3rd floor
(617) 536-4650

Nielsen Gallery
179 Newbury Street
(617) 266-4835

www.nielsengallery.com

Pepper Gallery
38 Newbury Street
(617) 236-4497

www.peppergalleryboston.com

Pucker Gallery
171 Newbury Street
(617) 267-9473

www.puckergallery.com

Paintings, graphics, sculpture, and carvings from around the world.

Beth Urdang Gallery
14 Newbury Street, 3rd floor
(617) 424-8468

Specializing in American art between 1915 and 1945.

Howard Yezerski Gallery
14 Newbury Street, 3rd floor
(617) 262-0550

www.howardyezerskigallery.com

ELSEWHERE

Bromfield Art Gallery
560 Harrison Avenue
South End
(617) 451-3605

www.bromfieldartgallery.com

A gallery run by the artists it represents.

Gallery @ Green Street

141 Green Street
Jamaica Plain
(617) 522-0000

www.jameshull.com

Gallery funded and run by artists in an Orange Line subway station.

Gallery Bershad

99 Dover Street
Davis Square, Somerville
(617) 629-9400, ext. 3

www.bershad.com/gb/

Bernard Toale Gallery

450 Harrison Avenue
South End
(617) 482- 2477

www.bernardtoalegallery.com

United South End Artists

www.useaboston.org

A group of South End artists.

Theatre

Boston's Theatre District is a Broadway in miniature. In fact, Broadway-bound plays often open here first. Beyond the theatre district, a number of troupes offer everything from avant-garde to classical plays. BosTix offers half-price tickets the day of a performance at booths at Quincy Market and at the corner of Boylston and Dartmouth streets in Copley Square, Back Bay: (617) 723-5181, www.boston.com/artsboston/Bostix.htm.

THEATRE DISTRICT

Broadway in Boston

(617) 880-2400

www.broadwayinboston.com

Operates the Colonial and Wilbur Theatres and the Charles Playhouse.

Emerson Majestic Theatre

219 Tremont Street
(617) 824-8000

www.maj.org

Lyric Stage Company

140 Clarendon Street
(617) 437-7172

www.lyricstage.com

Shear Madness
Charles Playhouse Stage II
74 Warrenton Street
(617) 426-5225

www.shearmadness.com/
boston.html

The longest-running play in U.S. history. The audience decides the outcome of this comic whodunit each night.

Wang Center for the Performing Arts
270 Tremont Street
(617) 482-9393

www.boston.com/wangcenter

Consists of two theatres: the Wang and the Shubert.

ELSEWHERE

American Repertory Theatre
Loeb Drama Center
64 Brattle Street
Cambridge
(617) 547-8300

www.fas.harvard.edu/~art

Boston Center for the Arts
539 Tremont Street
South End
(617) 426-5000

www.bcaonline.org

Nonprofit group that sponsors a variety of performances and exhibitions in several South End buildings, including the historic Cyclorama.

Boston Children's Theatre
321 Columbus Avenue, South End
(617) 424-6634

www.bostonchildrenstheatre.org

Plays for and by children.

Boston Theatre Works
(617) 728-4321

www.bostontheatreworks.com

Performs classical and contemporary plays at several Boston-area locations.

Footlight Club
7A Eliot Street
Jamaica Plain
(617) 524-3200

www.footlight.org

The oldest community theatre in the United States.

Huntington Theatre Company
264 Huntington Avenue
(617) 266-0800

www.huntingtontheatre.org

New Repertory Theatre
1155 Walnut Street
Newton Highlands
(617) 332-1646

www.newrep.org

Publick Theatre
165 Friend Street
Brighton
(617) 782-5425

www.publick.org

Performances in an open-air amphitheater on the banks of the Charles River.

SpeakEasy Stage Company
Boston Center for the Arts
539 Tremont Street
South End
(617) 426-2787

www.speakeasystage.com

Specializes in plays never before done in New England.

Spingold Theatre
Brandeis University
415 South Street
Waltham
(781) 736-3400

www.brandeis.edu/theater/boxoffice.html

Wheelock Family Theatre
200 The Riverway
Fenway
(617) 879-2000

www.wheelock.edu/wft.htm

Classical/Early Music

Boston Lyric Opera
Shubert Theatre
265 Tremont Street
Theatre District
(617) 482-9393

www.blo.org

Boston Modern Orchestra
Jordan Hall, New England
Conservatory
30 Gainsborough Street
Back Bay
(617) 363-0396

www.bmop.org

Performs twentieth- and twenty-first-century works.

CITY FACT

Parker House rolls are named for the historic Omni Parker House Hotel, where Ho Chi Minh worked as a busboy and Malcolm X as a waiter.

Boston Symphony Orchestra
Symphony Hall
301 Massachusetts Avenue
(617) 266-1492

www.bso.org

Actually two world-famous orchestras, made up of many of the same musicians but with different directors. Both play in Symphony Hall, acoustically one of the country's best performance halls. The BSO plays serious classical music; the Boston Pops Orchestra plays lighter fare. The BSO performs in the summer at Tanglewood in the Berkshires; the Pops are famous for the free Fourth of July concert on the Charles River Esplanade.

Cantata Singers
Jordan Hall, New England
Conservatory
30 Gainsborough Street
Back Bay
(617) 267-6502

www.cantatasingers.org

Chameleon Arts Ensemble
First and Second Church
Marlborough and Berkeley Streets
Back Bay
(617) 427-8200

www.chameleonarts.org

Chamber music.

Handel & Hayden Society
(617) 266-3605

www.handelandhaydn.org

One of the country's oldest period orchestra and chorus groups. Performs in both Boston and Cambridge.

Jordan Hall
New England Conservatory
of Music
290 Huntington Avenue
(617) 585-1100

www.newenglandconservatory.
edu/calendar

Scores of free solo and ensemble concerts.

Longwood Symphony
Orchestra
Jordan Hall
New England
Conservatory of Music
290 Huntington Avenue
(617) 332-7011

www.longwoodsymphony.org

Orchestra composed entirely of doctors, nurses, and other medical professionals from the Longwood Medical Area.

**Pro Arte Chamber Orchestra
of Boston
Sanders Theatre**
*Kirkland and Quincy Streets
Cambridge*
(617) 661-7067

www.proarte.org

Dance

Boston Ballet
*19 Clarendon Street
Back Bay*
(617) 695-6955

www.bostonballet.com

Boston Conservatory
8 The Fenway
(617) 536-6340

www.bostonconservatory.edu

This music, theatre, and dance
college offers numerous free
performances.

Dance Umbrella
Emerson Majestic Theatre
*219 Tremont Street
Theatre District*
(617) 824-8000

www.danceumbrella.org

Contemporary and "culturally
diverse" dance.

Comedy

Boston has long been a comedy hotbed. Jay Leno, for example, got
his start doing standup here. Other Boston alumni include Conan
O'Brien (who grew up in Brookline), Dennis Leary, Janeane Garo-
falo, Bobcat Goldthwaite, and Jonathan Katz.

Boston Comedy Festival
(617) 327-3048

www.bostoncomedyfestival.com

Annual series of shows held in
various Theatre District locations in early spring.

Comedy Connection
245 Quincy Market Place
Faneuil Hall
(617) 248-9700

www.comedyconnectionboston.
com

When big names from out of town play Boston, they often play here.

Comedy Studio
1236 Massachusetts Avenue
Cambridge
(617) 661-6507

www.thecomedystudio.com

Comedy and Chinese food Thursday through Sunday nights in Harvard Square.

Dick Doherty Comedy
124 Boylston Street
(800) 401-2221

www.dickdoherty.com

Shows Thursday through Saturday nights. Sunday is open-mike night.

Improv Asylum
216 Hanover Street
North End
(617) 263-6887

www.improvasylum.com

Shows Thursday, Friday, and Saturday nights. As the name implies, improvisational comedy.

ImprovBoston
1253 Cambridge Street
Inman Square, Cambridge
(617) 576-1253

www.improvboston.com

The Boston area's oldest improv troupe, performs Wednesdays, Fridays, Saturdays, and Sundays.

Ideas

You won't want for intellectual stimulation in Boston. All those colleges offer free lectures to the public. But even when school's out, you can count on bookstore talks, lectures, and other events. The *Boston Globe*'s Calendar section (in Thursday's paper) and the *Boston Phoenix* (which comes out on Thursday as well) offer extensive listings.

Ford Hall Forum

(617) 373-5800

www.dac.neu.edu/fordhallforum

Free lectures on a variety of topics. It's the nation's oldest public lecture series. Typical lectures include a forty-five-minute speech and a forty-five-minute period for audience questions. Held in several locations across Boston.

Movies

Boston and surrounding towns have as many googolplexes as you could need. Look in the daily paper or call MovieFone at (617) 333-3456 to see what's playing. The Boston area also has a number of art and second-run cinemas, many housed in classic pre-war theatres, as well as special film series.

Brattle Theater

40 Brattle Street
Cambridge
(617) 876-6837

www.beaconcinema.com/brattle

Screens a wide variety of classic, foreign, and independent films (and hosts the annual Bugs Bunny Film Festival).

Capitol Theater

204 Massachusetts Avenue
Arlington
(781) 648-4340

Coolidge Corner Theater

290 Harvard Street
Brookline
(617) 734-2500

www.coolidge.org

Screens everything from '30s films to science-fiction classics. Has special midnight shows on Fridays and Saturdays. Owned by a nonprofit organization that helped save it from the wrecking ball in the mid-1980s.

Dedham Community Theater

580 High Street
Dedham
(781) 326-1463

**Harvard Film Archive
Carpenter Center for the
Visual Arts**
24 Quincy Street
Cambridge
(617) 495-4700

www.harvardfilmarchive.org

Independent, rare, classic, political, and just plain esoteric films from all over the world.

**Mugar Omni Theater
Museum of Science**
Science Park
(617) 723-2500

www.mos.org/
whats_happening/index.html

3-D IMAX surround movies.

**Museum of Fine Arts
Film Program**
465 Huntington Avenue
(617) 369-3300

www.mfa.org/film

Contemporary international movies, restored classics, and independent U.S. films.

Studio Cinema
376 Trapelo Road
Belmont
(617) 484-1706

www.studiocinema.com

Second-run films. On Tuesdays, two get in for the price of one.

West Newton Cinema
1296 Washington Street
(617) 964-6060

www.westnewtoncinema.com

Foreign and second-run films. Best popcorn in the Boston area—uses real butter.

Restaurants

Once known mainly for seafood and boiled things, Boston has exploded as a restaurant town over the past decade. Today the city has a number of celebrity chefs (beyond Julia Child, who recently moved to California) and foodies follow their exploits as avidly as other Bostonians watch the Red Sox. In addition, Boston is now home to numerous ethnic restaurants—and even seafood restaurants that do more than just broil up some whitefish (although, truth be told, nothing is quite as satisfying as a bowl of thick, creamy New England clam chowder on a cold day).

Although there are restaurants all over the place, three areas stand out in particular for their cuisine. If you're hungry but can't decide where to eat, you could do worse than walking around these areas scoping out menus until you find one you like.

THE NORTH END

This heavily Italian neighborhood is home to a mouth-watering succession of restaurants (both northern and southern cuisine), caffes (where you can watch Italian soccer as you sip your expresso), and bakeries. Walk down Hanover Street and some of its side streets and just keep looking until you find the little restaurant that best suits your mood. You can get a good, inexpensive pizza at Pizzeria Regina or blow a week's paycheck on dinner at Mamma Maria's.

Wherever you eat, don't get dessert. Instead, go back up Hanover Street to Mike's Pastry at (617) 742-3050, or the Modern Bakery at (617) 523-3783, for some cannoli or other treats. Or stop in Caffe Vittoria at (617) 227-7606, for some expresso.

HARVARD STREET, ALLSTON

Attracted by cheap rents, numerous immigrants have set up ethnic restaurants here, serving such fare as Brazilian and Vietnamese. (One of the area's few kosher delis is just over the line in Brookline.) The Sunset Grill has what could be one of the world's largest beer selections (hundreds of brands).

MOODY STREET, WALTHAM

Once something of a forlorn area, this shopping street about ten miles west of Boston has also become an ethnic-dining mecca, lined with everything from Mexican to Indian restaurants, as well as Watch City Brewing Company, which makes its own beers.

KEEPING UP WITH THE FOODIES

To keep up with the Boston food scene, look for reviews in the Calendar section of the Thursday *Boston Globe* and the weekly *Boston Phoenix*. The following are some online resources:

The Boston Bagel FAQ

www.boston-online.com/
bagels.html

Answers the all-important question of where to get good bagels. Also explains the difference between Boston and New York bagels.

bostondine.com

www.bostondine.com

Search for restaurants by price, cuisine, or location.

bostonchefs.com

www.bostonchefs.com

Has local restaurant news and bios of local chefs.

Irish Pubs and Restaurants

www.celticweb.com/pubs.html

Kosher Resources in the Boston Area

www.kashrut.com/travel/Boston/

Mayor's Food Court

www.mayorsfoodcourt.com

Look up the most recent inspection report for Boston restaurants.

Phantom Gourmet

www.phantomgourmet.com

Restaurant reviews by both a reviewer and diners.

RESTAURANTS TO TRY

What follows is a list of restaurants that will get you started in Boston dining. It's hardly a complete list, so if you don't see something you'd like to try, or are looking for a restaurant closer to home, check out the *Globe* and *Phoenix* reviews (see previous), or ask your new neighbors. Restaurants are rated on their costs—with one star being inexpensive and four stars being the kind of place you'll definitely need a valid credit card for.

Abe & Louie's ★★★
793 Boylston Street
Back Bay
(617) 536-6300

www.abeandlouies.com

Solid, unpretentious steakhouse.

Addis Red Sea ★
544 Tremont Street
South End
(617) 426-8727

Ethiopian fare—no forks.

Ali's Roti Restaurant ★

1188 Blue Hill Avenue
Mattapan
(617) 298-9850)

1035 Tremont Street
Roxbury
(617) 427-1079

25 Poplar Street
Roslindale
(617) 325-8079

Ali's serves West Indian curried dishes, from chicken and shrimp to goat and oxtail. You can get them as entrées or as rotis, which is basically a curry wrap.

Amrhein's ★

80 West Broadway
South Boston
(617) 268-6189

The quintessential Southie restaurant; if you want to get a good feel for the neighborhood, eat here. Huge Sunday brunch.

Aujourd'hui ★★★★

Four Seasons Hotel
200 Boylston Street
Park Square
(617) 338-4400

Haute cuisine in a four-star hotel.

B&D Delicatessen ★★

1653 Beacon Street
Brookline
(617) 232-3727

A classic Jewish deli. Chopped liver? Of course. And everything from knishes to kishke. Weekends feature brunch.

Bangkok Bistro ★

1952 Beacon Street
Cleveland Circle, Brighton
(617) 739-7270

Shoehorned into a narrow space, this is the place for good, inexpensive Thai food—just the thing to eat before or after a movie at the nearby Cleveland Circle Cinema.

Bangkok Cuisine ★★

177A Massachusetts Avenue
(617) 262-5377

Old-timers remember when Thai food was something exotic—and this restaurant was the only place in Boston to get it.

Barcode ★★★

955 Boylston Street
Back Bay
(617) 421-1818

barcode.citysearch.com

French-Asian cuisine in a dining room meant to suggest a British colonial outpost.

Barking Crab ★

88 Sleeper Street
Northern Avenue Bridge
South Boston
(617) 426-2722

As close as Boston gets to a
Maine lobster shack: waterside
picnic tables for boisterous families and lobster bibs all around.
Large portions, cheap.

Bartley's Burger Cottage

1245 Massachusetts Avenue
Harvard Square
Cambridge
(617) 354-6559

Rub elbows with Harvard students in this old-time college
burger joint.

Bay Tower Room ★★★★

60 State Street
Financial District
(617) 723-1666

www.baytower.com

Floor-to-ceiling windows over-
look Boston Harbor from the
thirty-third floor of a downtown skyscraper. Good spot for
a romantic dinner.

B.B. Wolf ★

109 Brookline Avenue
Fenway
(617) 247-2227

Pack the napkins as you plow
into the hearty ribs at this unpretentious place near Fenway Park.

Biba ★★★

272 Boylston Street
Back Bay
(617) 426-7878

Expect the unexpected here.
Chef Lydia Shire likes to experi-
ment with Native American
food, so the menu is constantly
changing.

Blue Diner ★

150 Kneeland Street
South Station
(617) 695-0087

Not really a diner, but the place
to go for meatloaf at 3 A.M. It's
open around the clock.

Bob the Chef's ★

604 Columbus Avenue
South End
(617) 536-6204

www.bobthechefs.com

Classic Southern soul food with
some Louisiana-style dishes.
Jazz brunch on Sundays.

Bomboa ★★

35 Stanhope Street
South End
(617) 236-6363

www.bomboa.com

Fusion of Brazilian and French
food, eaten to a pounding
Brazilian beat.

Bon Appetit Restaurant ★

1132 Blue Hill Avenue
Dorchester
(617) 825-5544

Haitian food.

Bricco ★★★

241 Hanover Street
North End
(617) 248-6800

An Italian grill with a large wine list.

Bukhara ★★

701 Centre Street
Jamaica Plain
(617) 522-2195

Both northern and southern Indian cuisine in a serene atmosphere.

Buzzy's Fabulous Roast Beef ★

327 Cambridge Street
Charles Circle
Beacon Hill
(617) 242-7722

Hole-in-the-wall serves roast beef throughout the night— open twenty-four hours.

Cafe Budapest ★★★★

90 Exeter Street
Back Bay
(617) 266-1979

Hungarian food, served in an Old World dining room.

Cafe St. Petersburg ★★★

236 Washington Street
Brookline Village
(617) 277-7100

Russian food, from blini to blintzes. Closed Mondays.

Chau Chow City Restaurant ★★

83 Essex Street
Chinatown
(617) 338-8158

Three-story Chinese restaurant. The first two floors specialize in seafood, the third in dim sum.

China Pearl ★

9 Tyler Street
Chinatown
(617) 426-4338

When you think of Chinese restaurants, the China Pearl is what would come to mind. You could seriously OD on fried things, but it also serves dim sum in the late-night hours.

DeNo's Pizza and Subs ★

2040 Centre Street
West Roxbury
(617) 469-3220

Good thin-crust pizza.

Dottie's ★

5 Fairmount Avenue
Hyde Park
(617) 364-9814

Old-time soda fountain and lunch place (but it also serves breakfast all day).

Durgin Park ★★

340 Faneuil Hall Market Place
(617) 227-2038

www.durginpark.com

A Boston tradition. Hearty American food, eaten at communal long tables and served by waitresses who aren't as surly as they used to be. One of the few restaurants in Boston that still serves Boston baked beans.

Dynasty Restaurant ★★

33 Edinboro Street
Chinatown
(617) 350-7777

Basic, satisfying Chinese food.

Elephant Walk ★★

900 Beacon Street
Beacon Hill
(617) 247-1500

2067 Massachusetts Avenue
Cambridge
(617) 492-6900

Mixture of French and Cambodian cuisine.

The Federalist ★★★★

15 Beacon Street
Beacon Hill
(617) 670-2515

Dress up for this restaurant, where you'll find flavorful, small dishes (with an emphasis on seafood). Has a huge wine list.

Fontaine's ★

1436 VFW Parkway
West Roxbury
(617) 327-7600

The giant neon chicken waving at passing motorists gives you an idea of what's in store. Fontaine's serves chicken in every conceivable style and not much else. You'll feel like you've stepped into a '50s roadhouse (well, one that serves only chicken).

John Harvard's Brew House ★★

33 Dunster Street
Harvard Square
Cambridge
(617) 868-3585

Basic American pub food served with beer brewed on the premises.

Kashmir

279 Newbury Street
Back Bay
(617) 536-1695

www.kashmirspices.com/
KashmirRestaurant/
kashmirhome.html

Elegant Indian restaurant.

Legal Seafood ★★★

26 Park Plaza
(617) 426-4444

100 Huntington Avenue
Copley Place
Back Bay
(617) 266-7775

800 Boylston Street
Prudential Center
Back Bay
(617) 266-6800

255 State Street
Long Wharf
(617) 227-3115

43 Boylston Street
Chestnut Hill Shopping Center
Newton
(617) 277-7300

5 Cambridge Center
Kendall Square
Cambridge
(617) 864-3400

www.lsf.com

When out-of-towners think of Boston seafood, this local chain often springs to mind. Indeed, the food is fresh and, in recent years, more varied than your standard baked and broiled whitefish. But it can be pricey. It's the classic expense-account restaurant. If somebody is trying to sell your company something, make him take you to Legal.

Maison Robert ★★★★

45 School Street
Downtown Crossing
(617) 227-3370

www.maisonrobert.com

Upstairs, traditional French cuisine (jacket and tie required). Downstairs, Ben's Café offers less formal (and less expensive) fare. Housed in the old Boston City Hall.

Mamma Maria

3 North Square
North End
(617) 523-0077

www.mammamaria.com

Elegant northern Italian cuisine.

Mistral ★★★

223 Columbus Avenue
South End
(617) 867-9300

www.mistralbistro.com

French dining with a New England accent; also offers thin-crust pizzas.

Naked Fish ★★

16-18 North Street
(opposite Quincy Market)
(617) 742-3333

725 Cochituate Road (Route 30)
Framingham
(508) 820-9494

516 Adams Street
Quincy
(617) 745-9700

455 Totten Pond Road
Waltham
(781) 684-0500

114 Beacon Street
Newton
(617) 965-0110

343 Arsenal Street
Watertown
(617) 924-6400

215 Broadway (Route 1 north)
Lynnfield
(781) 586-8300

www.nakedfish.com

One of the few restaurants you'll find that has a formal philosophy of life: If you just want to eat the food, lie when your server asks you if this is your first visit; otherwise, he or she will recite it. The fish in these Cuban-accented restaurants is cooked on wood-fired grills, using simple ingredients such as olive oil, lemon juice, and herbs.

Olives ★★★

10 City Square
Charlestown
(617) 242-1999

Like Biba, another restaurant with a celebrity chef, in this case, Todd English. Modern American cuisine packs them in. Expect a wait because reservations aren't accepted for parties smaller than six.

Pandan Leaf ★★

250 Harvard Avenue
Coolidge Corner
Brookline
(617) 566-9393

Serves Malaysian food, which is an interesting mix of Chinese, Indian, and Thai influences.

Pizzeria Regina ★

11 Thatcher Street
North End
(617) 227-0565

www.pizzeriaregina.com

Classic thin-crust Boston pizza, nice and oily. There are Pizzeria Reginas in Quincy Market and the Burlington Mall, but make the original North End one (with the brick oven built in 1888) your first Boston pizza stop.

Redbones Barbecue ★

55 Chester Street
Somerville
(617) 628-2200

Texas-style ribs. The upstairs dining room is great for kids; downstairs, you'll find the bar.

Rubin's Kosher Restaurant ★

500 Harvard Street
Brookline
(617) 566-8761

As close as you'll get to a New York kosher deli. Work up an appetite before you go. Closed Friday evenings and Saturdays.

Samia's ★

1894 Centre Street
West Roxbury
(617) 323-5181

When you need to satisfy your kebob and hummus fixes, head to Samia's. Chances are, you'll want to get your food to go— it has only three tables.

Santarpio's ★

111 Chelsea Street
East Boston
(617) 567-9871

Some would argue this neighborhood joint has better pizza than any place in the North End.

Sunset Grill ★

130 Brighton Avenue
Allston
(617) 254-1331

Basic American fare, from burgers to ribs, with a huge selection of beers (hundreds of different brands).

Tex's Barbecue Express ★

888 South Street
Roslindale
(617) 327-0304

www.texsbbqexpress.com

The best ribs in the Roslindale/West Roxbury area are at this takeout-only place.

CITY FACT

Buzzy's Fabulous Roast Beef at Charles Circle sits next to what used to be the Charles Street Jail. When the jail was in use, people would sometimes buy sandwiches and throw them over the wall to the prisoners.

Turner Fisheries ★★★★

10 Huntington Avenue
Copley Place
Back Bay
(617) 424-7425

Similar to Legal Seafood in the quality—and price—of its seafood.

Union Oyster House ★★

41 Union Street
near Quincy Market
(617) 227-2750

www.unionoysterhouse.com

Solid seafood served in the historic dining rooms of the oldest restaurant in the country. While waiting for a table, suck down some oysters (or just watch) at the old wooden oyster bar.

Jacob Wirth ★★

31–37 Stuart Street
Theatre District
(617) 338-8586

go.boston.com/sites/
jacobwirth8/home.html

German food, eighteen beers on tap, Friday-night sing-alongs.

Ice Cream

One sin Bostonians indulge in heavily is ice cream. The whole concept of "mix-ins" started at the late, lamented Steve's Ice Cream in Somerville.

Herrell's Ice Cream

350 Longwood Avenue
Longwood Medical Area
(617) 731-9599

15 Dunster Street
Cambridge
(617) 497-2179

155 Brighton Avenue
Allston
(617) 782-9599

224 Newbury Street
Back Bay
(617) 236-0857

J. P. Licks

352 Newbury Street
Back Bay
(617) 236-1666

659 Centre Street
Jamaica Plain
(617) 524-6740

311 Harvard Street
Brookline
(617) 738-8252

46 Langley Road
Newton
(617) 244-0666

Best ice cream in Boston (and egg creams for you homesick New Yorkers). Be sure to visit the original and largest J. P. Licks in Jamaica Plain. You can't miss it—it's in the converted firehouse with the fiberglass cow's head gazing out from the second floor.

The Bar and Club Scene

In addition to the *Globe* and *Boston Phoenix* listings, bostonclubs.com (www.bostonclubs.com) and Boston Night Guide (www.boston nightguide.com) provide online coverage of the local club and bar scene. Because of Boston's large student population, many clubs have under-twenty-one nights. Bostonclubs.com has a listing of hours and age limits. In Boston, clubs can stay open until 2 A.M.; in some suburbs, bars can't stay open later than 1 A.M.

There are four main bar-hopping areas in Boston: Quincy Market, Kenmore Square/Landsdowne Street, Harvard Avenue in Allston, and The Alley off Tremont Street near the Public Garden.

Quincy Market is the place to go if you want to meet out-of-town businesspeople. Kenmore Square (and Landsdowne Street, a couple of blocks from the square) is where college students and recent grads tend to go—especially rich college students from Europe and the Middle East. Harvard Avenue is a mixture of college students and older adults, drawn by everything from blues at Harper's Ferry to the yupscale Jazz at the Wonder Bar to the old-time college hangout Great Scott. The Alley tends to attract young professionals.

Abbey Lounge
3 Beacon Street
Somerville
(617) 441-9631

www.schnockered.com/abbey/abbey.htm

Rock. *Boston* magazine named it the best dive in town.

An Tua Nua
835 Beacon Street
Kenmore Square
(617) 262-2121

Irish bar and dance club.

Aria

246 Tremont Street
(617) 338-7080

www.ariaboston.com

Every night a different theme, from hip-hop on Tuesdays to international house on Sundays.

Atlas Dance

3 Lansdowne Street
(617) 437-0300

www.jilliansboston.com/ atlasdance.htm

Part of the Landsdowne Street complex of clubs. Dancing Fridays and Saturdays.

Avalon

15 Lansdowne Street
(617) 262-2424

DJs, large dance floor, and a balcony for surveying the scene. Thursday is Eurohaus night.

Axis

13 Lansdowne Street
(617) 262-2437

www.axisnightclub.com

Dance to alternative and techno music.

Bill's Bar

5 Lansdowne Street
Kenmore Square
(617) 421-9678

Live bands, moderate drink prices.

Bishop's Pub

21 Boylston Place
(617) 351-2583

Acoustic rock.

Bob the Chef's

604 Columbus Avenue
South End
(617) 536-6204

www.bobthechefs.com

Live jazz Thursday through Saturday.

Brendan Behan Pub

378 Centre Street
Jamaica Plain
(617) 522-5386

Worth the visit if you want good conversation with your Guinness (no TV sets at this neighborhood bar). Also has live Irish and folk nights.

The Burren

247 Elm Street
Davis Square
Somerville
(617) 776-6896

www.burren.com

Irish pub with live Irish music.

Cantab Lounge

738 Massachusetts Avenue
Central Square
Cambridge
(617) 354-2685

R&B, plus bluegrass on Tuesdays and open-mike nights on Mondays.

Cheers

84 Beacon Street
Beacon Hill
(617) 227-9605

www.cheersboston.com

Go if you must, but be prepared to stand in line with all the other tourists. Aside from the fact that it's in a basement, the actual bar bears absolutely no resemblance to the one in the TV show. If you need to see an exact replica of the TV set, there's now one (complete with working bar) at Faneuil Hall.

Club Passim

47 Palmer Street
Harvard Square
Cambridge
(617) 492-7679

www.clubpassim.com

Long-time folk club.

Common Ground

83-87 Harvard Avenue
Allston
(617) 783-2071

Irish sports bar that also offers up reggae every Thursday.

Druid Pub

1357 Cambridge Street
Inman Square

Cambridge
(617) 497-0965

Irish pub. English football on the telly every Saturday.

Embassy

30 Lansdowne Street
Kenmore Square
(617) 536-2100

The place to go to mingle with all those rich foreign students. Thursday is Latin Night.

Emily's

48 Winter Street
Downtown
(617) 423-3649

DJs and a dance floor.

Harper's Ferry

158 Brighton Avenue
Allston
(617) 254-9743

www.newboston.net/harpers

Blues, blues, and more blues, including the annual February Blues Fest. Also has food and bar games to keep you busy.

House of Blues

96 Winthrop Street
Harvard Square
Cambridge
(617) 491-2583

www.hob.com

Live blues every night; Sunday gospel brunch.

Jillian's

145 Ipswich Street
Kenmore Square
(617) 437-0300

www.jilliansboston.com

Billiard, video games, giant screen TVs, and six bars.

Johnny D's

17 Holland Street
Davis Square
Somerville
(617) 776-2004

www.johnnyds.com

Eclectic mix of music, including Cajun, folk, and blues.

Jose McIntyre's

160 Milk Street
Downtown
(617) 451-9460

www.irishconnection.com/jose.html

Claims to be Boston's only Mexican/Irish bar. Live music and pool tables.

The Kells

161 Brighton Avenue
Allston
(617) 782-9082

www.thekells.com

Possibly Boston's largest Irish bar, it also has a floor with DJs who play everything from reggae to rock. Thursday is the weekly dance and beach party.

Kinvara Pub

34 Harvard Avenue
Allston
(617) 783-9400

www.kinvarapub.com

Live Irish music on Sunday nights.

Lava Bar

575 Commonwealth Avenue
Kenmore Square
(617) 267-7707

www.lavabar.com

DJs spin music for this large dance floor seven stories above Kenmore Square.

Lilli's

608 Somerville Avenue
Porter Square
Somerville
(617) 591-1661

Live rock and jazz.

Lizard Lounge

1667 Massachusetts Avenue
Cambridge
(617) 547-0759

Alternative rock, jazz, and folk at this intellectual (MIT is right nearby) lounge.

Man Ray

21 Brookline Street
Central Square
Cambridge
(617) 864-0400

Goth central.

Middle East

472 Massachusetts Avenue
Central Square
Cambridge
(617) 497-0576

www.mideastclub.com

This club started out as a Middle Eastern restaurant and belly-dancing spot. You can still see the belly dancing, but the club has also become a local mecca for live alternative rock.

Milky Way Lounge & Lanes

401 Centre Street
Jamaica Plain
(617) 524-3740

Live music, including lounge, Latin, and rockabilly. Bowling, too.

Our House

1277 Commonwealth Avenue
Allston
(617) 782-3228

Good second-date spot. Have dinner, then snuggle in on one of the couches for a game of backgammon.

The Paradise

967 Commonwealth Avenue
Allston
(617) 562-8800

www.dlclive.com/venues/
paradise.asp

Live rock music in a club setting.

Plough & Stars

912 Massachusetts Avenue
Cambridge
(617) 441-3455

Live music, including folk, bluegrass, and Celtic, in a room that hasn't changed much in decades.

Pravda 116

116 Boylston Street
Back Bay
(617) 482-7799

Look for a loud beat on the dance floor in this Soviet-influenced club, with a large selection of vodkas.

Purple Shamrock

1 Union Street
Downtown
(617) 227-2060

www.irishconnection.com/
purplesham.html

Live music nightly in this Irish-themed bar.

The Rack

24 Clinton Street
Faneuil Hall
(617) 725-1051

www.therackboston.com

Billiards and two bars.

Regattabar
Charles Hotel
Harvard Square
Cambridge
(617) 661-5000

www.regattabar.com

Upscale jazz.

The Roxy
279 Tremont Street
Downtown
(617) 338-7699

Boston's largest dance floor, with room for 3,000 people. DJs and Latin music.

Ryles Jazz Club
212 Hampshire Street
Inman Square
Cambridge
(617) 876-9330

www.rylesjazz.com

Two floors of live jazz.

Scullers
400 Soldiers Field Road
Allston
(617) 562-4111

www.scullersjazz.com

Jazz nightly.

Sophia's
1270 Boylston Street
Kenmore Square
(617) 351-7001

Indoor and rooftop salsa.

Sports Depot
353 Cambridge Street
Allston
(617) 783-2300

TVs are all over the three bars that now make up this former train station, and they're all showing sports.

Tir Na Nog
366A Somerville Avenue
Union Square
Somerville
(617) 628-4300

Neighborhood Irish bar with nightly live music, including traditional Irish fare on Sundays.

T.T. the Bear's
10 Brookline Street
Central Square
Cambridge
(617) 492-0082

www.mindspring.com/
~ttthebears/

A key spot on the local underground music circuit.

Vapor
100 Warrenton Street
Back Bay
(617) 695-9500

A popular gay dance club. Old-timers remember it as Chaps.

Venu

100 Warrenton Street
Downtown
(617) 338-8061

Four bars and a heavy concentration of Europeans. Sunday is Brazilian night.

Wally's Cafe

427 Massachusetts Avenue
South End
(617) 424-1408

www.wallyscafe.com

Live jazz. Established in 1947, when Boston was a major stop on the national jazz circuit.

Western Front

343 Western Avenue
Cambridge
(617) 492-7772

Best known for its Friday and Saturday live reggae, also has hip-hop, funk, and poetry performances.

Wonder Bar

(617) 351-COOL
186 Harvard Avenue
Allston

Dinner and live jazz.

CITY FACT

A common dish at Boston seafood restaurants is sometimes spelled "scrod" and sometimes "schrod." Some claim the former is young cod; the latter young haddock. In fact, it's whatever flaky white fish happened to have been cheapest at the pier.

Shopping

When it comes to shopping, Boston has something for everyone. Some particular areas stand out.

CHINATOWN

In addition to the obvious (Chinese groceries), the area has numerous fabric shops.

CONCORD CENTER

The heart of this historic town has numerous little boutiques, well worth a stop after your visit to Old North Bridge. Note: There are no public restrooms in Concord Center, so be prepared. Easily accessible by car (Route 2 west) and commuter rail.

COPLEY PLACE

Imagine taking a suburban shopping mall, building a wall around it, and then dropping it, Wizard of Oz style, in the middle of the country's best walking city. That's basically Copley Place, home to Neiman-Marcus. Although pedestrians aren't completely barred from entering the mall, it's clearly a destination for suburbanites who want to go into the city without ever having to leave their cars and walk on the streets (it's built right over a Massachusetts Turnpike exit). Human hamster tubes connect the mall with nearby hotels and the similar, if slightly less upscale, Prudential Center mall (Lord & Taylor's).

DOWNTOWN CROSSING

Unlike those in other downtowns, Boston's main shopping district mostly thrives. Be sure to check out Filene's Basement for discount clothes, but get out of the way of the stampede when the doors open for the semiannual wedding dress sale. The regular Filene's (now owned by another company) and Macy's anchor the area. Jewelers' buildings on Washington Street offer floor after floor of jewelry. Many have "wholesale only" signs, but you never know. My girlfriend stopped in one such place to ask for directions to a restroom; she got to talking to the owners and I wound up getting her engagement ring there.

FRAMINGHAM/NATICK

New England's second-largest retail area (after Downtown Crossing), it's everything you'd expect in suburbia: malls, malls, and more malls. A few minutes from the malls, though, is downtown Framingham, home to the Fabric Place, a magnet for people looking for fabrics and sewing supplies. Downtown Natick is home to Debsan Wallpaper and Paint, which claims to have the world's largest supply of wallpaper samples.

The malls are on Route 9. Route 135 connects downtown Natick and downtown Framingham; both are also accessible via commuter rail.

HARVARD AVENUE, ALLSTON

You've just spent all your money moving to Boston, but you don't have any furniture. What to do? Head to Harvard Avenue, the used- and discount-furniture capital of Massachusetts. The street also has several antiques shops to complete the look, as well as places to get such items as used CDs and used books. Several ethnic markets also make this the place to go for those exotic spices you've been wanting to try.

HARVARD SQUARE, CAMBRIDGE

Tweedy Harvard professors, college students from all over the Boston area, street performers, and skate punks all combine to give this square a distinctive feel. The square's once unique stores are rapidly disappearing under the onslaught of generic chains, but it remains the best place in the Boston area to browse for books, from the huge collection of history books at the Harvard Book Store to stores that specialize in mystery, foreign-language, and poetry books.

HARVARD STREET, BROOKLINE

Actually the same street as Harvard Avenue in Allston, just with a slightly different name. It's the center of Boston's Jewish community, and here you'll find Jewish and Israeli bookstores, restaurants, and galleries. Paperback Booksmith is a great bookstore at Coolidge Corner; there's also a competing Barnes & Noble.

NEWBURY STREET, BACK BAY

Fancy galleries and boutiques, outdoor cafes, and the Ritz Carlton. The Massachusetts Avenue end features a Virgin Megastore, the Avenue Victor Hugo used bookstore, and the original Newbury Comics, the place to go for alternative, indie, and import music. Boylston Street, which parallels Newbury, also has extensive shopping.

QUINCY MARKET

Like Harvard Square, Quincy Market used to be home to unique, locally owned shops. And like Harvard Square, it's been overrun by chains—the marketplace has both Disney and Warner Bros. stores. A few homespun shops hang on, such as Whippoorwill Crafts.

Sports

BASEBALL

Boston Red Sox
Fenway Park
Yawkey Way
(617) 267-1700

www.redsox.com

Fenway Park is one of the last of the original ballparks left. The Red Sox want to build a new park, so see a game before they tear the old park down (or join Save Fenway Park, www.savefenwaypark.com). Bring some cash; even without a new ballpark, the Sox have the highest ticket prices in the major leagues.

BASKETBALL

Boston Celtics
FleetCenter
Causeway Street
(617) 523-3030

www.nba.com/celtics

The bad news is the Celtics aren't what they used to be. The good news is this means it's easier to get seats these days.

FOOTBALL

New England Patriots
Foxboro Stadium
Route 1
Foxboro
(617) 931-2222

www.patriots.com

In 2002 the Patriots move into a brand-new stadium right next to the current one. Unlike Fenway Park, however, nobody is fighting to save Foxboro Stadium—a soulless and uncomfortable place to watch football.

HOCKEY

Boston Bruins
FleetCenter
Causeway Street
(617) 931-2222

www.bostonbruins.com

HORSE RACING

Foxboro Park (trotting)
Route 1
Foxboro
(508) 543-3800

Suffolk Downs (Thoroughbred)
Route 1A
East Boston
(617) 567-3900

www.suffolkdowns.com

SOCCER

Boston Renegades (women)
Bowditch Field
475 Union Avenue
Framingham
(508) 872-8998

www.bostonrenegades.com

Revolution
Foxboro Stadium
Route 1
Foxboro
(617) 931-2222

www.revolutionsoccer.net

Recreational Sports

In Boston, the city Parks and Recreation Department issues permits for use of city fields at (617) 635-4505. The parks and recreation departments in most cities and towns in eastern Massachusetts organize adult sports leagues. Contact your local city or town hall for more information.

Boston Baseball League
(617) BASEBAL

www.bostonbaseball.com

Two divisions, for ages 18–29 and 30 and older. Teams play at fields throughout Greater Boston.

Boston Park League Baseball

www.bostonparkleague.org

America's oldest amateur baseball league. Teams play thirty-two-game seasons at fields in Dorchester, Roslindale, Brighton, and East Boston.

Boston Ski and Sports Club Softball Leagues
(617) 789-4070

www.bssc.com/softball.html

Coed indoor and outdoor slow pitch.

Boston Volleyball Association
(617) 332-2320

www.bostonvolleyball.com

Indoor and outdoor leagues in Newton.

Massachusetts State Cricket League

www.mscl.org

Cricket May through September.

Massachusetts State Soccer Association

www.mass-soccer.org

Oversees men's, women's, and coed soccer leagues.

M Street Softball

www.geocities.com/
Colosseum/Park/1022/
softball.html

Competitive softball in South Boston.

Yankee Volleyball Association

(617) 491-7102

www.ultranet.com/~yankee/
menu.html

Indoor men's, women's, and coed tournaments September through May.

Beaches

Boston has a number of beaches, but there are many more beaches along the shore both to the north and south. Boston Harbor is far cleaner than it used to be, so the local waters are far safer to swim in, although there are still times when local beaches are closed because of sewage runoffs after heavy rains. However, if you've grown up south of Cape Cod or in California, you may find the water way too cold for more than toe-dipping; only hardy—and I mean hardy—natives dive right in.

Boston Harbor Beaches

The Boston Harbor Association maintains a listing of Boston Harbor beaches: www.tbha.org/boston.htm.

Revere Beach

(617) 727-8856

www.reverebeach.com

Muscle guys in muscle cars, girls with big hair, and Kelly's Roast Beef. Bring a towel and an appetite to this free beach only a couple of blocks from the Revere Beach subway station.

Bowling

Bostonians don't bowl with giant balls with three holes in them. Instead, they go candlepin bowling, a game invented by Justin White of Worcester in 1880 because he thought ten pins was just too easy. In candlepins, you use softball-size balls to try to knock down tiny cylindrical pins. You get three tries per frame, and you leave fallen pins down to try to knock down the others. Perfect scores are almost impossible, but the game is a lot easier for little kids (some lanes even put bumpers in the gutters on Saturday mornings to make it even easier for them). Read more about the game at www.bowlcandlepin.com, then head out to the lanes.

Big League Bowling

1834 Centre Street
West Roxbury
(617) 323-7291

Boston Bowl Family Fun Center

820 Morrissey Boulevard
Dorchester
(617) 825-3800

www.bostonbowl.com

Also has ten pins. Open 24 hours.

Central Park Lanes

10 Saratoga Street
East Boston
(617) 567-7073

Lanes & Games

195 Concord Turnpike
Cambridge
(617) 876-5533

Giant two-story structure that has more than enough room for ten-pins lanes.

Milky Way Lounge & Lanes

401 Centre Street
Jamaica Plain
(617) 524-3740

Not just bowling—the Milky Way also books live music, from lounge to Latin to rockabilly.

Ron's Gourmet Ice Cream and Bowling Alley

1231 Hyde Park Avenue
Hyde Park
(617) 364-5274

Yes, what could be better than homemade ice cream and some candlepins? This is basically an ice-cream parlor with several candlepin lanes.

South Boston Candlepin

543 East Broadway
South Boston
(617) 464-4858

Cross-Country Skiing

City
FACT

On September 3, 1988, Paul Tavilla of Arlington, Massachusetts, set a world record by using his mouth to catch a grape tossed from the top of the sixty-story John Hancock Building. Asked how it felt to catch the 110-mile-per-hour grape, he said, "It hurts."

Lincoln Guide Service
152 Lincoln Road
Lincoln
(781) 259-1111

Rents skis and sells maps of nearby trails (fifty-seven miles) on town conservation land.

Weston Ski Track
Martin Golf Course
200 Park Road
Weston

www.ski-paddle.com/skitrack/skitrack.shtml

Ten miles of groomed trails.

George Wright Golf Course
420 West Street
Hyde Park
(617) 361-8313

Varied terrain; minimal facilities.

Ice Skating

Frog Pond
Boston Common
(617) 635-2120

Outdoor skating and hot chocolate on the Common. Quintessential Boston right there!

MDC Rinks

www.state.ma.us/mdc/psschd.htm

The Metropolitan District Commission runs public skating rinks in Brighton, Charlestown, Dorchester, East Boston, Hyde Park, Medford, Milton, Quincy, Somerville, South Boston, Waltham, and West Roxbury. Public hours are limited, though; the rinks are home to the Boston area's numerous youth hockey leagues. Some rinks offer instructions.

Skating Club of Boston

1240 Soldiers Field Road
Brighton
(617) 782-5900

users.erols.com/scob/

The club has its own rink; offers lessons.

Parks

The crown jewel of the Boston park system is the Emerald Necklace. Designed by Frederick Law Olmsted (yes, the Central Park guy) in the 1870s, this seven-mile-long stretch of park encircles Boston like, well, a necklace. It starts at the Boston Common and wends through the Back Bay, Fenway, Jamaica Plain, and Roxbury. The parks are maintained by the Boston Parks Department. For more information on specific parks and programs, call the department at (617) 635-4505. Among the parks that make up the Emerald Necklace:

Boston Common

Between Boylston, Charles, Tremont, and Beacon Streets

Ball fields, statues, people feeding squirrels, and Frog Pond (a wading pool in the summer, ice skating in the winter).

Public Garden

Across Charles Street from the Common

Beautiful flower beds that get new plantings throughout the summer, the world's smallest suspension bridge, and the Swan Boats—people-powered boats that take you for a leisurely ride around the lagoon. There's something particularly soothing about a Swan Boat ride, which takes you around the island where Mr. Mallard was waiting for Mrs. Mallard and her brood in "Make Way for Ducklings." Kids enjoy sitting on the brass statues of Mrs. Mallard and the ducklings.

Muddy River

Along the Riverway

Paths along this creek provide a quiet respite from the hurly-burly of the neighboring Longwood Medical Area.

Jamaica Pond

Walk or jog around this pond, rent a sailboat or rowboat, or just cast a line into the water (it's stocked with trout).

Arnold Arboretum

Arborway and VFW Parkway
Jamaica Plain
(617) 524-1718

www.arboretum.harvard.edu

Maintained by Harvard University, this botanical museum features trees from temperate regions across the world and a huge collection of lilac bushes.

Franklin Park

The largest park in the chain, it's home to a zoo and a golf course in addition to ball fields and winding paths.

In total, the city Parks and Recreation Department runs 215 parks and playgrounds throughout the city. City park rangers give free summer tours of the Boston Common, Public Garden, and Freedom Trail. ParkArts sponsors art workshops for children across the city. Contact (617) 635-4505 or www.cityofboston.com/parks/.

The Metropolitan District Commission, a state agency, operates a number of parks and "reservations" in and around Boston. For a complete listing, see www.state.ma.us/mdc/reserv.htm. The parks include:

Blue Hills Reservation

Hillside Street
Milton
(617) 698-1802

www.state.ma.us/mdc/blue.htm

An 8,500-acre park centered on the Great Blue Hill, the highest point on the Atlantic coast south of Maine. Among its attractions: miles of hiking and cross-country ski trails, prehistoric and historic sites, winter skiing on the Great Blue Hill, and swimming at Ponkapoag Pond.

Boston Harbor Islands National Recreation Area and Boston Harbor Islands State Park

(617) 223-8666

www.state.ma.us/dem/parks/bhis.htm

Long ignored by almost everybody, the Boston Harbor islands offer windswept vistas of the city and the ocean and several historic sites. Today, most of the islands are owned by the state and the National Park Service, which are developing them as parks. A ferry from Long Wharf takes you to George's Island, from which you can take a free water taxi to five other harbor islands. See wildflowers and the remains of abandoned hospitals and forts. Several of the islands have picnic areas and beaches. Four islands have camping facilities (by permit only).

Charles River Reservation

www.state.ma.us/mdc/charlesr.htm

A seventeen-mile linear park that runs along both sides of the Charles River. The Esplanade on the Boston side is home to the Hatch Shell, where you can frequently find free concerts (including the Fourth of July Pops concert). It's a great place to walk, bike, or skate—or to just spread out a beach towel and soak up the sun. The Cambridge side features stunning views of Beacon Hill and the Back Bay.

Stony Brook Reservation

www.state.ma.us/mdc/stony.htm

A 475-acre forest within the city limits. Paths lead visitors through glacier-shaped landscapes to Turtle Pond, which becomes truly gorgeous when the leaves change.

Sledding

Wherever there's a hill, you'll find sledders. The Boston area has a lot of hills. Some prime spots:

- Olmsted Park along the Jamaicaway in Jamaica Plain.
- President's Golf Course in Quincy.
- Brae Burn Golf Course, Newton—the hill across from the clubhouse.
- Danehy Park, Cambridge (on the Sherman Street side).
- Hynes Field, VFW Parkway, West Roxbury. There's a small hill that's especially good for little kids.

Youth Sports

In addition to Little League, soccer and ice hockey are particularly big youth sports in the Boston area. The Metropolitan District Commission runs a number of skating rinks throughout the Boston area; most have youth hockey leagues (see under Ice Skating for more information).

Little League

www.littleleague.org/finder/massachusetts.htm

Massachusetts Premier Soccer League
(508) 655-7113

www.maplesoccer.org

Teen leagues in the suburbs.

Health Clubs

Beacon Hill Athletic Clubs

261 Friend Street
North Station

3 Hancock Street
Beacon Hill

1089 Washington Street
West Newton

(617) 720-2422

www.beaconhillathletic.com

Boston Racquet Club

10 Post Office Square
Financial District
(617) 482-8881

www.fitcorp.com

Dedham Health and Athletic Complex

Route 1 north
Dedham
(781) 326-2900

www.dedhamhealth.com

If they don't have it, you don't need it. Everything from exercise and weight equipment to racquetball, tennis, and basketball courts—and a wave pool.

Gold's Gym

71 Landsdowne Street
Kenmore Square
(617) 536-6066

1600 VFW Parkway
West Roxbury
(617) 327-4653

30 Park Avenue
Arlington Heights
(617) 646-4653

There are additional suburban locations.

Leave your mascara at home; these clubs specialize in serious weight training. They have separate women's gyms.

No Frills Aerobics and Martial Arts

624 Somerville Avenue
Somerville
(617) 626-2700

www.nofrillsaerobics.com

Live music and DJ to work out to.

YMCA

www.ymcaboston.org/branches.html

With branches throughout Greater Boston, the Y offers an economical way to stay in shape. Many have both exercise equipment and pools.

Free and Touristy Stuff

One of the great things about living in a tourist town is, well, being able to play tourist without going too far. Many local hotels offer discount rates on weekends, perfect for when you need a break or a quick romantic getaway.

The key Boston attraction is the Freedom Trail, a three-mile path that connects colonial and Revolutionary sites downtown and in Charlestown (just look for the red line painted on the sidewalk). Rangers from both the National Park Service and the Boston Parks and Recreation Department give free talks and tours. The park service provides free maps and other information at a storefront next to the Old State House and in Faneuil Hall. The city runs a tourist information kiosk on Tremont Street by the Boston Common.

Boston National Historic Park

(617) 242-5642

www.nps.gov/bost

Duck Tours

(800) 242-5642

www.bostonducktours.com

Get a tour of the city in a converted World War II amphibian landing craft, then splash into the Charles River for a cruise. Along the way, you'll be asked to quack at Bostonians.

Old Town Trolleys

(617) 269-7150

www.trolleytours.com/boston.htm

You buy a day pass that let's you get on and off as often as you want along the route through downtown. Apply online for a Boston resident's pass that lets you take a friend along for free.

Free Stuff

Many of the college museums are free, as are many of the talks and lectures there. The Museum of Fine Arts has a voluntary-fee admission policy on Wednesdays, starting at 4:45 P.M. In the summer, several radio stations sponsor free concerts at the Hatch Shell on the Charles River Esplanade and at City Hall Plaza.

Beyond organized events, there's something to be said for just hanging out. Take the subway to Harvard Square for people watching. Set a towel down on the Esplanade and get some sun (the strip between the river and the lagoon is particularly popular) or take the subway up to Revere Beach for both people-watching and sun. Walk around the Financial District on a Sunday and soak up the architecture and gargoyles.

Calendar of Events

JANUARY

What could be more bracing than a dip in the ocean on New Year's Day? The L Street Brownies take their annual New Year's swim in Dorchester Bay, L Street Bathhouse, South Boston.

Get out on the road with the New England Camping & RV Show, Bayside Expo Center at (800) 225-1577.

Boston Cooks is an annual series of culinary events featuring the Boston Cooks Kitchen and Culinary Expo at the World Trade Center, www.bostoncooks.com.

FEBRUARY

The North American Home Show gets you in the right mindset for all those spring renovation projects, Bayside Expo Center at (800) 225-1577, www.naexpo.com/homeshow/Homeshowindex.htm.

If you're feeling nautical, visit the New England Boat Show, also at the Bayside Expo Center at (800) 225-1577, www.naexpo.com/boatshow.

Greater Boston car dealers hold President's Day sales.

What's up, Doc? The Brattle Theater in Cambridge hosts an annual Bugs Bunny Film Festival at (617) 876-6837, www.beaconcinema.com/brattle.

The Beanpot Tournament determines the best college hockey team in Boston as Boston College, Boston University, Harvard University, and Northeastern University compete at the FleetCenter at (617) 931-2000.

MARCH

Forget the robins. The first real sign of spring in Boston is always the Massachusetts Horticultural Society's New England Spring Flower Show at the Bayside Expo Center at (617) 536-9280, ext. 248, or www.masshort.org. Featuring elaborate gardens and floral displays, it typically runs eight or nine days. Get there early to see the flowers at their peak (but expect crowds!).

South Boston hosts the largest St. Patrick's Day parade outside of New York. It's held the Sunday before St. Patrick's Day. Cambridge also hosts a parade. In Boston, city and state offices are closed on March 17—not to honor St. Patrick but to commemorate Evacuation Day—the day the British fled Boston during the Revolution.

The New England Film & Video Festival—(617) 536-1540 or www.bfvf.org/festival—brings to the Boston area independent films made entirely by New England directors. Screenings at the Coolidge Corner Theater and the Museum of Fine Arts.

APRIL

Hope springs eternal as the Red Sox hold their home opener at Fenway Park.

Patriots' Day, celebrated only in Massachusetts and Maine, commemorates the battles of Lexington and Concord. Lexington Minutemen reenact their town's battle at the crack of dawn at the Lexington Common.

CITY FACT

A popular kids' game is ghouls, which is like tag. A kid who sticks too closely to the ghoul, or home base, is a "ghoulsticka."

Groups of Minutemen in other towns start marching at dawn toward the Old North Bridge in Concord for a 9 A.M. reenactment of that battle (there's always a troop of Redcoats; for some reason, they always lose). Then it's off to Arlington for a parade down Massachusetts Avenue.

Outside Massachusetts, Patriots' Day is better known for the annual running of the Boston Marathon (www.bostonmarathon. com) from Hopkinton to Copley Square in Boston. Some 1 million people line the race route cheering on not only the pack-leading Kenyans but the thousands of other people who run the race. If you don't want to brave the throngs at the finish line, you can get an excellent view along Beacon Street in Brookline.

MAY

The "Make Way for Ducklings" Parade on Mother's Day is almost too cute for words. Hundreds of kids, many dressed as ducks or as Officer Mike, retrace the route taken by Mrs. Mallard and her ducklings through Beacon Hill to the lagoon in the Public Garden.

Lilac Sunday at the Arnold Arboretum (www.arboretum. harvard.edu) in Jamaica Plain brings thousands of people out to enjoy one of the world's largest lilac collections. It's also the only day you're allowed to have a picnic at the arboretum. Stick your face in the lilacs, watch the Morris dancers, and, yes, bring a picnic basket and stretch out on the big hill in the center of the arboretum.

Go fly a kite at the annual kite-flying festival in Franklin Park.

JUNE–AUGUST

Almost every Sunday brings another saint's festival in the North End. Societies dedicated to specific saints parade a statue around the neighborhood. Hanover Street is closed off for celebrations.

Radio stations sponsor free concerts at the Esplanade and City Hall Plaza. Check the Globe Calendar section for details.

JUNE

Join the AIDS Walk, an annual fundraising event for the AIDS Action Committee at (617) 437-6200. It starts with calisthenics on the Boston Common, then winds through Boston and Brookline before ending in a free concert at the Hatch Shell on the Charles River Esplanade.

Framingham celebrates Flag Day with a parade though downtown Framingham.

The Scooper Bowl lets you sample a wide variety of ice creams on City Hall Plaza. Proceeds go to the Jimmy Fund, which sponsors research into childhood cancers.

The Boston Dragon Boat Festival—(617) 426-6500, ext. 778., or www.bostondragonboat.org—celebrates a form of rowing unique to Hong Kong. Teams of twenty (eighteen rowers, a steerperson, and a drummer) compete in slim teakwood boats with hand-painted dragon's heads and tails on the Charles River between Brighton and Cambridge. On shore, learn about and participate in a variety of Chinese arts, including face painting and music.

JULY–AUGUST

Free concerts are held at Christopher Columbus Park on the North End waterfront, Fridays at 7 P.M.

JULY

Several hundred thousand people jam the banks of the Charles River in Boston and Cambridge for the Boston Pops concert and fireworks. If you want a really good seat (in front of the Hatch Shell, where you can actually see the Pops), plan on getting there several hours early (like, that morning). Forget about driving—take the subway! Many towns in the Boston area have their own, albeit smaller, fireworks displays; check the *Boston Globe* a few days before for a listing.

In addition to the Pops concert, Harborfest gives Bostonians a week's worth of Independence Day celebrations, including a reading of the Declaration of Independence at the Old State House. During Chowderfest, a most distinctive Boston festivity, several Boston restaurants (and any Navy ships that happen to be in the harbor) compete on City Hall Plaza for the title of Best Clam Chowder. (Only in Boston would people stand in line in the hot July sun to eat steaming clam chowder.) On the Fourth of July, you can also listen to a re-reading of the Declaration of Independence at the Old State House—and boo the troop of Redcoats as they beat a hasty retreat to Quincy Market. Or head on over to Charlestown to watch the annual turnaround of the U.S.S. *Constitution*. The world's oldest commissioned warship is towed out into the harbor, where she fires a cannon salute, is brought back to her dock, and is turned around to let her hull weather evenly.

Celebrate Bastille Day at the French Library's annual dinner and block party in the Back Bay at (617) 912-0400.

SEPTEMBER

Like the swallows to San Juan Capistrano, college students return to Allston/Brighton, Cambridge, and Somerville on Labor Day weekend.

The Boston Blues Festival is a free two-day series of concerts at the Hatch Shell on the Charles River Esplanade, www.bluestrust.com.

The Boston Folk Festival is an annual, multi-stage concert series at the University of Massachusetts–Boston.

OCTOBER

What the Boston Marathon is to running, the Head of the Charles Regatta, www.hocr.org, is to rowing. Teams from around the world compete over two days in races on the Charles River.

Foliage in the Boston area peaks roughly around Columbus Day (the exact timing varies each year depending on the weather), www.mass-vacation.com/foliage.html.

The North End and East Boston take turns hosting the Columbus Day Parade on the Sunday closest to October 12.

The Ringling Bros. Barnum & Bailey Circus returns to the FleetCenter: (617) 931-2000.

Roslindale celebrates itself at the annual Roslindale Day Parade.

CITY FACT

Don't let those Boston parking tickets pile up—the city has an active "Denver boot" program—anybody with five more tickets could find his car immobilized. You can pay those tickets online, though, at www.cityofboston.com/parking/default.asp.

NOVEMBER

Kick the tires and see what's new in driving at the annual International Auto Show at the Bayside Expo Center. (800) 258-8912.

The Boston Jewish Film Festival features films by or about Jews from around the world: (617) 244-9899, www.bjff.org.

DECEMBER

Boston has a number of Christmas-related traditions, including:

- The lighting of the Christmas tree at the Prudential Center. The city's largest tree is an annual gift from Halifax, Nova Scotia, in honor of aid Boston rendered that city after a munitions explosion destroyed much of it in 1918.
- The Enchanted Village. Housed in a tent outside City Hall, it's an animatronic re-creation of a turn-of-the-century New England village.
- The Boston Ballet's performances of *The Nutcracker* at the Wang Center: (617) 695-6955.

Boston ushers in the New Year with First Night, www.firstnight.org. Every December 31, people flock to the Back Bay and downtown for performances of all types, ice sculptures, a parade, and fireworks. Indoor events require the purchase of a First Night button; outdoor events are free. Fireworks go off twice: once at 7 P.M. on the Boston Common, once at midnight over Boston Harbor.

Public Transportation

Boston has an extensive, relatively inexpensive, and efficient public transportation system of subways (the oldest system in the country), buses, and commuter rail. Known collectively as "the T" (subway and commuter-rail stops are marked by large black Ts in white circles), the system is particularly effective in getting people to and from downtown Boston. More than 800,000 people ride the T daily, including some 4,000 on a nascent ferry system around Boston Harbor.

The basic fare is $1 for the subway (some of the more distant stations, such as Quincy and Braintree, require another $1); 75 cents for buses (free transfers between bus and subway lines are available).

Commuter-rail rates depend on the distance traveled. Monthly passes eliminate the need to fumble for tokens or exact change and get you a discount on auto insurance. You can also buy weekly passes.

The subway is divided into four main color-coded lines: Red, Green, Orange, and Blue. Commuter rail terminates at South Station (from the south and west) and North Station (from the north and northwest).

The T has two main drawbacks. One is hours. Although bars and clubs in Boston stay open until 2 A.M., the T shuts down at 12:45 A.M. However, the T now offers "Night Owl" bus service along the subway lines and some bus routes between 1 and 2:30 A.M. on Fridays and Saturdays. Buses depart Government Center downtown every half hour. The second drawback is that the system is not terribly efficient for going across town or from north to south in the suburbs.

Driving

Everything you may have heard about Boston drivers is true: They are among the nation's most aggressive and obnoxious. Driving around here is especially fun in winter snowstorms. Drivers who figure they can't stop will just sail through intersections, regardless of whether they have the light or not. Speaking of intersections, it's a good idea always to look both ways, even if you have a green light and even if you're crossing a one-way street.

But maybe Boston drivers are a product of their environment. Roads are often poorly marked, if at all (many towns don't even post the names of main streets, so if you get lost on one, you won't know where you are). Roads change names frequently and apparently at random (in a span of two miles, the Riverway turns into the Jamaicaway, the Arborway, Centre Street, and finally the VFW Parkway). Many towns use the same name for roads in different parts of town (Boston has several unconnected Washington Streets, for example). Never rely on online mapping services to get you from A to B in the Boston area—they just can't deal with it all.

On some highways, such as Route 128 and Route 93, you're legally allowed to drive in the "breakdown lane" (what Bostonians call shoulders) during rush hour. Along Route 128, the state has built a series of emergency turnouts for anyone unlucky enough to actually break down in the breakdown lane.

And then there are rotaries. After a few years, you'll get used to them and come to appreciate these traffic circles as more efficient than traffic lights in moving traffic. Until then, you will approach them with fear. Legally, a car in a rotary has the right of way over a car entering the rotary. In practical terms, whichever car has the least to lose in an accident has the right of way. An '81 Omni with a dented hood trumps a late-model Lexus every time (SUV drivers often ignore this rule, however, so watch out).

Now add to all this the disruption caused by the Big Dig project (the state is building a tunnel to replace the current elevated Central Artery that splits downtown Boston), the most expensive road project in U.S. history. An engineering marvel to be sure, it has meant a never-ending series of changes in roads and traffic patterns downtown—as many as fifty a week. The *Boston Globe*'s "Starts and Stops" column on Sunday lists upcoming Big Dig–related changes. The whole project is scheduled for completion in late 2004. State officials promise it will end the regional traffic bottleneck through downtown Boston. Of course, they said the same thing about the Central Artery in the 1950s, so we'll see.

Taxis

Downtown and in the Back Bay, you can usually just hail a taxi on the street. Elsewhere, however, you generally have to call ahead for one. Boston cabs work on meters—$1.50 for the first quarter of a mile and then $.25 for each eighth of a mile. There are additional charges to and from Logan Airport.

Boston Cab
(617) 536-5010

City Cab
(617) 536-5100

Checker Cab
(617) 536-7000

ITOA
(617) 825-4000

Metro Cab

(617) 782-5500

Town Taxi

(617) 536-5000

The Boston Police Hackney Carriage Unit oversees cab service and complaints: (617) 343-4475; www.cityofboston.gov/transportation/ CABS.ASP.

Airport Transportation

Logan Airport is closer to downtown Boston than almost any other major airport is to its downtown. That's the good news. The bad news is that if you get stuck in traffic, a ten-minute ride can turn into an hour-long ordeal. Also, parking is fairly limited at the airport and difficult at peak travel times, such as around Thanksgiving and Christmas. However, there are parking lots in East and South Boston that offer shuttle-bus service to the airport. The Massachusetts Port Authority's Logan Web site offers live updates on parking and traffic as well as on incoming and outbound flights: www. massport.com/logan.

If you're looking for discount prices, Southwest Airlines flies out of Providence's T. F. Green Airport and Manchester Airport in New Hampshire: (800) 435-9792, www.southwestair.com.

BY CAR

Take the Callahan Tunnel, then follow the signs for the airport. Parking, when available, is $21 a day.

BY TAXI

Expect to pay $10 to $15 from downtown locations to the airport, plus various fees and tolls depending on whether you're coming or going. Allow time to account for traffic.

BY SUBWAY

The Blue Line's airport stop gets you most of the way there. A free Massport shuttle will take you from there to your terminal.

BY BUS

Logan Express provides bus service from parking lots in Braintree, Framingham, and Woburn. The bus costs $14 round trip; parking is $7 a day: (800) 23-LOGAN.

Logan DART connects the South Station train and bus terminal with the airport, Sunday through Friday from 6 A.M. to 8 P.M., $5 per ride: (800) 23-LOGAN.

BY VAN

A number of companies provide van service from areas across Greater Boston:

www.massport.com/logan/getti_typeo_share.html

CHAPTER 7

What's Out of Town

Boston may not really be the hub of the universe, but it is the hub of New England. Drive an hour or so in any direction (well, except east) and you'll find yourself in another state.

Although geographically small when compared to the rest of the country, New England packs a wallop. From the ocean to mountains, the region has many destinations to keep you busy year-round. If you want to lounge by the beach, you can do it from Rhode Island up to Maine (but be aware that the ocean north of Cape Cod will be cold no matter what time of year). In the summer, Route 3 south of Boston gets jammed with people heading off for a weekend on the Cape. In the winter, Route 93 north and sometimes even Route 128 north slow down as Bostonians drive up to New Hampshire for some skiing. Ski areas in Vermont and Maine are also an easy drive (and they're increasingly becoming summertime destinations as well, as the resorts keep their facilities open year-round). Take a cruise from Gloucester to see whales. Or break out the credit card and head off to the southern coast of Maine for outlet-store shopping.

An essential part of life in New England is, of course, the fall foliage. All of the six New England states run fall hotlines to keep you abreast of the latest conditions. In the Boston area, peak foliage tends to be around Columbus Day. A great day trip is to drive west on Route 2. Drive into Concord Center for some window-shopping, then drive back to Route 2 to pick up a pumpkin or two at Arena

Farms (there are numerous other farm stands along Route 2, but Arena Farms has the largest collection of both pumpkins and cute little kids scampering around them).

Foliage hotlines

Connecticut: (800) CT-BOUND

Maine: (800) 777-0317

Massachusetts: (800) 533-9595

New Hampshire: (800) 258-3608

Rhode Island: (800) 556-2484

Vermont: (800) VERMONT

A note on driving in northern New England (Maine, New Hampshire, and Vermont). Unlike in Massachusetts, there is no major east-west highway. People from other parts of the country, especially the West, often look at a map of New England and think they can quickly traverse the region. But, as they say in Maine, "you can't get theah from heah." If you want to see Maine and Vermont, it's best to do it in separate trips. Otherwise you'll spend far more time than you thought was possible on smallish back roads and highways.

NewEngland.com

www.newengland.com

This Yankee magazine Web site has comprehensive information on timeless attractions in all six New England states, along with seasonal and calendar information and forums to discuss everything from foliage to travel.

Massachusetts

Beyond Greater Boston, there's a whole state to explore, from the ski hills of the Berkshires to the surf of Cape Cod. Outdoor activities abound. Massachusetts has the fifth-largest state park system in the country, even though it's the fifth smallest state.

Massachusetts Department of Environmental Management
Division of Forests and Parks
(617) 626-1250

www.massparks.org

Massachusetts Office of Travel and Tourism
(800) 447-MASS

www.mass-vacation.com

THE BERKSHIRES

About two and a half hours west of Boston, the Berkshires offer natural beauty and sophisticated culture. Wintertime means skiing; summertime brings the Boston Symphony Orchestra to Tanglewood for concerts. Williamstown and Northampton offer boutiques and dining.

Take Route 2 west for the scenic route (be sure to stop at the Golden Eagle Restaurant at the Famous Hairpin Turn for the view of the Berkshires) or take the Massachusetts Turnpike if time is of the essence.

Berkshire Visitors Bureau
(800) 237-5747

www.berkshires.org

Hidden-Hills.com

www.hidden-hills.com

Detailed information on one of Massachusetts's more remote areas. There's no way to get to any of the hills by interstate.

Massachusetts Museum of Contemporary Art
(413) 664-4481

www.massmoca.org

A work in progress: The museum is gradually converting a twenty-seven-building, thirteen-acre former mill into an arts complex featuring everything from giant sculptures to theatre and dance space.

Mohawk Trail Region

www.mohawktrail.com

CAPE ANN

Drive (or take commuter rail) an hour north of Boston for Gloucester and Rockport, quintessential New England fishing villages.
Gloucester is still a hardworking fishing town (think *Perfect Storm*),
right down to the "Gorton's of Gloucester" memorial overlooking the
harbor. Rockport has become a vibrant artists' community centered
on Bearskin Neck, a small peninsula jutting into the ocean that is
lined with galleries and boutiques. It's also home to Motif No. 1, a
lobster shack and artistic icon that was rebuilt after it fell into the harbor during the Blizzard of '78, and numerous B&Bs and motels.
Drive a bit farther north for fried clams at Woodman's in Ipswich,
where they were first made. For an odd diversion, check out the Paper
House in Pigeon Cove. Ellis Stenman used 100,000 newspapers to
build it in the 1920s.

To get to Cape Ann, take Route 93 north to Route 128 north, or take
the Rockport line (which has a stop in Gloucester) from North Station.

cape-ann.com

www.cape-ann.com

Information on all the communities of Cape Ann.

Rockport Chamber of Commerce

(978) 546-6575

www.rockportusa.com

Seven Seas Wharf

(888) 283-1812

www.cape-ann.com/7seas

This 350-year-old wharf has an anchor museum and is the starting
point for whale-watch cruises.

CAPE COD AND ISLANDS

Massachusetts has two capes, but only Cape Cod is "the Cape."

The Cape has something for everyone, from the windswept
dunes of Cape Cod National Seashore and the quiet beaches along

Cape Cod Bay to the endless miniature golf courses and gift shops along Route 138 (I once saw one with a sign that read "Last gift shoppe for 1/10th mile").

The traffic can be murder getting across the Cape Cod Canal (there are only two bridges connecting the Cape with the mainland; don't believe those Cape Cod Tunnel resident stickers), but when you get settled into your cottage or hotel and head out to the beach, it'll be worth it.

CITY FACT

Bostonians don't just go somewhere— they go down somewhere; for example, down Cape or down cellar.

Each Cape town has its own character. Barnstable, the largest town, is best known for its Hyannis section, where the Kennedys still have their famous compound. Truro is quiet; most of the town is actually part of the National Seashore. Visit Marconi Beach for some unforgettable views and what is now the cliffside site where Marconi transmitted the first transatlantic radio signals. Provincetown is a boisterous fishing village that has an active gay and arts community.

Offshore, Martha's Vineyard and Nantucket offer another way to get away from it all. Martha's Vineyard is the bigger of the two and is a well-known destination for celebrities and politicians. The smaller Nantucket is quieter and retains the feel of the nineteenth-century whaling outpost it once was. The Steamship Authority provides a ferry between the Cape and the two islands. The ferries carry cars, but you'll have to reserve a spot well in advance.

One tip for the Cape and Islands: Visit after Labor Day. The water and air will still be warm, but there'll be a lot less traffic and fewer people.

By car, drive south on Route 3, which takes you to the Cape bridges. Cape Air provides service between Logan and Hyannis, Provincetown, and Martha's Vineyard: (800) 352-0714. Nantucket Air flies between Hyannis and Nantucket: (800) 635-8787. Bay State

Cruises provides summertime ferry service from Boston to Province-town at the tip of the Cape: (617) 748-1428.

Cape Cod Beaches

www.capecodusa.com/beachstart.asp

Database that lists beaches as well as their facilities and services.

Cape Cod Recreation

www.capecodrec.com

Cape Cod Travel

www.capecodtravel.com

Martha's Vineyard Chamber of Commerce

(508) 693-0085

www.mvy.com

Nantucket.net

www.nantucket.net/indexlong.html

Nantucket Online

www.nantucketonline.com

LOWELL

You could argue that the American industrial revolution began in this gritty mill town on the banks of the Merrimack River. Attracted by its ample water power, a group of Boston Brahmins built a planned community centered on mills. Today the Lowell National Historical Park commemorates this history at the Boott Cotton Mills Museum and related buildings along a five-mile stretch of canal. At these sites, you can see power looms and learn about the ramifications of the change from agrarian to industrial society.

Another reason to visit Lowell is the annual Lowell Folk Festival, held each July. It's a three-day event featuring six outdoor stages, parades, dance parties, and craft demonstrations held throughout the city.

Lowell is about an hour north of Boston on Route 93. There is also commuter-rail service between Lowell and North Station.

Lowell Folk Festival

www.lowellfolkfestival.org

Lowell National Historical Park

(978) 970-5000

www.nps.gov/lowe

SPRINGFIELD

If you're a serious basketball fan, the Basketball Hall of Fame might be worth the two-and-a-half-hour drive.

September brings the Eastern States Exposition, or the Big E, to neighboring West Springfield. The Big E is essentially a state fair for all of New England; each state has its own hall to show off its foods and crafts. The Big E runs for two weeks and features concerts, a daily parade, exhibits of giant vegetables, and a hall that consists mainly of pitchmen (and women) trying to sell you the latest miracle mop or frying pan.

Six Flags Over New England, formerly Riverside Park, is right across the Connecticut River from Springfield. As New England's only gigantic amusement park, it has everything from roller coasters some of us just look at and go "Ohmigod!" to a water park to such characters as Bugs Bunny strolling around. Open seven days a week from late April through October; weekends in October; closed November through April.

Take the Massachusetts Turnpike west to Springfield.

Basketball Hall of Fame

(877) 4HOOPLA

www.hoophall.com

The Big E

(413) 787-0271

www.thebige.com

Six Flags Over New England

(413) 786-9300

www.sixflags.com/newengland

STURBRIDGE

This town right off the Massachusetts Turnpike is best known for Old Sturbridge Village, a working re-creation of an 1830's New England farming community. Watch craftsmen make candles and candle-holders. See farmers yoking oxen and a housewife making bread in a "beehive" oven.

Open daily from 9 A.M. to 5 P.M., March 31 to October 28; 10 A.M. to 4 P.M. February 19 to March 30; and 10 A.M. to 4 P.M. on weekends only January 2 to February 18. Closed in November and December.

In addition to the village, Sturbridge has a number of crafts, antiques, and clothing stores worth a visit. It's not far from Brimfield, which hosts a huge antiques show three times a year. Dealers from across the country set up tents to offer their wares.

Take the Massachusetts Turnpike to the Sturbridge exit. It'll take you forty-five minutes or so from Boston.

Brimfield Antiques Show

www.brimfield-antiqueshow.com

Old Sturbridge Village

(508) 347-3362

www.osv.org

Sturbridge Chamber of Commerce

(800) 628-8379

www.sturbridge.org

WACHUSETT MOUNTAIN

About eighty minutes west of Boston, Wachusett—(978) 464-2300, www.wachusett.com—offers family-friendly skiing and snowboard-ing. It has nowhere near the vertical drop of mountains in northern New Hampshire, so this isn't the place for expert skiers.

Take Route 2 west to the Westminster/Princeton exit.

WORCESTER

Tell a native Bostonian you're traveling to Worcester by choice and he'll look at you like you've just grown a third eye. But New England's second-largest city has a decent art museum, a kind of oddball but interesting museum of armor, and the redundantly named Centrum Center, which is where many arena bands play when they come to Massachusetts.

Take Route 9 west into Worcester or take the Massachusetts Turnpike to Route 146 north or Route 290 north. It'll take you forty-five minutes to an hour via the turnpike. Commuter-rail service is available from South Station; however, it's geared to getting people from Worcester into Boston in the morning and then from Boston to Worcester in the evening.

Higgins Armory Museum
100 Barber Avenue
(508) 853-6015

www.higgins.org

Worcester Art Museum
55 Salisbury Street
(508) 799-4406

www.worcesterart.org

New York City

Okay, okay, it's not part of New England, but it's not all that far from Boston, either—four to five hours by car or bus, three and a half hours by Amtrak, or an hour by air shuttle (plus as much as another hour to get into Manhattan, depending on traffic)—so you can see what all the fuss is about.

Amtrak
(800) USA-RAIL

www.amtrak.com

Bonanza Bus Lines
(888) 751-8800

www.bonanzabus.com

Delta Shuttle
(800) 221-1212

www.delta.com/prog_serv/
delta_shuttle/ds_schedule/

Greyhound
(800) 229-9424

www.greyhound.com

US Airways Shuttle
(800) 245-4882
www.usair.com/shuttle

Maine

Maine is the largest state in New England—it's as large as the rest of the region put together—and it offers attractions to match.

Shoppers will love the outlet shops in Kittery and Freeport. Many of the same chains are in both towns; if you stop in Kittery first, the main reason to continue on to Freeport is L.L. Bean, the sporting goods and clothing store open twenty-four hours a day, 365 days a year. Besides L.L. Bean, the main difference between the two areas is that Kittery is just a series of strip malls, and Freeport is an old-time New England fishing village whose main-street stores have been converted into outlets (for the complete shopping experience in Freeport, stay at one of its B&Bs to give yourself more time).

The Maine coast really is rockbound and rugged. It's dotted with lighthouses, small fishing villages, and, of course, waves crashing on rocks. Acadia National Park is the most visited park in the country. Maine also has some of the best skiing and fishing in the East. Just north of the New Hampshire line, you'll find some nice beaches, although, as in Massachusetts, only the grizzled natives actually go swimming because of the water temperature.

To get to Maine, drive north on Route 1 (the scenic route once you cross into New Hampshire) or Route 95 (the fast route; it parallels Route 1 through southern Maine, then turns north). Count on a two to two-and-a-half hour trip.

CITY
FACT

A frappe is ice cream, milk, and chocolate syrup. The "e" is silent. If you get an ice cream cone, ask for jimmies—chocolate sprinkles.

Acadia National Park

(207) 288-3338

www.nps.gov/acad

Maine Fall Foliage

www.state.me.us/doc/
foliage/index.html

Current reports and tips on where to get the best views.

Maine Office of Tourism

(888) 624-6345

www.visitmaine.com

Ski Maine

(207) 761-3774

www.skimaine.com

Information on Maine ski areas and resorts.

New Hampshire

Bostonians have a love-hate relationship with the Granite State. Maybe it's the politics (Massachusetts has a reputation as one of the most liberal states in the country; New Hampshire as one of the most conservative), but whatever the reason, some Bostonians would rather drive the extra miles to get to Vermont than spend time in New Hampshire. Others, however, love the skiing, the boating on Lake Winnipesaukee, and even the discount booze at the state liquor stores.

The Kancamagus Highway, which winds through the heart of the White Mountains, has some of the best foliage viewing in New England. On either end of the highway are kid-friendly places: on one end, Clark's Trading Post, which has everything from trained bears to buildings full of antique cars (and antique batteries, of all things); on the other, Storyland, an amusement park geared to the under-six set.

From Boston, take Route 93 north for ski country; Route 95 north for the New Hampshire sea coast. Unless you get stuck in rush-hour traffic, you'll hit the New Hampshire line in forty-five minutes to an hour.

Lake Winnipesaukee Home Page

www.winnipesaukee.com

New Hampshire Division of Travel

(800) FUNINNH

www.visitnh.gov

Ski New Hampshire

(800) 88SKINH

www.skinh.com

Information on New Hampshire ski areas and resorts.

Storyland

(603) 383-4186

www.storylandnh.com

White Mountains Attractions Association

(800) 346-3687

www.visitwhitemountains.com

Rhode Island

Sure, it's the smallest state in the country, but it has a distinct feel and even a dialect that sets it apart from everyplace else (whereas New Yorkers drink milk shakes and Bostonians frappes, Rhode Islanders down cabinets). Large parts of Providence are every bit as lovely as shown on the TV show named for it, and the city has some excellent Italian restaurants. Newport has amazing turn-of-the-century mansions built by robber barons (many now open to the public), the annual Newport Folk Festival, and the oldest synagogue in the United States. Block Island is a one-hour ferry ride off the coast.

Take Route 95 south from Boston and forty-five minutes later, you're in Providence. Both Amtrak and the MBTA provide train service between Providence and Boston (Amtrak is faster, but it costs more). Bonanza Bus Lines also provides regular service between the two cities.

The Preservation Society of Newport County

(401) 847-1000

www.newportmansions.org

Helps restore and preserve Newport mansions.

Rhode Island Tourism Division

www.visitrhodeisland.com

Vermont

On a map, Vermont and New Hampshire sort of look like upside-down images of each other. You could be forgiven for thinking the states really are mirror images. Whereas New Hampshire has an anything-goes attitude toward development and a conservative reputation, Vermont has some of the strictest land-use regulations in the country, as well as the nation's only socialist congressman, not to mention Ben & Jerry's. And instead of state liquor stores and fireworks stands, the first thing you see upon entering Vermont on Route 7 is a sign advertising Vermont cheddar cheese. Like New Hampshire, though, Vermont has beautiful mountains and, of course, the skiing to go with them, at resorts such as Killington, Stowe, Sugarbush, and Stratton.

Manchester Village is a cute little town in some danger of being overrun by chain stores. Further north, the state's biggest city (Burlington, with all of 30,000 residents) is a small but surprisingly sophisticated city overlooking beautiful Lake Champlain. You can take a ferry ride across the lake or drive up into Canada—Montreal is only two-and-a-half hours away.

From Boston, it'll take you three hours or so by car to get to southern Vermont. Take Route 2 west to Route 7 north.

Ben and Jerry's Factory Tour

(866) BJ-TOURS

www.benjerry.com/tourinfo.tmpl

Thirty-minute tours of the ice cream plant. The cost is $2, but you get free samples, and part of the proceeds goes to a group that builds safer playgrounds.

Discover Burlington

www.discoverburlington.com

Vermont Department of Tourism

(800) VERMONT

www.1-800-vermont.com

Vermont Ski Areas Association

(800) VERMONT

www.skivermont.com

Information on Vermont ski areas and resorts.

CHAPTER 8

Volunteer and Community Involvement

Think of "Boston charity" and the first thing that may spring to mind is debutantes at a charity ball. And, indeed, the *Boston Globe* Living section runs photos of Bostonians at fancy balls several times a week. But community involvement in the Boston area is really a grassroots affair. From volunteering for town boards to marching in the annual AIDS Walk and Walk for Hunger to helping to build houses with Habitat for Humanity, Bostonians have plenty of opportunities for getting involved with their community.

General Resources

Attorney General's Division of Public Charities
(617) 727-2200

www.ago.state.ma.us/charity.asp

Provides tips on charitable giving, such as what questions to ask before making a donation.

CITY FACT

When you register to vote in Massachusetts, you'll have a choice of enrolling as a Democrat, Republican, or Independent. Independents can vote in either party's primary elections.

Boston Better Business Bureau Charity Info

www.bosbbb.org/charity.htm

Look up reports on specific charities and get more information on donations.

Boston Cares

167 Milk Street
Boston
(617) 263-CARE

www.bostoncares.org

Matches would-be volunteers with organizations that can use their help.

United Way of Massachusetts Bay

245 Summer Street, Suite 1401
Boston
(617) 624-8000

www.uwmb.org

Umbrella group for nonprofit organizations in the Boston area.

Volunteer Solutions

www.volunteersolutions.org/boston/volunteer

Online database that lists volunteer opportunities in the Boston area.

Volunteer and Nonprofit Organizations

AIDS Action Committee

131 Clarendon Street
Back Bay
(617) 437-6200

www.aac.org

Provides a variety of support and educational programs and sponsors the annual AIDS Walk through Boston and Brookline every June.

Alianza Hispana

409 Dudley Street
Roxbury
(617) 427-7175

www.laalianza.org

Provides health and social resources for Hispanics in Roxbury and Dorchester.

Alliance Française de Boston et Cambridge

53 Marlborough Street
Back Bay
(617) 912-0400

www.afboston.org

Promotes French language and culture in the Boston area. Offers French classes and cultural events.

American Red Cross of Massachusetts Bay

285 Columbus Avenue
Boston
(617) 375-0700

www.bostonredcross.org

Benevolent and Protective Order of Elk, Mother Lodge of New England

1 Morrell Street
(off Spring Street)
West Roxbury
(617) 327-1618

www.elks.org/lodges/home.cfm

Big Brothers of Massachusetts Bay

55 Summer Street
Downtown Crossing
Boston
(617) 542-9090

www.bbmb.org

America's largest Big Brother group.

Big Sister Association of Greater Boston

161 Massachusetts Avenue
Boston
(617) 236-8060

www.bigsister.org

Black and White Boston Coming Together

One Exeter Plaza
Boston
(617) 247-9300

www.bwboston.com

Works for increased goodwill between blacks and whites. Sponsors an annual Caddie Scholar Program.

Boston Adult Literacy Fund

3 School Street
Boston
(617) 720-0181

www.tiac.net/users/balf

Helps adults learn to read.

Boston Coalition

105 Chauncy Street
Boston
(617) 451-1441

www.bostoncoalition.org

Antidrug, antiviolence group.

Boston Institute for Arts Therapy

90 Cushing Avenue
Boston
(617) 288-5858

www.biat.org

Art programs for the elderly, the disabled, and others.

CITY FACT

If you want to stay enrolled as a voter in Massachusetts, you'll have to fill out a yearly resident's census form. This census, which lists your age, address, and occupation, is a public record available for perusal or sale at your local city or town clerk's.

Boston Jaycees

1 Beacon Street
Beacon Hill
(617) 367-5710

www.bostonjaycees.org

A charitable and individual development organization for young people (twenty-one to forty) in the Greater Boston area.

Boston Jewish Coalition for Literacy

126 High Street
Boston
(617) 457-8661

www.jcrcboston.org/bjclcoal.htm

Runs literacy programs and book drives. Organized by the Jewish Community Relations Council of Greater Boston.

Boston Minuteman Council, Boy Scouts of America

199 State Street, 3rd Floor
Boston
(617) 723-0007

www.bsaboston.org

Boston Partners in Education

44 Farnsworth Street
Boston
(617) 451-6145

www.bostonpartners.org

Helps students in the Boston public schools gain the academic skills they need to become successful learners.

Boston Rescue Mission

39 Kingston Street
Boston
(617) 482-8819

members.bellatlantic.net/
~vze24y94

"To help change broken lives
with Christian service and com-
passion." Started in 1899.

Boys and Girls Clubs of Boston

50 Congress Street, Suite 730
Boston
(617) 994-4700

www.bgcb.org

Clubhouses in Charlestown,
Dorchester, Chelsea, Roxbury,
and South Boston.

Canine Connections

25 East Hoyle Street
Norwood
(781) 793-7879

www.mousemagic.net/
canineconnections

Animal rescue group that promotes pet adoption from local
shelters.

Catholic Charities

75 Kneeland Street
Boston
(617) 482-5440

www.ccab.org

The Archdiocese of Boston's
charitable wing provides services such as adoption, summer
camps, and family counseling.
Started in 1903.

Christmas in the City

P.O. Box 24
Charlestown, MA 02129
(617) 242-3534

www.ultranet.com/~citc/

Started as an effort to give
memorable Christmases to
homeless children. Now works
to help families move from
homelessness to homes.

Citizen Schools

Museum Wharf
308 Congress Street
Boston
(617) 695-2300, ext. 130

www.citizenschools.org

After-school program located in
eleven Boston public schools.
Volunteers from different pro-
fessions teach small groups of
children, ages nine to fourteen,
about their careers.

City Year

285 Columbus Avenue, 4th Floor
South End
(617) 927-2600

www.cityyear.org/boston

CITY FACT

A giant natural-gas tank off Route 93 in Dorchester sports a rainbow-like mural by Corita Kent that is the largest copyrighted piece of art in the world. Look at the blue stripe for what could be the world's largest profile of Ho Chi Minh.

Boston's pioneering volunteer program for young adults, sort of an urban Peace Corps.

Combined Jewish Philanthropies of Greater Boston
126 High Street
Boston
(617) 457-8500

www.cjp.org

The CJP is the central fundraising and planning arm of Boston's Jewish community, supporting more than eighty local and international humanitarian, educational, cultural, and health care agencies.

Dante Alighieri Society of Massachusetts
41 Hampshire Street
Cambridge
(617) 876-5160

www.dantealighieri.net/cambridge

Promotes Italian language and culture.

FIERI Boston
16 LeBlanc Drive
West Peabody, MA 01960

www.fieri-boston.org

Students and young professionals celebrating Italian culture.

The Food Project
Box 25641
Dorchester, MA 02125
(617) 442-1322

www.thefoodproject.org

Plants food in Lincoln for hungry people in Dorchester and Roxbury.

Goethe Institute
170 Beacon Street
Beacon Hill
(617) 262-6050

www.goethe.de/uk/bos/enindex.htm

Promotes German culture in New England.

Greater Boston Food Bank

99 Atkinson Street
Boston
(617) 427-5200

www.gbfb.org

Seeks to ease hunger in the
Boston area.

Habitat for Humanity Boston

455 Arborway
Jamaica Plain
(617) 524-8891

www.habitatboston.org

Dedicated to building simple
low-cost homes by forming
working partnerships with
families with very low incomes
in desperate need of decent
housing.

Helping Hands

541 Cambridge Street
Allston
(617) 787-4419

www.helpinghandsmonkeys.org

Provides trained monkeys to the
disabled.

Homeless Empowerment

1151 Massachusetts Avenue
Cambridge
(617) 497-1595

www.homelessempowerment.org

Publisher of *Spare Change*, a
newspaper sold by homeless

people, this group also runs
computer training and writing
programs.

Horizons Initiative

90 Cushing Avenue
Dorchester
(617) 287-1900

www.horizonsinitiative.org

Helps homeless children and
their families.

iAbolish

198 Tremont Street, # 421
Boston
(617) 426-8161

www.anti-slavery.org

Fights slavery around the world.

International Institute of Boston

1 Milk Street
Boston
(617) 695-9990

www.iiboston.org

Has provided aid to new immigrants since 1924.

Irish Immigration Center

59 Temple Street, Suite 1105
Boston
(617) 542-7654

www.iicenter.org

Self-help organization for Irish
immigrants in the Boston area.

Japan Society of Boston
1 Milk Street
Boston
(617) 451-0726

www.us-japan.org/boston

Promoting cultural ties between Japan and the United States since 1904.

Jewish Big Brother and Big Sister Association of Greater Boston
333 Nahanton Street
Newton
(617) 965-7055

www.jbbbs.org

Jimmy Fund
375 Longwood Avenue
Boston
(800) 52-JIMMY

www.jimmyfund.org

Boston's unique cancer fund, founded in 1948 by the Variety Club of Boston and the Boston Braves to help a child with cancer known only as "Jimmy." The group raises millions each year through the efforts of the Boston Red Sox, the Massachusetts Chiefs of Police, local movie theatres, and annual events such as the Scooper Bowl ice cream festival.

Junior League of Boston
117 Newbury Street
Back Bay
(617) 536-9640

www.jlboston.org

Women's group that trains volunteers.

Kiwanis International
Kiwanis Club of Danvers
Box 92
Danvers, MA 01923

www.geocities.com/ Colosseum/Bleachers/9638/ danverskiwanis

Kiwanis Club of Medford
Box 478
Medford, MA 02155

www.medkiwanis.org

Other Kiwanis clubs:

www.homestead.com/ newenglandkiwanis/files/ Divisions.htm

Knights of Columbus, Massachusetts State Council
470 Washington Street
Norwood
(781) 551-0628

www.massachusettsstatekofc.org

Massachusetts Alliance of Portuguese Speakers

92 Union Square
Somerville
(617) 628-6065

www.maps-inc.org

Provides services to people from Portuguese-speaking countries.

Patriots' Trail Girl Scout Council

95 Berkeley Street
Back Bay
(617) 482-1078

www.ptgirlscouts.org

Umbrella group for Girl Scouts in Greater Boston.

Polish American Congress of Eastern Massachusetts

360 Huntington Avenue
Boston
(617) 889-6730

pages.prodigy.net/j.goclowski

Project Bread

160 North Washington Street
Boston
(617) 723-5000

www.projectbread.org

Dedicated to alleviating, preventing, and ending hunger in Massachusetts. Sponsors the annual springtime Walk for Hunger.

Rotary International

You can get a listing of Boston Rotary clubs at

www.rotary.org/cgi-bin/rbox/List-Clubs.cgi?city=boston

Other Boston-area Rotary clubs:

Rotary Club District 7910

www.rotary7910.org

Includes several clubs in the western suburbs.

Samaritans of Boston

654 Beacon Street, 6th Floor
Boston
(617) 536-2460

www.samaritansofboston.org

Helps the depressed and people thinking of suicide.

Sons of Italy in Massachusetts

93 Concord Avenue
Belmont
(617) 489-5234

www.osiama.org

TecsChange

83 Highland Street
Roxbury
(617) 442-4456

www.tecschange.org

Provides recycled computers and computer assistance to nonprofit groups in the Boston area and around the world.

Tibetan Association of Boston

Box 381256
Cambridge, MA 02238
(617) 864-6433

www.bostontibet.org

Preserves and promotes Tibetan language, culture, and religion.

Vietnamese American Civic Association

1452 Dorchester Avenue
3rd Floor
Dorchester
(617) 288-7344

Volunteers of America— Massachusetts

441 Centre Street
Jamaica Plain
(617) 522-8086

www.voamass.org

Nonprofit, spiritually based organization providing local human service programs and opportunities for individual and community involvement.

Women's Educational and Industrial Union

356 Boylston Street
Back Bay
(617) 536-5651

www.weiu.org

Founded in 1877, the union seeks to enhance the lives of women and their families. Has resources on work, housing, and families. Its Boylston Street women's craft store, with a large brass swan atop the front door, is a local landmark.

YMCA of Greater Boston

316 Huntington Avenue
Boston
(617) 927-8060

www.ymcaboston.org

The country's first Y. Has thirty-six branches in eastern Massachusetts, providing everything from children's day camps to swimming to job training. Branches include Dorchester, East Boston, Framingham, Hyde Park, Needham, Quincy, Roxbury, West Roxbury/Roslindale, Wakefield, and Waltham.

Youth Tech Entrepreneurs

389 Main Street, Suite 404
Malden
(781) 321-0594

www.yte.org

Prepares high school students for leadership and further education by helping them develop technology enterprises that serve their schools and communities.

Finding the Essentials

CHAPTER 9

Important Places to Know

Boston's a big city. If you need it, chances are you can find it, whatever it is (you just might not be able to find it at 3 A.M., though, but see the following section on late-night Boston). Here are some resources to get you started in your new life in Boston.

Cleaners/Laundry

Dry cleaners in the Boston area are still sometimes called "cleansers" (or, more properly, "cleansas"; they're wheah you get your clothes Mahtinized). Can't stand to wash your clothes? Wait until you get an SUV's worth, then drive the whole thing over to Fern Cleansers, 128 Brighton Avenue in Allston, where they'll wash it in their industrial-size machines and charge you by the pound: (617) 254-9649.

Anton's Cleaners
(617) 247-8887

Has locations in Boston, Braintree, Burlington, Reading, Malden, Melrose, Needham, Wakefield, and Canton.

Birch Coin Laundromat
10 Corinth Street
Roslindale
(617) 323-8516

Bubbles Coin Laundry
1230 VFW Parkway
(617) 323-9533

Bush Cleaners
60 State Street
Financial District
(617) 248-0374

Christo's Cleaners
473 Harvard Street
Brookline
(617) 566-8079

Clean Brite Laundromat
321A Centre Street
Jamaica Plain
(617) 983-8468

Crimson Cleaners
1609 Massachusetts Avenue
Cambridge
(617) 876-0268

Dependable Cleaners
110 Newbury Street
Back Bay
(617) 267-1235

www.dependablecleaners.com

Also has locations in Braintree, Brookline, and Watertown.

Esplanade Cleaners
109 Charles Street
Beacon Hill
(617) 523-6925

Holly Cleaners
1314 Centre Street
Newton
(617) 527-0770

Leisure Laundries
4549 Washington Street
Roslindale
(617) 469-3602

Missing Sock Laundromat & Dry Cleaning
1846 Commonwealth Avenue
Brighton
(617) 566-4777

MOVING TIP

Moving from a warmer climate? You'll need plenty of warm clothes for New England winters. But if your state levies a sales tax on clothing, try to wait until you get here to buy—Massachusetts excludes most clothing from the state sales tax.

**Mr. Clean Laundromat &
Dry Cleaners**
220 Somerville Avenue
Somerville
(617) 625-2862

Neponset Cleaners
610 Gallivan Boulevard
Dorchester
(617) 288-6100

Regent Tailors and Cleaners
463 Massachusetts Avenue
Arlington
(781) 648-2439

**Royal White Laundry &
Dry Cleaners**
13 Warwick Street
Somerville
(617) 776-1500

**South End Neighborhood
Laundry**
135 West Canton Street
South End
(617) 424-1199

South End Suds
1407 Washington Street
South End
(617) 266-8126

Swan Laundry and Cleaners
535 Washington Street
Brighton
(617)254-9730

Zoots Dry Cleaning
1833 Centre Street
West Roxbury
(617) 469-2022

Health Care

Boston has a well-deserved reputation as a medical mecca, thanks to its heavy concentration of teaching hospitals. The Longwood Medical Area alone has several world-renowned facilities, including Beth Israel Deaconess Hospital, Brigham and Women's Hospital, Children's Hospital, the Joslin Diabetes Clinic, and the Dana-Farber Cancer Institute. Add in Massachusetts General Hospital, Tufts New England Medical Center in Chinatown, and Boston Medical Center, and you can see why people from around the world often fly into Boston for care—and why Boston often brings in more federal research dollars than any other city. Also unusual is that almost all hospitals in Massachusetts are run by nonprofit organizations.

At the same time, however, health care in Massachusetts is more expensive than in other parts of the country. Perhaps that's one of the reasons why HMOs took hold here earlier than in many other places. Recent years have seen considerable consolidation in hospitals, as smaller community facilities either close, merge with neighboring hospitals, or get acquired by teaching hospitals.

INSURERS AND DOCTORS

The state Division of Insurance offers a series of online guides to buying health insurance in Massachusetts, including overviews of HMOs and tips on buying nongroup health insurance: www.state.ma.us/doi/Consumer/CSS_health.html. The state Managed Care Advisory Board has a guide to HMOs that has more tips and results of a survey of member satisfaction at Massachusetts managed-care plans: www.state.ma.us/dhcfp/pages/dhcfp_87.htm. The board also has an ombudsman to hear consumer complaints: (800) 436-7757.

CITY FACT

A five-foot-long carved wooden codfish known as the Sacred Cod hangs over the entrance to the House of Representatives chamber in the State House on Beacon Hill.

Blue Cross Blue Shield of Massachusetts
401 Park Drive
Boston
(800) 262-BLUE
www.bcbsma.com

Delta Dental Plan of Massachusetts
465 Medford Street
Boston
(800) 872-0500
www.deltamass.com

Harvard Pilgrim Health Care
93 Worcester Street
Wellesley
(888) 888-4742
www.harvardpilgrim.org

Neighborhood Health Plan
253 Summer Street
Boston
(800) 433-5556
www.nhp.org

Tufts Health Plan
333 Wyman Street
Waltham
(800) 462-0224
www.tufts-healthplan.com

In addition to lists provided by insurers, most hospitals (see below) have physician referral services. So does the Massachusetts Medical Society at www.massmed.org/referrals.

The Massachusetts Board of Registration in Medicine runs an online database that lets you see if a doctor has ever faced disciplinary or malpractice action in the state: www.docboard.org/ma/df/masearch.htm. The board also has suggestions for questions to ask your doctor before an exam or test: www.massmedboard.org/ccu1.htm.

The Boston area has a large number of support groups for people with particular conditions and their families. You can find a listing at www.boston-online.com/Health/.

HOSPITALS AND HEALTH CENTERS

Beth Israel Deaconess Hospital
330 Brookline Avenue
Longwood Medical Area
Roxbury
(617) 667-7000
www.bidmc.harvard.edu

Boston Medical Center
88 East Newton Street
Boston
(617) 638-8000
www.bmc.org
Formerly Boston City Hospital and University Hospital.

Beverly Hospital
85 Herrick Street
Beverly
(978) 922-3000
www.beverlyhospital.org

Brigham and Women's Hospital
75 Francis Street
Longwood Medical Area
(Roxbury)
(617) 732-5500
www.brighamandwomens.org

Caritas Norwood Hospital

800 Washington Street
Norwood
(781) 769-2950

www.caritasnorwood.org

Carney Hospital

2100 Dorchester Avenue
Dorchester
(617) 296-4000

www.carneyhospital.org

Children's Hospital

300 Longwood Avenue
Longwood Medical Area
(617) 355-6000

www.childrenshospital.org

Dana-Farber Cancer Institute

44 Binney Street
Longwood Medical Area
(617) 632-3000

www.dfci.harvard.edu

Outpatient services only.

Deaconess-Waltham Hospital

Hope Avenue
Waltham
(781) 647-6000

www.waltham.caregroup.org

Emerson Hospital

133 Old Road to Nine Acre Corner
Concord
(978) 369-1400

www.emersonhospital.org

Faulkner Hospital

1153 Centre Street
Jamaica Plain
(617) 983-7000

www.faulknerhospital.org

Fenway Community Health Center

7 Haviland Street
Fenway
(617) 267-0900

www.fchc.org

One of Boston's oldest health centers. Specializes in medical and mental-health care for gays, lesbians, and bisexuals.

Franciscan Children's Hospital and Rehabilitation Center

30 Warren Street
Brighton
(617) 254-3800

www.fchrc.org

Greater Roslindale Medical & Dental Center

6 Cummins Highway
Roslindale
(617) 323-4440

www.bmc.org/roslindale

Community health and dental center.

Harvard Street Neighborhood Health Center
632 Blue Hill Avenue
Dorchester
(617) 825-3400

www.harvardstreet.org

Joslin Diabetes Center
1 Joslin Place
Longwood Medical Area
(617) 732-2400

www.joslin.harvard.edu

Outpatient services only.

Lahey Clinic
41 Mall Road
Burlington
(781)744-5100

www.lahey.org

Massachusetts Eye and Ear Infirmary
243 Charles Street
West End
(next to Massachusetts General)
(617) 573-5520

www.meei.harvard.edu

Massachusetts General Hospital
55 Fruit Street
Beacon Hill/West End
(617) 726-2000

www.mgh.harvard.edu

MetroWest Medical Center
115 Lincoln Street
Framingham
(508) 383-1000

www.mwmc.com

Leonard Morse Hospital
67 Union Street
Natick
(508) 650-7000

www.mwmc.com

Mount Auburn Hospital
330 Mount Auburn Street
Cambridge
(617) 492-3500

www.mountauburn.
caregroup.org

CITY FACT

Bostonians drink a lot of tonic; it's what the rest of the country calls soda or pop. You can buy it at a "spa," a mom-and-pop convenience store or lunch counter.

New England Baptist Hospital

125 Parker Hill Avenue
Mission Hill
(617) 754-5800

www.nebh.caregroup.org

New England Medical Center

750 Washington Street
Chinatown
(617) 636-5000

www.nemc.org

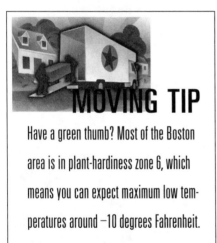

MOVING TIP

Have a green thumb? Most of the Boston area is in plant-hardiness zone 6, which means you can expect maximum low temperatures around −10 degrees Fahrenheit.

Newton-Wellesley Hospital

2014 Washington Street
Newton
(617) 243-6000

www.nwh.org

North End Community Health Center

332 Hanover Street
North End

(800) 711-4MGH

www.mgh.harvard.edu/
primarycare/locations/nend.html

Shriners Hospital

51 Blossom Street
Beacon Hill/West End
(617) 722-3000

www.shriners.com/shc/boston

Children's burn hospital.

Joseph M. Smith Community Health Center

287 Western Avenue
Allston
(617) 783-0500

www.josephsmith.org

St. Elizabeth's Medical Center

736 Cambridge Street
Brighton
(617) 789-3000

www.semc.org

Uphams Corner Health Center

500 Columbia Road
Dorchester
(617) 287-8000

www.uphamscornerhealthctr.
com

Winchester Hospital

41 Highland Avenue
Winchester
(781) 729-9000

www.winchesterhospital.org

Markets/Grocery Stores

No matter how exotic your tastes, chances are there's a market in the Boston area that can satisfy you. In particular, Harvard Avenue in Allston has a number of ethnic markets. However, buying international foods no longer necessarily requires a long trip: A number of Star Markets now have large international food sections, stocking everything from Vietnamese spices to gefilte fish.

One trend of recent years has been supermarket chains rediscovering inner Boston neighborhoods. From Jamaica Plain to Dorchester, chains have opened up stores in areas that had long gone without a decent supermarket.

For the cheapest produce, you need to get to Haymarket. Every Friday and Saturday throughout the year, vendors loudly hawk fresh fruits and vegetables in this outdoor marketplace around the corner from Quincy Market (you can also pick up fish and meat). Don't just go for the fruit, though; go for the street theatre. The last time I was there, I listened as two competing vendors had an impromptu duet:

"Buck a box!"

"Dollar a pound!"

"Buck a box!"

"Dollar a pound!"

Buck a box of what? Dollar a pound for what? Doesn't really matter. The key was to get the jostling pedestrians to stop and look.

You generally can't check out individual fruits (these vendors are feisty; they'll call you on it), so don't be surprised if you come home with a couple of spoiled ones, but the prices more than make up for it.

Many neighborhoods and towns also have regular farmer's markets throughout the summer, where you can pick up fresh produce and plants from New England farms. The state Department of Food and Agriculture puts together an annual listing of these markets at www.massdfa.org.

YOUR BASIC CHAINS

BJ's Wholesale Club

6 Hutchison Drive
Danvers
(978) 777-0469

26 Whittier Street
Framingham
(508) 872-2100

273 Middlesex Avenue
Medford
(781) 396-0451

85 Cedar Street
Stoneham
(781) 279-1499

www.bjs.com

When you need five-pound bags of chicken wings or gallon jugs of mayonnaise, go to BJ's. Although you can save quite a bit by buying in bulk, savvy shoppers know to compare prices; sometimes the regular supermarkets still have better prices.

Johnny's Foodmaster

(617) 660-1300

www.foodmaster.baweb.com

Supermarkets in Arlington, Charlestown, Lynn, Medford, Melrose, Revere, Somerville, South Weymouth, and Swampscott.

Roche Bros.

www.rochebros.com

Stores in Acton, Millis, Natick, Needham, Quincy, Wellesley, West Roxbury, and Westwood. The Westwood store has a gigantic deli and prepared-meals section.

Shaw's

www.shaws.com

Supermarkets all over the place, but mostly in the suburbs (although that is changing as it absorbs Star Market).

Star Market

www.starmarket.com

Has supermarkets all over Boston and the inner suburbs. Star is now owned by Shaw's, which is slowly converting the stores to Shaw's. Newer Star Markets tend to have add-ons such as juice bars and Starbucks outlets, as well as Wild Harvest areas for natural foods.

Stop & Shop

www.stopandshop.com

Has supermarkets all over the place. Immortalized in the song "Roadrunner" by Jonathan Richman and the Modern Lovers.

SPECIALTY CHAINS AND STORES

Abruzzese Meat Market
94 Salem Street
North End
(617) 227-6140

Babushka Deli
62 Washington Street
Brighton
(617) 731-9739

Russian foods, videos, and CDs.

Berezka International Food Store
1211 Commonwealth Avenue
Allston
(617) 787-2837

Russian foods, videos, and CDs.

Bread & Circus

Stores in downtown Boston, Bedford, Brighton, Cambridge, Newton, Wayland, and Wellesley Hills.

www.breadandcircus.com

Natural foods.

The Butcherie
428 Harvard Street
Brookline
(617) 731-9888

www.butcherie.com

A kosher grocerie, um, grocery and meat store.

Cardullo's Gourmet
6 Brattle Street
Harvard Square
Cambridge
(617) 491-8888

www.cardullos.com

Gourmet foods from around the world.

Cibao Market
3936 Washington Street
Roslindale
(617) 524-7708

Puerto Rican foods.

DeLuca's Market
11 Charles Street
Beacon Hill
(617) 523-4343

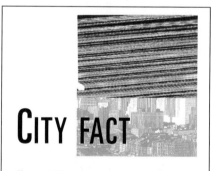

CITY FACT

Human billboards are people who stand at intersections or on overpasses waving political signs. Three or more of them make up a standout.

Formaggio Kitchen

244 Huron Avenue
Cambridge
(617) 354-4750

www.formaggiokitchen.com

All kinds of cheese from around the world.

Harvest Co-op Supermarkets

581 Massachusetts Avenue
Cambridge

57 South Street
Jamaica Plain
(617) 661-1580

www.harvestcoop.com

Member-owned markets, specializing in organic and bulk foods. Membership starts at $10 a year.

Hilltop Steakhouse Butcher Shop

855 Broadway (Route 1 south)
Saugus
(781) 233-7700

www.hilltopsteakhouse.com/
butcher.html

Meat, meat, and more meat. You can't miss it; just look for the fiberglass cows and the giant neon cactus.

International Market

433 Cambridge Street
Brighton
(617) 254-7440

Brazilian food.

James Hook & Co.

15–17 Northern Avenue
Waterfront
(617) 423-5500

Lobsters, lobsters, lobsters.

Kotobukiya

1815 Massachusetts Avenue
Cambridge
(617) 354-6914

A Japanese grocery in the Porter Exchange Mall, which has a number of Japanese restaurants and food outlets.

Ming's Supermarket

1102–1108 Washington Street
Chinatown
(617) 338-1588

Chinese foods.

Mirim Trading Co.

152 Harvard Avenue
Allston
(617) 783-2626

Korean foods.

Salumeria Italiana

151 Richmond Street
North End
(800) 400-5916

www.italian-gourmet-foods.com

Italian foods.

Savenor's
160 Charles Street
Beacon Hill
(617) 723-6328

Meats.

See Sun Co.
25 Harrison Avenue
Chinatown
(617) 426-0954

Chinese meats and produce.

Shalimar India Food & Spices
571 Massachusetts Avenue
Cambridge
(617) 868-8311

Super 88
101 Allstate Road
Dorchester
(617) 989-8895

Supermarket specializing in Chinese foods and medicinal herbs.

Trader Joe's
Stores in Arlington, Brookline, Cambridge, Framingham, Needham, and Swampscott.

www.traderjoes.com

Eclectic mix of food products; the kind of place you'd expect to see on the West Coast (which is where it started).

Tropical Market
280 Centre Street
Jamaica Plain
(617) 524-1312

Hispanic and Caribbean foods.

Vien Dong Fareast Supermarket
1159 Dorchester Avenue
Dorchester
(617) 265-9131

Vietnamese and Asian foods.

Wild Oats
2151 Mystic Valley Parkway
Medford
(781) 395-4998

Natural foods.

Wulf's Fish Market
407 Harvard Street
Brookline
(617) 277-2506

CITY FACT

Boston clam chowder is made with cream and bacon, not tomatoes.

ONLINE GROCERY SHOPPING

The Boston area currently has one grocery-delivery service:

Peapod

www.peapod.com

Affiliated with Stop & Shop.

Farm Stands and Orchards

What could be better than some corn on the cob fresh from the farm? How about some apples you picked yourself? There are numerous farm stands, apple orchards, and you-pick farms only a short drive outside Boston. In particular, the towns along Route 2, such as Lincoln, Concord, Stow, Bolton, and Harvard, have numerous farm stands and orchards. All are an hour or less from Boston.

The Massachusetts Association of Roadside Stands maintains a complete listing of farm stands and orchards: (413) 529-0386 or www.massfarmstands.com. The state agriculture department lists other "Massachusetts Grown" sites, including turkey and Christmas-tree farms, at www.massgrown.org/farms_products.

Allandale Farm
259 Allandale Road
Brookline
(617) 524-1531

Arena Farms
Route 2
Concord
(978) 369-4769

Bolton Orchards
Junction of Routes 117 and 110
Bolton
(978) 779-2733

Capasso Farms
118 Framingham Road
Southborough
(508) 485-1680

Carver Hill Orchards
101 Brookside Avenue
Stow
(508) 897-6117

Connors Farm
30 Valley Road (Route 35)
Danvers
(978) 777-1245

www.connorsfarm.com

Doe Orchards
327 Ayer Road
Harvard
(978) 772-4139

Hanson's Farm
20 Nixon Road
Framingham
(508) 877-3058

Honeypot Hill Orchard
144 Sudbury Road
Stow
(978) 562-5666

Idylwilde Farm
366 Central Street
Acton
(978) 263-1662

Nicewicz Farm
116 Sawyer Road
Bolton
(978) 779-6423

Nourse Family Farm
80 Nourse Street
Westboro
(508) 870-0803

www.noursefamilyfarm.com

Shelburne Farm
106 West Acton Road
Stow
(978) 897-9287

Tougas Family Farm
246 Ball Street
Northboro
(508) 393-6406

Verrill Farm
11 Wheeler Road
Concord
(978) 369-4494

Wade Orchard
62 Westcott Road
Harvard
(978) 456-3926

Liquor Stores

Boston-area liquor stores are often called "packies" or "package stores." By law, they are closed on Sunday, unless they are within ten miles of the New Hampshire state line (where Massachusetts granted an exemption due to competition from New Hampshire's state-owned liquor stores). Most supermarkets do not sell alcohol; those that do are limited to beer and wine (and they also have to obey the Sunday restriction). In another Massachusetts quirk, a few drug stores that have been in business since Prohibition are allowed to sell hard liquor (strictly for medicinal purposes, of course). Speaking of

Prohibition, to this day, some towns prohibit the sale of alcohol. Wellesley, for example, is a "dry" town (although it does allow liquor sales at some local restaurants). Fortunately for thirsty Wellesleyites, there's a liquor store just over the town line in Natick.

Atlas Liquors
156 Mystic Avenue
Medford

661 Adams Street
Quincy

591 Hyde Park Avenue
Roslindale
(781) 395-4400

www.atlasliquors.com

Blanchard's Liquors
418 LaGrange Street
West Roxbury

288 American Legion Highway
Revere

741 Centre Street
Jamaica Plain
(617) 327-1400

www.blanchardsliquor.com

Brookline Liquor Mart
1354 Commonwealth Avenue
Brighton
(617) 734-7700

www.blmwine.com

Has frequent wine tastings.

Buy Rite Liquors
2440 Massachusetts Avenue
Cambridge
(617) 354-1100

www.buyritemassave.com

Martignetti's
1650 Soldiers Field Road
Brighton
(617) 782-3700

64 Cross Street
North End
(617) 227-4343

Parkway Plaza Mall
Chelsea
(617) 884-3500

www.martignetti.com

Marty's Liquors
193 Harvard Avenue
Allston
(617) 782-3250

Large selection of international beers and wines.

Murray's Wines and Spirits
747 Beacon Street
Newton Centre
(617) 964-1550

Pharmacies

The big chains in the Boston area are Brooks, CVS, Osco, and Walgreens. Many Star Market and Stop & Shop supermarkets also have pharmacies.

Brooks Pharmacy
www.brooks-rx.com/stores.htm

CVS
(800) SHOP-CVS
www.cvs.com/storeloc/
StoreLocator1.asp

Osco
(888) 443-5701
www.oscodrug.com

Walgreens
(800) 925-4733
www.walgreens.com

Other Pharmacies

You can get a more complete listing of independent pharmacies at www.irxplus.com/main/states/massachusetts/massleft.shtml.

Allston Pharmacy
177 Allston Street
Brighton
(617) 277-5125

Casper Pharmacy
611 East Broadway
South Boston
(617) 268-5457

Gary Drug
59 Charles Street
Beacon Hill
(617) 227-0023

Huron Drug
356 Huron Avenue
Cambridge
(617) 547-6400

Inman Pharmacy
1414 Cambridge Street
Cambridge
(617) 876-4868

Maida Pharmacy
121 Massachusetts Avenue
Arlington
(781) 643-7840

CITY FACT

Massachusetts's famous blue laws have largely been repealed; however, liquor sales are still illegal on Sunday except within ten miles of the New Hampshire line (where an exception was made because of the presence of state-run liquor stores across the line).

Strand Pharmacy
533 Columbia Road
Dorchester
(617) 436-0155

Sullivan's Pharmacy and Medical Supply
1 Corinth Street
Roslindale
(617) 323-6544

Sutherland Pharmacy
1690 Commonwealth Avenue
Brighton
(617) 232-3513

Village Pharmacy
1 Brookline Place
Brookline
(617) 735-9094

West Roxbury Pharmacy
1868 Centre Street
(617) 325-0017

Late-Night Boston

"Late-night Boston" is something of an oxymoron. The clubs and bars close by 2 A.M. (1 A.M. in many surrounding towns), and the subways stop at 12:45 A.M., although the MBTA now runs "Night Owl" buses between 1 and 2:30 A.M. along subway and some bus routes on Friday and Saturday nights.

Still, if you are up and around at 4 A.M., you do have a few options for eating and shopping, if not dancing and drinking.

BOWLING

Boston Bowl Family Fun Center

820 Morrissey Boulevard
Dorchester
(617) 825-3800

www.bostonbowl.com

Has both candlepins and ten pins. Open twenty-four hours.

RESTAURANTS

Blue Diner

150 Kneeland Street
South Station
(617) 695-0087

Bar and diner food twenty-four hours a day. Often crowded; don't be surprised if you have to wait for a table at 3 A.M.

Buzzy's Fabulous Roast Beef

327 Cambridge Street
Charles Circle
Beacon Hill
(617) 242-7722

This Boston institution is a twenty-four-hour takeout stand specializing in—tah-dah—roast beef (as well as onion rings).

Café Pompeii

280 Hanover Street
North End
(617) 523-9438

Italian food and desserts until 4 A.M.

East Ocean City Restaurant

27 Beach Street
Chinatown
(617) 542-2504

Chinese seafood until 3:30 A.M. most nights (4 A.M. Friday and Saturday).

Ginza

16 Hudson Street
Chinatown
(617) 338-2261

Japanese food until 3:30 A.M. on weekends.

Hi-Fi Pizza and Giant Sub

469 Massachusetts Avenue
Cambridge
(617) 492-4600

Pizza until 4 A.M., Friday and Saturday; 3 A.M. Monday through Thursday; and 2 A.M. on Sunday.

International House of Pancakes

1850 Soldiers Field Road
Brighton
(617) 787-0533

All pancakes, all the time.

McDonald's

There are two all-night McDonald's on Route 128: southbound, just past Route 16 in Newton, and northbound, just past Route 2 in Lexington.

Redneck's Roast Beef

140 Brighton Avenue
(corner Harvard Avenue)
Allston
(617) 782-5775

Roast-beef sandwiches and fries until 3 A.M.

SoundBites

708 Broadway
Somerville
(617) 623-8338

Breakfast served until 3 A.M.

CITY FACT

Because of a design flaw, the windows in the sixty-story glass-encased John Hancock Building started falling out as it was nearing completion in 1972. Until replacements could be installed, the building briefly became the world's tallest plywood structure.

PHARMACIES

CVS

590 Middlesex Fells Parkway
Medford
(781) 391-5150

210 Border Street
East Boston
(617) 567-3236

600 Southern Artery
Quincy
(617) 472-7592

27–43 Main Street
Watertown
(617) 926-6662

35 White Street
Porter Square
Cambridge
(617) 876-4037

Walgreens

757 Gallivan Boulevard
Dorchester
(617) 282-3880

317 Ferry Street
Everett
(617) 389-2186

1228 Broadway
Saugus
(781) 233-4660

SUPERMARKETS AND CONVENIENCE STORES

Many Star Markets and some Stop & Shops are now open twenty-four hours.

www.starmarket.com

Store 24

www.store24.com

A chain of Boston-area convenience stores. Due to local regulations, many Store 24s outside Boston could more accurately be called Store 18s. Vies with Cumberland Farms ("Cumbie's"), White Hen Pantry, Li'l Peach, and Christy's for dominance of the Boston convenience-store market.

Places of Worship

Few cities have had as profound an effect on American religion as Boston. The Puritans who founded the city begat Congregationalists and Unitarians. Rhode Island was founded in part by refugees from the harsh Puritans (who executed Quakers when they refused to leave the "city on a hill"). Mary Baker Eddy founded Christian Science in Boston, which is home to the religion's mother church. Today Boston is one of the most heavily Catholic cities in the country.

CATHOLIC
Archdiocese of Boston
2121 Commonwealth Avenue
Brighton
(617) 436-3113

www.rcab.org

The archdiocese covers has 373 parishes, more than 130 parochial schools, and ten hospitals. You can look up Mass times at www.masstimes.org.

Cathedral of the Holy Cross
1400 Washington Street
South End
www.rcab.org/tourofcathedral/
default.html

Mother church for the archdiocese.

CHRISTIAN SCIENCE
The First Church of Christ, Scientist
175 Huntington Avenue
Back Bay
(617) 450-2000
www.tfccs.com

CONGREGATIONAL
Massachusetts Conference, United Church of Christ
Framingham
(508) 875-5233
www.macucc.org

Old South Church
645 Boylston Street
Back Bay
(617) 536-1970

www.scrollinggrid.com/osc

EPISCOPAL
Episcopal Diocese of Boston
131 Tremont Street
Boston
(617) 482-5800

www.diomass.org

GREEK ORTHODOX
Greek Orthodox Diocese of Boston
162 Goddard Avenue
Brookline
(617) 277-4742

www.boston.goarch.org/welcome.html

HINDU
Sri Lakshmi Temple
117 Waverly Street
Ashland
(508) 881-5775

www.srilakshmitemple.org

ISLAM
Islamic Society of Boston
204 Prospect Street
Cambridge
(617) 876-3546

www.isboston.org

JEWISH
Chabad House of Boston
491 Commonwealth Avenue
Back Bay
(617) 424-1190

Synagogue Council of Massachusetts
1320 Centre Street, Suite 306
Newton Centre
(617) 244-6506

www.synagoguecouncil.org

Represents Orthodox, Conservative, Reform, and independent congregations.

New England Region, United Synagogue of Conservative Judaism
1320 Centre Street, Suite 304
Newton Centre
(617) 964-8210

www.uscj.org/NEWENG

METHODIST
New England Conference, United Methodist Church
276 Essex Street
Lawrence
(978) 682-7676

www.neumc.org

MORMON
Boston Temple
86 Frontage Road
Belmont
(617) 993-9993

www.bostontemple.org

PAGAN
Society of Elder Faiths
Box 335
Boston University Station
Boston, MA 02215
www.elderfaiths.org

QUAKER
Beacon Hill Friends House
6 Chestnut Street
Beacon Hill
(617) 227-9118
www.bhfh.org

SEVENTH-DAY ADVENTIST
Boston Temple
105 Jersey Street
Fenway
(617) 536-5022
www.tagnet.org/bostontemple

UNITARIAN UNIVERSALIST
Massachusetts Bay District of Unitarian Universalist Churches
110 Arlington Street
Back Bay
(617) 542-3231
www.mbd.uua.org

Represents 55 congregations in the Boston area.

ZOROASTRIAN
Zoroastrian Association of the Greater Boston Area
53 Firecut Lane
Sudbury
(978) 443-6858
www.fas.harvard.edu/
~pluralsm/98wrb/zo_zoro.htm

Post Offices

The South Boston Postal Annex, 25 Dorchester Avenue (behind South Station), has extended hours. Consumer Affairs: (617) 654-5001. Express Mail information: (617) 654-5745.

Allston
47 Harvard Avenue
(617) 789-4273

Arlington
10 Court Street
(781) 648-1940

Back Bay
390 Stuart Street
(617) 236-1330

Prudential Center
800 Boylston Street
(617) 267-8162

Beacon Hill
136 Charles Street
(617) 723-1951

Brookline
1295 Beacon Street
(617) 738-1776

Cambridge
770 Massachusetts Avenue
(617) 876-0620

Dorchester
Fields Corner
218 Adams Street
(617) 288-1219

Uphams Corner
551 Columbia Road
(617) 287-0297

Hull
515 Nantasket Avenue
781-925-3300

Jamaica Plain
655 Centre Street
(617) 524-0420

Needham
1150 Great Plain Avenue
781-449-7524

Newton
2344 Washington Street
(617) 527-4045

North End
217 Hanover Street
(617) 723-5134

Somerville
237 Washington Street
(617) 666-0745

South Boston
444 East Third Street
(617) 269-0555

South End
59 West Dedham Street
(617) 266-8613

Watertown
126 Main Street
Watertown
(617) 924-0081

Weston
25 Colpitts Road
781-893-5280

West Roxbury
1970 Centre Street
(617) 325-0058

CHAPTER 10

Local Schools and Colleges

They don't call Boston the "Athens of America" for nothing. Boston is the ultimate college town: It has one of the highest concentrations of colleges and universities in the world, including world-famous institutions such as Harvard University and M.I.T. and an extensive network of community colleges. You see the influence of the high concentration of educational institutions in everything from the large number of clubs and music venues to apartment leases (which almost always start September 1). You also see it in the general population; a fair number of the people who go to school in Boston stay after they graduate.

And as with so much else in the Boston area, education has deep roots here. Harvard is the oldest college in the United States. Boston Latin School, founded in 1635, is the oldest public school in the United States (although Roxbury Latin School, founded in 1645, claims to be the oldest school "in continuous existence"). English High School is the oldest public high school in the country, founded in 1821. The Eliot School of Fine and Applied Arts has been offering art classes since 1676. And a scholarship fund started by Benjamin Franklin still aides Boston students.

At the same time, Boston parents have a sometimes wrenching decision when it comes to elementary and secondary education. Although Boston has one of the nation's best secondary schools—public or private—in Boston Latin School, the city as a whole has some of the lowest standardized test scores in the state. One of the perennial challenges facing whoever is mayor (who appoints the school committee) is trying to improve those schools.

Some parents opt for private or parochial schools (the Archdiocese of Boston has a large school system). A few take advantage of the state's "school choice" system, which lets them enroll their children in participating schools in neighboring communities (there is no charge; however, the parents have to figure out how to get their kids to school). Minority students are eligible for the Metco program, which buses students to a number of suburban schools. Some parents simply move to the suburbs.

CITY FACT

Don't like the offerings at your local library? Under state law, you can get a card at almost any library in the state. Any Massachusetts resident can get a Boston Public Library card.

In recent years, the Massachusetts Comprehensive Assessment System (MCAS) tests have become one way for incoming residents to decide where to live. These standardized tests, given in the fourth, eighth, and tenth grades, show how students perform in English, math, and science (eighth and tenth graders are also tested in history and social sciences). Starting in 2003, students will not be able to graduate unless they pass the tenth-grade test (they'll have five tries).

There are a number of online resources that let you compare school districts on both test results and other criteria (for example, spending).

Caliper MCAS Test Results Web Mapper

shiraz.caliper.com/Maptitude/mcas/find.asp

Lets you see MCAS results by town or district on a map. Can be handy for zeroing in on towns in particular geographic regions.

Massachusetts Department of Education Directory Profiles

profiles.doe.mass.edu

This Web site has profiles of individual school districts that include both MCAS and SAT scores.

MCAS Headlines

www.doe.mass.edu/mcas/

MCAS overview and information from the state Department of Education.

MCAS Tests

www.boston.com/mcas

Latest MCAS news from the *Boston Globe*.

Immunization

Under state law, the parents of children entering kindergarten have to show proof of vaccination against diphtheria, tetanus, pertussis, polio, mumps, measles, hepatitis B, and chicken pox (or proof that they've had chicken pox). Seventh-grade students need proof that they have gotten two MMR shots. Even college students are not exempt: All Massachusetts students must show proof of two MMR shots, a tetanus shot within the past ten years, and three doses of the hepatitis B vaccine. The state provides free vaccine to doctors and local boards of health (some doctors may charge a fee, however).

Child Care/Preschool/Kindergarten

As in other large metropolitan areas, parents in Greater Boston face a sometimes ludicrous fight to get their kids into the "right" preschool (because if they don't, they won't get into the right elementary school, and they'll eventually wind up living in cardboard boxes under highway overpasses). In particularly child-heavy neighborhoods, you'll need to line up several hours in advance just to get your child into a YMCA preschool program.

Boston now provides full-time kindergarten.

Note: In addition to the listings that immediately follow, see the section on private schools later in the chapter. Many private schools also have preschool programs.

GENERAL RESOURCES
Boston Child-Care Listings

www.ci.boston.ma.us/bra/child_care.asp

Lists a number of child-care services in Boston.

Child Care Choices of Boston

105 Chauncy Street
Boston, MA 02111
(617) 542-5437

www.bostonabcd.org/cccb

A child-care referral and resource agency for Boston, Brookline, Chelsea, Winthrop, and Revere.

Community Care for Kids

1509 Hancock Street
Quincy, MA 02169
(617) 471-6473, ext. 105
(800) 637-2011

Child-care referrals for the South Shore.

MaChildCare.com

www.machildcare.com/massachusetts.asp

This Web site has links to child-care agencies (listed by community) and relevant state departments, along with message areas for finding and discussing play groups, support services, and child-care facilities.

Massachusetts Office of Child Care Services

1 Ashburton Place, Room 1105
Boston, MA 02108
(617) 626-2000

www.qualitychildcare.org

Can provide guides on selecting a child-care provider; the Web site has a searchable database of state-licensed providers.

Pre-School/Child Care in Brookline

www.townofbrooklinemass.com/BCPC/preschoolchildcare.html

This town-run Web page lists and describes programs in Brookline, many of which are also open to residents of neighboring communities.

PRE-SCHOOL PROGRAMS

ABC Day School
319 Kittredge Street
Roslindale, MA 02131
(617) 325-6382

Apple Orchard School
282D Newton Street
Brookline, MA 02445
(617) 731-6463

Day care on a farm.

Beacon Hill Nursery School
74 Joy Street
Boston, MA 02114
(617) 227-0822

www.bhns.org

Busy Little Bees Family Day Care
26 Conant Road
Watertown, MA 02472
(617) 924-6157

www.machildcare.com/family/
busylittlebees.html

Cambridge Nursery School
6 Hillside Place
Cambridge, MA 02140
(617) 547-7288

www.machildcare.com/cns.html

The nation's oldest cooperative nursery school, founded in 1923.

The Child Care Center at Whitney Place
Three Vision Drive, Route 9 West
Natick, MA 01760
(508) 651-9306

www.salmonfamily.com/
child.html

Child Development Center
390 Rindge Avenue
Cambridge, MA 02140
(617) 491-0889

451 Lowell Street
Lexington, MA 02420
(781) 674-2595

200 Governors Avenue
Medford, MA 02155
(781) 395-9979

www.childdevelopmentcenter.org

The Children's Center of Brookline
59 Cypress Street
Brookline, MA 02445
(617) 566-0190

Staffers include early childhood students from local universities.

Clinton Path Pre-School
15 St. Paul Street
Brookline, MA 02445
(617) 731-8415

A co-op program.

Corner Co-op Nursery School

1773 Beacon Street
Brookline, MA 02445
(617) 738-4631

Dean Park Pre-School

1762 Beacon Street
Brookline, MA 02445
(617) 232-0465

Early Childhood Learning Laboratory

605 Commonwealth Avenue
Boston, MA 02215
(617) 353-3259

www.bu.edu/family/ecll.html

Half-day preschool that's part of the early childhood teacher education program at Boston University.

Etty's Child Development Center

33 Dwight Street
Brookline, MA 02445
(617) 730-5485

Happy Child Day Preschool/Day Care

1191 Chestnut Street
Newton
(617) 964-8231

www.machildcare.com/
happychild.html

Kehillath Israel Nursery School

384 Harvard Street
Brookline, MA 02446
(617) 731-9006

Based at a conservative synagogue.

Kiddie Country Club

16 Cohasset Street
Roslindale, MA 02131
(617) 325-2216

Lemberg Children's Center

415 South Street
Waltham, MA 02453
(781) 736-3000

www.brandeis.edu/lemberg

On the campus of Brandeis University; staff includes Brandeis professors and students.

Les Petits Nursery School

178 Mason Terrace
Brookline, 02445
(617) 232-7666

Longwood Medical Area Child Care Center

395 Longwood Avenue
Boston, MA 02215
(617) 632-2755

www.masco.org/childcare.htm

Serving the children of employees and students in the Longwood Medical Area.

**Mulberry Child Care
& Pre-School**
5 Brookline Street
Brookline, MA 02445
(617) 730-4311

N.I.C.E. Day Care
3297 Washington Street
Jamaica Plain, MA 02130
(617) 525-1439

Old South Preschool
645 Boylston Street
Back Bay, MA 02116
(617) 536-1970

At the Old South Congregational Church.

**PediCare Medical
Day Care Center**
*Franciscan Children's Hospital
& Rehabilitation Center*
30 Warren Street
Brighton, MA 02135
(617) 254-3800, ext. 5500

www.machildcare.com/
pedicare.html

Day care for children with special medical needs.

**Plowshares Education
Development Centers**
360 Lowell Avenue
Newtonville, MA 02460
(617) 527-3755

www.machildcare.com/
plowshares.html

Rainbow Preschool
240 Babcock Street
Brookline, MA 02446
(617) 277-9832

Small Fry Nursery School
15 Bellevue Street
West Roxbury, MA 02132
(617) 323-3200

**Theophany Orthodox
Christian School**
Box 920-376
Needham, MA 02492
(781) 444-3059

www.theophanyschool.org

Preschool and kindergarten programs.

**Tot Spot Child
Development Center**
1400 VFW Parkway
West Roxbury, MA 02132
(617) 363-5650

**Trinity Covenant Church
Christian Preschool**
7 Clematis Road
Lexington MA 02421
(781) 861-6868

home.att.net/~tcpreschool/

YMCA, North Suburban Branch
137 Lexington Street
Woburn, MA 01801
(781) 935-3270

www.ymcaboston.org/
branches_north.shtml

Offers toddler, preschool, and nursery-school day programs.

YMCA, Waltham Branch
725 Lexington Street
Waltham, MA 02452
(781) 894-5295

www.ymcaboston.org/
branches_wroxbury.shtml

Offers preschool and nursery-school programs.

YMCA, West Roxbury Branch
15 Bellevue Street
West Roxbury, MA 02132
(617) 323-3200

www.ymcaboston.org/
branches_wroxbury.shtml

Offers toddler, preschool, and kindergarten programs.

CITY FACT

The Harvard Bridge across the Charles River actually goes to M.I.T. It is exactly 364.4 smoots and an ear in length, the smoot being a unit of length derived from Oliver Smoot, an M.I.T. fraternity pledge used to measure the bridge in 1958. Today the bridge is marked every ten smoots.

Public Schools

Acton-Boxborough School District
16 Charter Road
Acton, MA 01720
(978) 264-4700

ab.mec.edu

Arlington Public Schools
869 Massachusetts Avenue
Arlington, MA 02476
(781) 316-3510

www.town.arlington.ma.us/
arschool.htm

Beverly Public Schools
20 Colon Street
Beverly, MA 01915
(978) 921-6100

www.beverlyschools.org

Boston School Department

26 Court Street
Boston, MA 02108
(617) 635-9000

www.boston.k12.ma.us

The Web site has profiles of individual schools. The city is divided into three geographic zones, and parents can choose any elementary or middle school within their zone (there are five lower-grade schools with special programs open to all city residents). All high schools are open to all city residents regardless of where they live. For more detailed information about how to select a school and special programs, go to www.boston.k12.ma.us/info/assign.asp. The site's school profiles show how schools did on the MCAS compared to citywide and state averages.

Boston Arts Academy

174 Ipswich Street
Fenway
(617) 635-6470

artsacad.boston.k12.ma.us

The city's school for the visual and performing arts. Prospective students must complete a written application and audition before a panel of teachers, instructors from local arts colleges, and local artists.

Boston Latin Academy

205 Townsend Street
Dorchester
(617) 635-9957

bla.boston.k12.ma.us

Has an entrance exam.

Boston Latin School

78 Avenue Louis Pasteur
Fenway
(617) 635-8895

www.bls.org

This is the oldest public school in America, founded in 1635. The school starts with grade seven. Students must pass a rigorous entrance exam to get in. The school boasts a 99 percent college-acceptance rate and MCAS scores far above the state average.

Braintree Public Schools

348 Pond Street
Braintree, MA 02184
(781) 380-0130

Brookline Public Schools

333 Washington Street
Brookline, MA 02445
(617) 730-2401

www.brookline.mec.edu

Cambridge Public Schools

159 Thorndike Street
Cambridge, MA 02141
(617) 369-6400

www.cps.ci.cambridge.ma.us

Cohasset Public Schools

143 Pond Street
Cohasset, MA 02025
(781) 383-6112

www.ssec.org/idis/cohasset/
highschool/main.htm

English High School

144 McBride Street
Jamaica Plain
(617) 635-8979

Founded in 1821, it's the oldest public high school in the country.

Franklin Public Schools

397 East Central Street
Franklin, MA 02038
(508) 541-5243

www.franklin.ma.us/
school/public

Hull Public Schools

7 Hadassah Way
Hull, MA 02045
(781) 925-0771

Marlborough Public Schools

17 Washington Street
Marlborough, MA 01752
(508) 460-3509

www.marlborough.k12.ma.us

Marshfield Public Schools

South River Street
Marshfield, MA 02050
(781) 834-5010

Medfield Public Schools

459 Main Street
Medfield, MA 02052
(508) 359-2302

Natick Public Schools

13 East Central Street
Natick, MA 01760
(508) 647-6500

www.natick.k12.ma.us

Needham Public Schools

1330 Highland Avenue
Needham, MA 02492
(781) 455-0435

Newton Public Schools

100 Walnut Street
Newtonville, MA 02460
(617) 552-7710

www.newtonpublicschools.com

Quincy Public Schools

70 Coddington Street
Quincy, MA 02169
(617) 984-8700

quincy.k12.ma.us

Somerville School Department

181 Washington Street
Somerville, MA 02143
(617) 625-6000

www.ci.somerville.ma.us/
departments/schools

Wakefield Public Schools
60 Farm Street
Wakefield, MA 01880
(781) 246-6400

www.wakefield.k12.ma.us

Wellesley Public Schools
40 Kingsbury Street
Wellesley, MA 02481
(781) 446-6210

Weston Public Schools
89 Wellesley Street
Weston, MA 02493
(781) 529-8080

www.weston.org/Schools

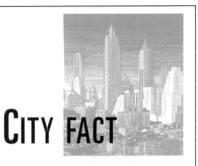

CITY FACT

Founded in 1635, the Boston Latin School is the oldest public school in America. Today, admission is determined by a rigorous entrance exam.

Charter Schools

Charter schools represent an attempt at innovation in publicly funded education. Instead of being run by a city or town, these publicly funded schools are run by boards of educators and parents. Many specialize in particular fields; some follow serious back-to-basics 3R curricula with extended school hours. Massachusetts has been relatively slow to approve charters, however.

Massachusetts Charter Schools

www.doe.mass.edu/cs.www

School listings, news, and overviews from the state Department of Education.

Academy of the Pacific Rim
1 Westinghouse Plaza
Boston, MA 02136
(617) 361-0050

www.pacrim.org

Grades 6–11.

Students must take Mandarin Chinese.

**Benjamin Banneker
Charter School**
21 Notre Dame Avenue
Cambridge, MA 02140
(617) 497-7771

www.banneker.org

Grades K–8.

**Boston Renaissance
Charter School**
250 Stuart Street
Boston, MA 02116
(617) 357-0900

Grades K–8. One of the largest
charter schools in the country.

City on a Hill Charter School
320 Huntington Avenue
Boston, MA 02115
(617) 262-9838

Grades 9–12.

**Conservatory
Lab Charter School**
50 West Broadway
South Boston, MA 02127
(617) 269-2408

Grades K–3, with an emphasis
on music.

Health Careers Academy
360 Huntington Avenue
Boston, MA 02115
(617) 373-8576

boston.k12.ma.us/schools/
rc648.asp

Grades 9–12.

**Media and Technology
Charter High School**
1187 Beacon Street
Brookline, MA 02446
(617) 232-0300

www.matchschool.org

Grades 9 and 10.

**Neighborhood House
Charter School**
197A Centre Street
Dorchester, MA 02124
(617) 825-0703

Grades K–8.

South Boston Harbor Academy
7 Elkins Street
South Boston, MA 02127
(617) 269-7557

www.sbha.org

Grades 5–10, with plans to
expand to grade 12. Uses Boston
Harbor as an educational
resource.

South Shore Charter School
2 A Street
Hull, MA 02045
(781) 925-2225

www.sscs-ma.org

Grades K–12.

Private and Parochial Schools

Arlington Catholic High School
16 Medford Street
Arlington, MA 02474
(781) 646-7770

www.achs.net

Back Bay Montessori
30 Fairfield Street
Boston, MA 02116
(617) 536-5984

Bartlett School
132 Lexington Street
Belmont, MA 02478
(617) 489-6007

www.bartlett.org

Preschool through grade 6.

Beaver Country Day School
Hammond Street
Chestnut Hill, MA 02467
(617) 738-2700

www.beavercds.org

Grades 6–12. Competitive admissions; tuition costs more than some colleges.

Boston College High School
150 Morrissey Boulevard
Dorchester, MA 02125
(617) 474-5010

www.bchigh.edu

Like Boston College, a Jesuit-run school. For boys, grades 9–12.

Brimmer and May School
69 Middlesex Road
Chestnut Hill, MA 02467
(617) 566-7462

www.brimmer.org

Nursery school through grade 12.

Buckingham Browne and Nichols School
10 Buckingham Street
Cambridge, MA 02138
(617) 800-2461

www.bbn-school.org

From preschool through grade 12. Divided into three grade-based campuses. One of the Boston area's most exclusive private schools.

Cambridge Friends School
5 Cadbury Road
Cambridge, MA 02140
(617) 354-3880

www.cambridgefriendsschool.org

Quaker elementary school.

Cambridge Montessori School
161 Garden Street
Cambridge, MA 02138
617 492-3410

Catholic Memorial High School

235 Baker Street
West Roxbury, MA 02132
(617) 469-8019

www.cath-mem.org

Catholic boys' school, grades 7–12.

Catholic School Office

2200 Boston Avenue
Boston, MA 02125
(617) 298-6555

Oversees parochial schools in Greater Boston. You can see a listing of Catholic schools at www.archbosk-12.org/boston.htm.

City Fact

In 1789 Benjamin Franklin left 100 pounds for a scholarship fund for Boston students. With wise investments, the fund grew and today continues to provide scholarships.

Chestnut Hill School

428 Hammond Street
Chestnut Hill, MA 02467
(617) 566-4394

www.tchs.org

Elementary and preschool classes.

Children's Montessori School

376 Hale Street
Beverly, MA 01915
(978) 922-3938

www.cmschool.org

Concord Academy

166 Main Street
Concord, MA 01742
(978) 369-6080

www.concordacademy.org

Exclusive, small high school with boarding and day students.

Dana Hall School

45 Dana Road
Wellesley, MA 02482
(781) 235-3010

www.danahall.org

Girls' college-preparatory school, grades 6–12.

Delphi Academy

564 Blue Hill Avenue
Milton, MA 02186
(617) 333-9610

www.delphiboston.org

Preschool through grade 8.

Ecole Bilingue

45 Matignon Road
Cambridge, MA 02140
(617) 499-1451

www.ecolebilingue.org

Offers French/English education, grades K–12 (preschool and kindergarten are in Arlington, which borders Cambridge).

Eliot Montessori School

5 Auburn Street
South Natick, MA 01760
(508) 655-7333

Fessenden School

250 Waltham Street
West Newton, MA 02465
(617) 964 5350

www.fessenden.org

Boys' school, grades K–9, with boarding school for grades 5–9.

Fontbonne Academy

30 Brook Road
Milton, MA 02186
(617) 696-3241

www.mec.edu/fontbonn

Private, Catholic college-preparatory school for young women.

Harborlight Montessori School

243 Essex Street
Beverly, MA 01915
(978) 922-1008

www.harborlightmontessori.org

Islamic Academy of New England

84 Chase Drive
Sharon, MA 02067
(781) 784-0519

www.ia-ne.org/iane

Islamic education, K–8.

Japanese Language School of Boston

361 Massachusetts Avenue
Arlington, MA 02474
(781) 641-2370

www.comed.org/boston

Japanese classes, K–12.

Kingsley Montessori School

30 Fairfield Street
Back Bay, MA 02116
(617) 536-5984

Maimonides School

34 Philbrick Road
Brookline, MA 02445
(617) 232-4452

www.maimonides.org

Orthodox Jewish day school.

Mesivta High School of Greater Boston

184 Chiswick Road
Brighton, MA 02135
(617) 254-6914

Orthodox Jewish high school.

Milton Academy
170 Centre Street
Milton, MA 02186
(617) 898-1798
www.milton.edu

Grades K–12, both boarding and day. Founded in 1798.

Mother Caroline Academy
515 Blue Hill Avenue
Dorchester, MA 02121
(617) 427-1177
www.mothercaroline.org

Catholic girls' school, grades 5–8.

New Jewish High School of Greater Boston
8 Prospect Street
Waltham, MA 02453
(781) 642-6800
www.njhs.org

Coeducational college-track high school featuring intensive Judaic studies.

Newman Prep School
245 Marlborough Street
Back Bay, MA 02116
(617) 267-4530
www.newmanprep.org

College-preparatory school, grades 9–12.

Noble and Greenough School
10 Campus Drive
Dedham, MA 02026
(781) 326-3700

www.nobles.edu

Grades 7–12, day and boarding.

The Park School
171 Goddard Avenue
Brookline, MA 02445
(617) 277-2456

www.parkschool.org

Preschool through grade 9.

Pincushion Hill Montessori School
30 Green Street
Ashland, MA 01721
(508) 881-2123

www.pincushion.com

Preschool through age twelve.

Rashi School
15 Walnut Park
Newton, MA 02458
(617) 969-4444

www.rashi.org

A reform Jewish day school, from preschool to grade 8.

The Rivers School
333 Winter Street
Weston, MA 02493
(781) 235-9300

www.rivers.org

College-preparatory secondary school.

Roxbury Latin School

101 St. Theresa Avenue
West Roxbury, MA 02132
(617) 325-4920

www.roxburylatin.org

Small (275 students) boys'
college-preparatory secondary
school. Founded in 1645.

Shady Hill School

178 Coolidge Hill
Cambridge, MA 02138
(617) 868-1261

www.shs.org

Pre-kindergarten through
grade 8.

Solomon Schechter Day School of Greater Boston

60 Stein Circle
Newton Centre, MA 02459
(617) 964-7765

www.ssdsboston.org

A conservative Jewish day
school.

Summit Montessori School

283 Pleasant Street
Framingham, MA 01701
(508) 872-3630

www.summitmontessori.org

Preschool through grade 6.

Thayer Academy

745 Washington Street
Braintree, MA 02184
(781) 843-3580

www.thayer.org

College-preparatory secondary
school.

The Waldorf School

739 Massachusetts Avenue
Lexington, MA 02420
(781) 863-1062

www.thewaldorfschool.org

Day school based on the work
of Rudolf Steiner. Nursery
school through grade 12.

Walnut Hill School

12 Highland Street
Natick, MA 01760
(508) 650-5020

www.walnuthillarts.org

Secondary school focusing on
music and art. Day and boarding students.

Archbishop Williams High School

80 Independence Avenue
Braintree, MA 02184
(781) 843-3636

www.awhs.org

Four-Year Colleges and Universities

Babson College
Babson Park
Wellesley, MA 02457
(781) 235-1100

www.babson.edu

Business education.

Bentley College
175 Forest Street
Waltham, MA 02452
(781) 891-2000

www.bentley.edu

Business education.

Berklee College of Music
1140 Boylston Street
Boston, MA 02215
(800) 421-0084

www.berklee.edu

Boston Architectural Center
320 Newbury Street
Boston, MA 02115
(617) 262-5000

www.the-bac.edu

Bachelor's and master's degrees
in architecture.

Boston College
140 Commonwealth Avenue
Chestnut Hill, MA 02467
(617) 552-8000

www.bc.edu

Jesuit-sponsored university.

Boston Conservatory
8 The Fenway
Boston, MA 02215
(617) 536-6340

www.bostonconservatory.edu

Undergraduate programs in
music, dance, and musical
theater.

Boston University
121 Bay State Road
Boston, MA 02215
(617) 353-2000

www.bu.edu

Brandeis University
415 South Street
Waltham, MA 02454
(781) 736-2000

www.brandeis.edu

Curry College
1071 Blue Hill Avenue
Milton, MA 02186
(617) 333-0500

www.curry.edu/welcome

Eastern Nazarene College
23 East Elm Avenue
Quincy, MA 02170
(617) 745-3000

www.enc.edu

Emerson College
120 Boylston Street
Boston, MA 02116
(617) 824-8600

www.emerson.edu

Communications and performance arts.

Emmanuel College
400 The Fenway
Boston, MA 02115
(617) 277-9340

www.emmanuel.edu

Catholic liberal-arts college.

Harvard University
Cambridge, MA 02138
(617) 495-1000

www.harvard.edu

Hebrew College
43 Hawes Street
Brookline, MA 02446
(800) 866-4814

www.hebrewcollege.edu

Undergraduate and graduate degrees in Jewish Studies and Jewish Education.

Lasell College
1844 Commonwealth Avenue
Newton, MA 02466
(617) 243-2225

www.lasell.edu

Lesley College
29 Everett Street
Cambridge, MA 02138
(800) 999-1959

www.lesley.edu

Education, human services, management, and the arts.

Longy School of Music
1 Follen Street
Cambridge, MA 02138
(617) 876-0956

www.longy.edu

Massachusetts College of Art
621 Huntington Avenue
Boston, MA 02115
(617) 879-7000

www.massart.edu

CITY FACT

Bostonians often think about the long term. Harvard University has a 1,000-year lease from Boston for the Arnold Arboretum.

Massachusetts Institute of Technology

77 Massachusetts Avenue
Cambridge, MA 02139
(617) 253-1000

web.mit.edu

Newbury College

129 Fisher Avenue
Brookline, MA 02146
(617) 730-7007

www.newbury.edu

New England College of Optometry

424 Beacon Street
Boston, MA 02115
(617) 266-2030

www.ne-optometry.edu

New England Conservatory of Music

290 Huntington Avenue
Boston, MA 02115
(617) 585-1100

www.newengland
conservatory.edu

Northeastern University

360 Huntington Avenue
Boston, MA 02115
(617) 373-2000

www.neu.edu

Undergraduates take a five-year "cooperative" course of learning, in which they spend time working at "co-op" jobs at local businesses in their field of study.

Pine Manor College

400 Heath Street
Chestnut Hill, MA 02467
(617) 731-7000

www.pmc.edu

Regis College

235 Wellesley Street
Weston, MA 02493
(781) 768-7000

www.regis.edu

Catholic women's college.

School of the Museum of Fine Arts

230 The Fenway
Boston, MA 02115
(617) 267-6100

www.smfa.edu

Simmons College

300 The Fenway
Boston, MA 02115
(617) 521-2000

www.simmons.edu

Women's college, but with coed graduate courses.

Suffolk University

8 Ashburton Place
Boston, MA 02108
(617) 573-8000

www.suffolk.edu

Tufts University
Medford, MA 02155
(617) 627-3170
www.tufts.edu

University of Massachusetts–Boston
100 Morrissey Boulevard
Dorchester, MA 02125
(617) 287-5000
www.umb.edu

Wellesley College
106 Central Street
Wellesley, MA 02481
(781) 283-2270
www.wellesley.edu
Women's college.

Wentworth Institute of Technology
552 Huntington Avenue
Boston, MA 02115
(800) 556-0610
www.wit.edu

CITY FACT

In 2000, Boston began installing Paris-style street toilets in downtown areas.

Wheelock College
200 The Riverway
Boston, MA 02215
(617) 879-200
www.wheelock.edu

Two-Year Colleges

Bay State College
122 Commonwealth Avenue
Back Bay, MA 02116
(617) 236-8000
www.baystate.edu

Bunker Hill Community College
250 New Rutherford Avenue
Boston, MA 02129
(617) 228-2000
www.bhcc.state.ma.us

This is where Robin Williams worked as a professor in *Good Will Hunting*.

Fisher College
118 Beacon Street
Boston, MA 02116
(617) 236-8818

www.fisher.edu

Laboure College
2120 Dorchester Avenue
Dorchester, MA 02124
(617) 296-8300

www.labourecollege.org

Massachusetts Bay Community College
50 Oakland Street
Wellesley, MA, 02481

www.mbcc.mass.edu

Massachusetts Communications College
10 Brookline Place
Brookline, MA 02445
(800) 903-4425

Mt. Ida College
777 Dedham Street
Newton Centre, MA 02459
(617) 928-4500

www.mountida.edu

North Shore Community College
1 Ferncroft Road
Danvers, MA 01923
(978) 762-4000

www.nscc.mass.edu

Roxbury Community College
1234 Columbus Avenue
Roxbury, MA 02120
(617) 427-0060

www.rcc.mass.edu

Continuing Education

TakeAClass.com
www.takeaclass.com

Comprehensive online guide to continuing-education programs and one-day courses in eastern Massachusetts.

Boston Architectural Center
320 Newbury Street
Back Bay, MA 02116
(617) 262-5000

www.the-bac.edu/ce

Boston Center for Adult Education

5 Commonwealth Avenue
Beacon Hill, MA 02116
(617) 267-4430

www.bcae.org

Wide variety of noncredit classes.

Boston College, College of Advancing Studies

McGinn Hall
Chestnut Hill, MA 02467
(617) 552-3900

www.bc.edu/advancingstudies

Boston University Metropolitan College

755 Commonwealth Avenue
Boston, MA 02215
(617) 353-6000

www.bu.edu/met

Offers classes on the main BU campus, in downtown Boston, and in Tyngsboro (north) and Foxboro (south).

Brookline Adult & Community Education Program

115 Greenough Street
Brookline, MA 02246
(617) 730-2700

www.takeaclass.com/
brooklineadult

Wide variety of noncredit classes.

Cambridge Center for Adult Education

42 Brattle Street
Cambridge, MA 02138
(617) 547-6789

www.ccae.org

Wide variety of noncredit classes.

Cambridge College

1000 Massachusetts Avenue
Cambridge, MA 02138
(888) 868-1002

www.cambridge.edu

Nontraditional college for adult learners.

CITY FACT

Boston has a fair number of Triple Eagles, people who went to Boston College High School, Boston College, and Boston College Law School.

Eliot School of Fine and Applied Arts

24 Eliot Street
Jamaica Plain, 02130
(617) 524-3313

www.eliotschool.org

Arts classes. Founded in 1676.

Emerson College Division of Continuing and Advanced Education

120 Boylston Street
Back Bay, 02116
(617) 824-8280

www.emerson.edu/ce

Communications courses.

Harvard Extension School

51 Brattle Street
Cambridge, MA 02138
(617) 495-4024

www.harvard.edu/extension

Northeastern University Continuing Education Program

360 Huntington Avenue
Boston, MA 02136
(617) 373-2000

www.neu.edu/cont-ed

University of Massachusetts–Boston Continuing Education

100 Morrissey Boulevard
Dorchester, MA 02125
(617) 287-7900

www.conted.umb.edu

CHAPTER 11

Working in the City

Greater Boston today is the epitome of a service-oriented economy. Think high tech, mutual funds, health care, and tourism, and you've got a good snapshot of the dominant players in the Boston economy. A study by the Federal Reserve Bank of Boston found that 85 percent of jobs in Massachusetts are in the service sector. The dominance of such jobs continues: Each year, 93 percent of newly created jobs are in the service sector, with high tech and health care making up the bulk of the new jobs.

With relatively low unemployment rates, world-class universities constantly churning out new startups, and strong financial institutions, Boston has become an economic powerhouse for the Northeast.

Boston also continues its centuries-old involvement in international trade.

In colonial days, Boston was a major destination in the so-called triangular trade. British colonies in the West Indies shipped molasses to Boston, where it was distilled into rum and shipped to Africa, where it was used to buy slaves to be transported to the West Indies to grow more sugar cane to be turned into molasses. As the British government clamped down on the North American colonies, smuggling became a major industry in Boston.

Later, international trade and shipbuilding grew in importance. Clipper ships sped tea from China and India to Boston. You can still see echoes of the tea trade on Stuart Street at the corner of Berkeley Street in the Back Bay: The entrance to an office building consists of bronze and stone friezes commemorating the tea trade (look for the elephants above the doorway). There's also a restaurant at that corner; imagine it in the nineteenth century when it was a room where clerks measured out the tea fresh off the boat. Oceangoing has declined as a major Boston industry—Portland, Maine, now records more ship traffic than Boston—but the city remains at the forefront of the New England economy thanks to high tech and banking. Fleet-Boston, for example, is one of the largest lenders in South America. In the year 2000, Massachusetts exports totaled $21 billion, according to state statistics. Computer and electronic equipment accounted for about half the total.

The American industrial revolution started in Massachusetts. In the early nineteenth century, Boston Brahmin families started two new cities on the Merrimack River (Lawrence and Lowell) to create mass quantities of cloth and clothing. But before that, the first ironworks in British North America was built in Saugus, just to Boston's north, in 1650. Even today, the AFL-CIO remains a powerful force in Massachusetts politics. However, manufacturing started declining after World War II. Most of the mills fled to the South decades ago. And although Greater Boston still has a number of large industrial plants, manufacturing jobs continue to disappear even as other sectors grow at a rapid pace.

According to the Boston Redevelopment Authority, the turning point was the completion in 1965 of the Prudential Center, an apartment and office complex that included a fifty-story office building, the first major high-rise erected in Boston in several decades.

Wages and Cost of Living

Over the past few years, the Massachusetts economy has far outpaced the national economy. Although it was hit by the same economic downturn as the rest of the country in 2001, unemployment in the state in general, and in Greater Boston in particular, remains below the

CITY FACT

Set that radio dial! Boston has a variety of radio stations. Some include:

AM:

WRKO, 680: Talk radio

WEEI, 850: All sports

WBZ, 1030: News and traffic daytime, talk, and Bruins hockey at night

FM:

WZBC, 90.3: Alternative, indie rock

WBUR, 90.9: NPR, BBC news, and talk shows

WZLX, 100.7: Classic rock

WCRB, 102.5: Classical

WODS, 103.3 Oldies

WBCN, 104.1: Hard rock, Howard Stern in the morning

WNJL, 106.5: Smooth jazz

WMJX, 106.7: Soft rock

---

national average. In 2000, the unemployment rate in the Boston area dipped below 2 percent (it had risen to 3 percent by mid-2001).

Per capita income in Massachusetts is roughly 25 percent higher than the national average, although, as you saw earlier, you'll need a fair piece of that to make up for our higher-than-average housing

CITY
FACT

Many Chinese restaurants in Boston serve fluffy French rolls instead of chop-suey noodles.

costs. In fact, according to the ACCRA Cost of Living Index, Boston is about 33 percent more expensive to live in than the national average. Only New York, San Francisco, and Los Angeles are more expensive. Housing and health care costs in particular drive up Boston's cost of living. Housing in Boston costs 70 percent more on average than in the rest of the country, according to the survey, which also found that the average apartment in Boston rents for $1,331 a month, compared to $771 nationally, and that the average house sells for $332,985, compared to $229,228 in the rest of the country. You can compare Boston with other metropolitan areas at the ACCRA Web site: www.accra.org/costofliving.

Here are mean salary figures for some occupations in the Boston area, as compiled by the federal Bureau of Labor Statistics in 1999 (see the complete report at stats.bls.gov/oes/1999/oes_1120.htm):

Architect: $50,940

Auto-body worker: $38,940

Bartender: $16,440

Boilermaker: $33,630

Chef: $36,890

Chemical engineer: $66,180

Claims adjuster: $45,060

Coffee-shop counter worker: $14,450

Computer programmer: $61,220

Computer systems engineer: $75,400

Construction laborer: $42,080

Crossing guard: $17,000

Epidemiologist: $51,890

Financial manager: $90,400

Funeral director: $51,800

Graphic designer: $45,640

Home health aide: $20,470

Human resource manager: $67,090

Janitor: $21,250

Kindergarten teacher: $41,900

Landscape architect: $46,210

Lawyer: $109,290

Legal secretary: $39,220

Librarian: $41,780

Machinist: $37,130

Manicurist: $17,240

Marketing manager: $84,740

Market-research analyst: $55,790

Meeting planner: $38,630

Mental-health counselor: $28,510

Microbiologist: $62,150

Mangement Information Systems manager: $78,980

Movie projectionist: $24,200

Nutritionist: $40,810

Pediatrician: $110,040

Photographer: $27,610

Physics professor: $66,840

Preschool teacher: $24,430

P.R. specialist: $45,440

Real-estate agent: $45,060

Registered nurse: $51,620

Sales manager: $85,560

School principal: $67,930

School psychologist: $47,780

Substance-abuse counselor: $28,280

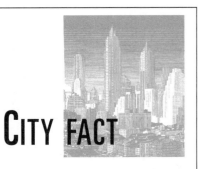

CITY FACT

When Patriots' Day (the Monday closest to April 19) falls on April 15, you can take an extra day to file both your state and federal income-tax returns.

Specific Industries

As mentioned previously, the Boston economy in recent years has far outpaced the national economy. Although 2000 and 2001 saw a slow-down, the region still has jobs that go unfilled. Let's take a look at some specific sectors. You can get state estimates for job growth in specific industries at www.detma.org/forms/pdf/1030N_601.pdf.

CONSTRUCTION

Visitors to Boston in 2001 could be forgiven if they couldn't recall the number of construction cranes they saw while they drove through the city. In recent years, few fields in Greater Boston have grown faster than construction, thanks to giant public-works projects and a red-hot real estate and office market (although it did begin to cool down with the dot-com collapse in late 2000). According to the Boston Redevelopment Authority, Boston saw $2.1 billion worth of new con-struction, and the number of construction jobs in the city increased 82 percent between 1992 (when the city began to emerge from a recession) and 1999.

In the heart of the city, the state highway department is spending $14 billion in federal and state money to replace the elevated Central Artery highway with a series of tunnels and a bridge. At the same time, the Massachusetts Water Resources Authority is nearing com-pletion of a $3.6-billion sewage-treatment system.

New homes continue to go up in the region, even if that means, at least in the richer suburbs, tearing down existing homes to put up even larger ones (after 350 years or so, there are few large tracts of land left for giant subdivisions). The Boston skyline has seen the addition of numerous new high-rise office and residential build-ings and hotels, from the downtown financial district out to the Prudential Center in the Back Bay.

And the city and state are in the midst of constructing a $700 million convention center on the South Boston waterfront, close to largely vacant parcels on which private developers have proposed a mini-city of offices, hotels, and high-priced apartments. City plan-ners expect 5,000 new hotel rooms to be built over the next few years.

Still, the state Division of Employment and Training now pro-jects that the demand for such jobs will stay relatively steady over the next ten years. It forecasts the number of people working as construction tradesmen to increase from 20,730 in 1998 to only 21,040 in 2008 (and it forecasts general contracting jobs to decrease from 24,340 in 1998 to 23,820 in 2008).

EDUCATION

With more than sixty colleges and universities and close to 200,000 students, Boston has more students per capita than any other city in the country. And that means it has no shortage of post-secondary teaching and educational positions. However, there is one key problem for newcomers: The reputation of Boston educational facilities means they attract the absolute best of the best and competition for those jobs can be fierce. Simply having a Ph.D. doesn't have the same cachet it might in other parts of the country. Still, the state expects the number of college professors to increase from 34,930 in 1998 to 40,530 in 2008. Although the large schools are no longer looking at major expansion (in fact, the largest, Northeastern University, has been deliberately cutting its enrollment), smaller colleges are still thinking big. Even the odd new school pops up, such as the Franklin W. Olin College of Engineering, which opened in the fall of 2001 in Needham as the first new engineering college in the United States in forty years.

The immediate outlook for openings is better at the elementary and secondary levels. The state Division of Employment and Training predicts the number of teaching positions in Greater Boston will increase from 136,250 in 1998 to 159,490 in 2008. Currently, teaching salaries average $27,000 a year in Massachusetts, but that can vary considerably from district to district and will depend on your educational level (most contracts provide raises for additional degrees). To help attract highly qualified educators, the state has a competitive grant program that awards $20,000 over three years to new teachers who pass a series of tests and interviews (only 500 of these grants are awarded each year). See eq.doe.mass.edu/mint for more information.

FINANCIAL

As New England's regional hub, you'd expect Boston to have a fair number of jobs in the financial sector. And, indeed, it does (the Federal Reserve Bank of Boston is a major employer), many clustered around State Street downtown.

But Boston's financial reach has long extended beyond New England. In the nineteenth century, Boston bankers provided much of the capital that built the nation's railroads. Today Boston banks are active overseas. Boston is also a leader in mutual funds and insurance. Fidelity Investments alone employs more than 8,000 people. John Hancock is headquartered here; Prudential has a large presence here (including the eponymous Prudential Center). All told, Boston is the third-largest money-management center in the world, behind only New York and London. The stock market bubble of the late 1990s helped these companies propel the Boston economy into the stratosphere; however, they were also hit by the stock market decline of 2000.

The past few years have seen major consolidation in the banking sector. Massachusetts banking today is dominated by FleetBoston. This bank is the result of a merger between Fleet Bank of Providence and BankBoston (itself the product of a merger between the Bank of Boston and BayBank). Citizens Bank and Sovereign Bank (which entered the market by buying up branches that FleetBoston had to sell off) are making a run at FleetBoston, though. Consolidation often leads to job losses; continued consolidation could mean the loss of still more.

HEALTH CARE

This sector is similar to education: The Boston area has plenty of health care jobs, but competition can be fierce because Boston institutions attract the best of the best. One key exception is nursing; Boston-area hospitals continually report problems finding enough nurses even as they attempt to save money by reducing overall nursing slots.

In addition to providing world-renowned medical care (patients fly in from around the world, drawn by the reputation of local hospitals and doctors), Boston hospitals have large research facilities that continue to do pioneering work in virtually every facet of medicine. One indication of the area's strength: Boston routinely pulls in more money in grants from the National Institutes of Health than any other city, including New York. In 1999, according to city statistics, Boston facilities won $947 million in federal grants (Massachusetts General Hospital alone won $158 million worth of grants).

All told, one out of every seven jobs within the city limits is in health care, according to the Boston Redevelopment Authority. Many are clustered in the Longwood Medical Area in Roxbury, but Massachusetts General Hospital, on the other side of Beacon Hill, is the city's largest employer, with more than 11,000 workers. Five of the city's ten largest employers are hospitals.

Recent years have seen the financial problems that have long squeezed community hospitals affect even the larger teaching facilities, which have responded in part by merging or affiliating with each other. Despite efforts to contract health care, however, the state Division of Employment and Training projects continued job growth in health care, from 341,320 in 1988 to 404,190 by the year 2008.

A related field that shows promise of growth is biotechnology. From Boston to Worcester, a number of pioneers are developing new drugs. Many local startups are spun out of the area's numerous colleges and universities.

HIGH TECH

The Boston area is one of the engines of global high tech. For more than forty years, the region has been a center for innovation in high tech, often spurred by startups created by M.I.T. professors and graduates. Close to 300,000 people in eastern Massachusetts make their living in high tech, according to state figures.

In the late 1990s, high tech in Massachusetts recovered from a serious slump in the late 1980s and early 1990s. Ironically, the slump was caused mainly by the failure of industry leaders to foresee the PC revolution (ironic because Massachusetts companies had earlier seen the need for mid-size computers ignored by the mainframe makers). Pioneers like Digital, Data General, and Prime disappeared, through either bankruptcy or acquisition by upstarts (Digital was bought by Compaq and Data General by EMC; Prime Computer simply disappeared). Wang Laboratories managed to survive bankruptcy by reducing its operations and getting out of the business of actually making computers.

The recovery came largely through innovations in computer networking. Eastern Massachusetts became a powerhouse in the development of equipment for high-speed networking, just the kind of equipment telephone companies and Internet service providers needed to handle increasingly large numbers of users and ever more complex applications.

Most of these new companies set up shop along Route 495, where the rents were cheap and the commute easy (although nowadays 495 often rivals Route 128 for traffic tie-ups). The Rte. 495 corridor, however, has been hit fairly hard by a slowdown in the telecommunications market.

Venture-funded dot-coms and boutique Web shops tended to settle closer to town, in Cambridge (already home to IBM's Lotus Development Corp.). Greater Boston is home to some 3,000 Internet- and software-related companies. Some of these companies, such as computer storage vendor EMC, quickly became leaders in their markets. Others seemed to get bought up for huge sums before they even shipped any product. In fact, the late 1990s saw many Massachusetts high-tech companies gobbled up by larger companies from outside the state (Cisco and Lucent in particular).

The stock bust of 2000 has slowed this sector. Web-related companies, such as CMGI, have been particularly hard hit. But whereas pure high-tech companies have been laying off, other, more staid companies have continued to hire programmers, network professionals, and other high-tech workers. Mutual fund companies have as much of a need for such workers as any startup.

A related field, computer consulting and market research, thrives in Boston. Consulting firms such as IDC, Forrester Research, and the Yankee Group provide advice to clients around the world.

MANUFACTURING

This is one of the few sectors on a long, slow decline in eastern Massachusetts (farming and fishing are others). To be sure, the area still has a fair number of traditional manufacturing jobs. Gillette's "world shaving headquarters" is in South Boston, and Raytheon and General Electric build defense systems and jet engines north of Boston. Within the city of Boston itself, manufacturing jobs have remained fairly steady. Outside the city, however, the decrease in jobs continues. Recent years have seen the loss of everything from New England's only auto-assembly plant (in Framingham) to the state's last major shipyard (in Quincy). Between 1989 and 1999, Massachusetts lost some 100,000 manufacturing jobs, according to state statistics.

The state projects the decline to continue. It forecasts the number of assembly jobs, for example, to shrink from 50,650 in 1998 to

49,990 in 2009, and the number of machine operators to go from 42,770 to 41,190.

However, it also forecasts an increase in the number of truck drivers, from 56,980 to 62,750.

PUBLISHING

Boston is no New York. Nevertheless, Boston is an important center for publishing. Book publishers Houghton Mifflin and Harcourt General are based in the Boston area. The region is also home to numerous magazines, in particular trade publications. For example, IDG, the world's largest publisher of technology-related publications, is headquartered in Boston. Competitor Cahners is next door in Newton. Ziff-Davis, another technology publishing firm, has a strong presence in the Boston area. The *Atlantic* and *Fast Company* magazines are also based here.

CITY FACT

Boston-area highways don't have shoulders; they have "breakdown lanes." This term is often an oxymoron because some of these lanes become legal driving lanes during rush hour. The state has built a series of emergency turnouts along Route 128 for people who actually break down in the breakdown lane.

TOURISM

Boston's key role in the Revolution keeps the tourists coming back year after year, although the September 11 attacks helped cool this market. More than 12 million people visit Boston and nearby attractions such as Lexington, Concord, and Plymouth each year (some studies show more tourists visit Quincy Market each year than Disney World). The city is also a popular convention destination, one reason the city is building a new, larger convention center.

All told, tourism is an $8 billion business in Greater Boston, so there are plenty of jobs everywhere. State officials are predicting continued growth in this sector, in part because of a new convention center that is supposed to attract larger conventions than the city can now support and because of the construction of new hotels. The state expects the number of people employed in restaurants and bars in Greater Boston to increase from 1998's 221,030 to 236,130 in 2008. Nearly 100,000 people are employed in other tourism jobs, according to state figures.

Employment Resources

In certain sectors, such as health care and education, fierce competition could mean challenges in finding the right job for you. And for other positions, thinking a bit outside the box might be helpful. For example, instead of trying for a programming job at a dot-com, look at programming positions at large insurance or mutual-fund companies. In the following section, you'll find listed numerous resources for help in finding a job. As always, however, the best way to find a job is often word of mouth. Talk to your friends and even friends of friends who might know about a cool job that hasn't been posted yet.

EXECUTIVE SEARCH FIRMS AND PERSONNEL AGENCIES

Never pay a fee to a search firm; reputable firms always collect their fees from the companies that use them to hire workers. In trying to decide on a firm to work with, ask lots of questions, such as how long the company has been around. Also ask whether the firm works on a retainer or contingency basis. Ask for references. If you don't feel comfortable, keep looking—there are plenty of agencies out there.

Alexander Group

10 Post Office Square
Boston
(713) 993-7900

www.thealexandergroup.com

Executive searches.

Association of Executive Search Consultants

www.aesc.org

This Web site has tips on working with a search firm as well as a service for submitting your resume to various search firms.

Burke, Hegan, Roessle and Associates

6 Beacon Street
Beacon Hill
(617) 720-0808

www.bhrassociates.com

Places office and financial support workers.

Capital Search Group

77 Summer Street
Boston
(617) 482-9800

www.capitalsearchgroup.com

Specializes in financial jobs.

Commonwealth Resources

262 Washington Street
Boston
(617) 250-1100

www.crijobs.com

Construction and engineering positions.

Essex Partners

1 Boston Place
Boston
(617) 720-7500

www.essexpartners.com

For senior executives looking to change companies.

Heidrick & Struggles

150 Federal Street
Boston
(617) 737-6300

www.heidrick.com/
office_boston.htm

Helps to fill senior management and board-of-director positions.

Isaacson, Miller

334 Boylston Street
Boston
(617) 262-6500

www.imsearch.com

Specializing in education, environmental, communications, health care, arts, and nonprofit positions.

Kenexa

18 Commerce Way
Woburn
(781) 932-0400

www.kenexa.com

Executive searches in finance and health care.

Korn/Ferry International

265 Franklin Street
Boston
(617) 345-0200

www.kornferry.com

Senior- and middle-management positions.

MAS New Hampshire

172 Route 101
Bedford, NH
(603) 472-8844

www.mas-jobs.com

High-tech recruiting for Greater Boston and New Hampshire.

Phoenix Placement Services

900 Massachusetts Avenue
Arlington
(800) 261-2858

www.phoenixplacement.com

Skilled tradesmen.

Positions, Inc.

1 Faneuil Hall Marketplace
Boston
(617) 367-9200

www.positionsinc.com

Accounting, administration, biotech, engineering, health care, information services, legal, operations/purchasing, human resources, and real estate.

Sullivan and Cogliano

230 Second Avenue
Waltham
(888) SULCOG1

www.sullivancogliano.com

Construction and engineering positions.

TMP Worldwide Executive Search

99 High Street
Boston
(617) 292-6242

www.tmpworldwide.com

Winter, Wyman & Co.

950 Winter Street
Waltham
(781) 890-7000

www.winterwyman.com/boston

Professional positions.

Egon Zehnder International

75 Park Plaza
Boston
(617) 535-3500

www.zehnder.com/offices/alphabet/boston.htm

Specializes in high technology, financial services, life sciences, consumer, and manufacturing.

TEMPORARY AGENCIES

Not quite ready to commit to a permanent job? Want more flexibility in your scheduling? There are plenty of opportunities for temporary and contract work in the Boston area.

Accountants On Call

121 High Street
Boston
(617) 345-0440

161 Worcester Road
Framingham
(508) 872-7800

Accountemps
(800) 803-8367

www.accountemps.com

Financial services positions.

Accounting Team
25 Corporate Drive
Burlington
(781) 505-1919

1250 Hancock Street
Quincy
(617) 479-1414

www.accountingteam-ari.com

Brattle Temps
50 Congress Street
Boston
(617) 523-4600

www.brattletemps.com

Specializes in placing temps
with local colleges, universities,
hospitals, and museums.

Budget Temps
415 Broadway
Chelsea
(617) 884-3050

Warehouse, factory, printing,
cafeteria, mail room, and construction positions.

Bulfinch Temporary Service
101 Merrimac Street
Boston
(617) 726-5858

Temporary positions at Massachusetts General and Brigham
and Women's Hospitals.

Cleary Consultants
21 Merchants Row
Faneuil Hall
Boston
(617) 367-7189

www.clearyconsultants.com

Management, office, travel,
banking, information services,
sales, financial, legal, and medical staffing.

Contemporaries, Inc.
18 Tremont Street
Boston
(617) 723-9797

www.bostoncontemporaries.
com

Marketing, online, publishing,
advertising, public relations, and
education.

Franklin-Pierce Temporaries
112 Water Street
Boston
(617) 722-0070

Office and customer service
positions.

Interstate Technical Services
170 Cambridge Street
Burlington
(781) 273-9121

www.itsstaffing.com

High-tech contract staffing.

Kelly Services
295 Devonshire
Boston
(617) 482-8833

222 Forbes Road
Braintree
(781) 932-3600

www.kellyservices.com

Kforce.com
155 Federal Street
Boston
(617) 482-8211

www.kforce.com/boston

Information technology, finance and accounting, human resources, and investment and insurance staffing.

KNF&T
133 Federal Street
Boston
(617) 574-8200

33 Lyman Street
Westborough
(508) 836-3355

Academic, advertising, communications, financial,

online, human-resources, public relations, and publishing positions.

LawCorps
20 Park Plaza
Boston
(617) 948-2170

www.lawcorps.com

Legal positions.

John Leonard
75 Federal Street
Boston
(617) 423-6800

www.johnleonard.com

Office, human resources, graphic arts, and information-services positions.

OfficeTeam
101 Arch Street
Boston
(617) 951-0036

14 Story Street
Cambridge
(617) 876-9000

15 Forbes Road
Braintree
(781) 356-0104

450 Bedford Street
Lexington
(781) 863-2744

www.officeteam.com

Manpower

101 Federal Street
Boston
(617) 443-4100

160 Gould Street
Needham
(781) 444-7160

www.manpower.com

Office and light industrial staffing.

MediTemp

264 Msgr. O'Brien Highway
Cambridge
(800) 526-7185

Allied health and medical office workers.

NSight

10 Fawcett Street
Cambridge
(617) 354-8328

www.nsightworks.com

Print and interactive communications positions: writers, editors, designers, and online content developers.

Onsite Companies

150 Wood Road
Braintree
(781) 794-9947

www.onsite-inc.com

Commercial, environmental, energy, aviation, and call-center staffing.

Preferred Temporaries

Sears Crescent Building
100 City Hall Plaza
Boston
(617) 723-1919

www.preferredtemps.com

Administrative and support staffing.

Professional Staffing Group

89 Devonshire Street
Boston
(617) 250-1000

www.psgboston.com

Administrative, financial, human resources, and print and online positions.

CITY FACT

A "bubbla" is a device that provides a jet of water when you're thirsty. A "coffee regula" is a cup of coffee with cream and two sugars.

Resource Partnership
251 West Central Street
Natick
(508) 647-1722

www.resourcepartnership.org

Temporary placement agency
for people with disabilities.

Daniel Roberts Temployment
175 Federal Street
Boston
(617) 262-5400

www.danielroberts.com

Office and human resources
staffing.

Routhier
160 State Street
Boston
(617) 742-2747

www.routhierplacement.com

Legal positions, from secretaries
to attorneys.

Sapphire Technologies
10 Presidential Way
Woburn
1-87-SAPPHIRE

www.newboston.com

Information-technology contract positions.

Sally Silver Companies
470 Totten Pond Road
Waltham
(781) 890-7272

www.sallysilver.com

High-tech contract staffing.

The Skill Bureau
129 Tremont Street
Boston
(617) 423-2986

www.skillbureau.com

Office help.

Spherion
18 Tremont Street
Boston
(617) 227-3113

www.spherion.com

Office, customer service, and
data entry positions.

Staffing Now
699 Boylston Street
Boston
(617) 451-5900

www.staffingnow.com

Office, accounting, legal, and
technology positions.

TAC Staffing Services
18 Tremont Street
Boston
(617) 523-3200

607 Boylston Street
Back Bay
(617) 266-1988

124 Mt. Auburn Street
Cambridge
(617) 354-5202

990 Washington Street
Dedham
(781) 329-1810

175 Highland Avenue
Needham
(781) 455-0745

100 Hancock Street
Quincy
(617) 984-2520

295 Weston Street
Waltham
(781) 899-7090

www.tacstaffing.com

TalentTree Staffing Services
260 Franklin Street
Boston
(617) 261-0717

Office, data entry, and customer service staffing.

Total Clerical Services
8 Winter Street
Boston
(800) 708-8367

www.total-cler.com

Office and light industrial positions.

Triad Engineering
132 Middlesex Turnpike
Burlington
(781) 273-1880

www.triad-eng.com

Contract engineering and programming positions.

Veritude
82 Devonshire Street
Boston
(617) 563-4915

www.veritude.com

Administrative, business, and technology positions at Fidelity Investments.

CITY
FACT

Boston frankfurt (not frankfurter) rolls are white on the outside.

JOB LISTINGS

The Internet may have its flaws, but when it comes to finding a job, it's wonderful, especially if you want to start looking before you move. Here are some Internet-based and more traditional jobs listing services.

Boston ComputerJobs.com

www.boston.computerjobs.com

Job listings for information-technology professionals.

Boston ComputeWork.com

boston.computerwork.com

Job listings and resume service for computer professionals.

Boston Globe

(617) 929-2000

bostonworks.boston.com

New England's largest classified section. The online version has a large advantage over the print version: The ads are grouped by category in alphabetical order and are searchable. The Web site also has a resume service, profiles of large employers, relevant *Globe* articles, and a salary calculator that lets you see how much you should get paid for a given job in the Boston area.

Boston's IT/Engineering Employment Web Site

www.high-techjobs.net

Job listings for information-technology professionals in Boston and eastern Massachusetts.

BostonEngineer.com

www.bostonengineer.com

Listings for engineering and technical jobs.

BostonHire.com

www.bostonhire.com

Job listings, resume service, and company profiles.

BostonSearch.Com

www.bostonsearch.com

A career site focused on professional and technical employment opportunities. Has an e-mail service to notify you of new jobs matching your criteria.

boston.techies.com

boston.techies.com

Yes, another job site aimed at high-tech professionals.

Commonwealth Employment Opportunities

www.state.ma.us/hrd/ceo

Searchable database of current openings at state agencies.

craigslist

boston.craigslist.org

Noncommercial bulletin board helping people find jobs. Has job listings and a forum for asking (and answering) questions about moving to Boston, finding work here, and the like.

Dice.com

marketing.dice.com/internet/bostonjobs/

Specializes in high-tech jobs.

Environmental Jobs in Massachusetts

www.ejobs.org/states/ma.html

Film Jobs and Television Employment in New England

www.newenglandfilm.com/jobs.htm

Government Jobs in Boston

bostonjobsource.com/magov.html

Links to job postings at city, state, and federal agencies.

HigherEdJobs.com

Calder Square
P.O. Box 10676
State College, PA 16805
(814) 861-3080

www.higheredjobs.com

Specializes in post-secondary jobs.

HotJobs

406 West 31st Street
New York
(212) 699-5300

www.hotjobs.com/htdocs/browse/job-browse-state-ma-flat.html

Another general-purpose job site that lets you submit resumes electronically and get e-mail notification of new jobs that match your criteria.

Jobfind

www.jobfind.com

The *Boston Herald*'s online classifieds and resume service.

Massachusetts College Employment Web Pages

www.webcrawler.com/education/teacher_resources/education_jobs/college_job_pages/massachusetts

Links to employment pages at Massachusetts colleges and universities.

Monster.com
(800) MONSTER

www.monster.com

Opportunity NOCs New England
87 Summer Street
Boston
(617) 357-0849

www.opnocsne.org

Openings at nonprofit organizations.

Vacancies in Massachusetts Community Colleges

www.tiac.net/users/mccc/
Vacancies.html

Working

www.townonline.com/working

Classifieds, job matching service, and articles from community newspapers, which cover Boston suburbs.

JOB FAIRS

A good job fair lets you compare numerous companies in one place. If the economy continues to cool, though, expect to see fewer of them.

Health Care Events

bostonworks.boston.com/events
/healthcare.shtml

Lists events for people looking for work in the field.

Job Fairs/Events

bostonworks.boston.com/events

Lists job fairs in Greater Boston.

Job Fairs in Massachusetts and New Hampshire
45-B Tosca Drive
Stoughton

www.carouselexpo.com

More listings.

JOB TRAINING AND NETWORKING

Maybe your job isn't working out. Or maybe you'd like to try another career. The Boston area has a number of resources to help you find a new type of job.

Boston Career Link
281 Huntington Avenue
Boston
(617) 536-1888

www.bostoncareerlink.com

Career center that helps people thinking about changing careers or looking for a new job.

BostonWorks Events Calendar

bostonworks.boston.com/events
/networking_events

Lists job-training opportunities and networking events and parties.

Career Source

185 Alewife Brook Parkway
Cambridge
(617) 661-7867

www.yourcareersource.com

Career center that strengthens and assists individuals and employers in attaining their social and economic goals.

Employment and Training Resources

300 Howard Street
Framingham
(508) 626-2545

288 Walnut Street
Newtonville
(617) 928-0530

275 Prospect Street
Norwood
(781) 769-4120

www.etrcc.org

Career center that helps people thinking about changing careers or looking for a new job.

Jewish Vocational Service

105 Chauncy Street
Boston
(617) 451-8147

www.jvs-boston.org

Nonprofit, nonsectarian organization dedicated to helping people from all walks of life overcome obstacles to employment.

Job Training Alliance of Massachusetts

www.bostonjobtraining.org

Umbrella site for a number of Boston-area agencies that provide vocational training and job placement services for adults.

Massachusetts School Information

www.detma.org/jobseeker/cis_maschools.htm

Online database maintained by the Massachusetts Division of Employment and Training that lists private job-training and vocational programs.

Veterans Technical Training Institute

17 Court Street
Boston

Free job-training and placement programs for veterans. Prospective students need to be referred from the local veteran's agent or the Massachusetts Department of Employment and Training office.

PROFESSIONAL GROUPS

Professional associations can be a great place to meet your peers and do a little career networking. Many host regular events, both formal and informal. Some also have job-listing services.

American Marketing Association—Boston Chapter

200 Reservoir Street
Needham
(781) 449-1555

www.amaboston.org

American Society of Women Accountants—Boston Chapter

35 Winchester Drive
Lexington
(781) 736-7890

Association for Computing Machinery, Greater Boston Chapter

(781) 862-1181

www.gbcacm.org

Association for Women in Computing

Box 68
Newton Upper Falls, MA 02464

www.awcboston.org

Audio Engineering Society, Boston Section

www.digitalbear.com/boston-aes.html

Boston Bar Association

16 Beacon Street
Boston
(617) 742-0615

www.bostonbar.org

Boston Press Photographers Association

Box 122
Boston, MA 02101

www.bostonpressphoto.com

Boston Psychoanalytic Association and Institute

15 Commonwealth Avenue
Boston
(617) 266-0953

www.bostonpsa.org

Boston Society of Architects

52 Broad Street
Boston
(800) 662-1235

www.architects.org

Commonwealth Institute

69 Newbury Street
Boston
(617) 859-0080

www.commonwealth
institute.org

Women CEO entrepreneurs.

Independent Computer Consultants Association, Boston Chapter

www.icca-boston.org

Institute of Industrial Engineers

www.iieboston.com

Institute of Management Accountants, Boston Chapter

www.bostonima.org

Massachusetts Bar Association

20 West Street
Boston
(617) 338-0641

www.massbar.org

Massachusetts Dental Society

2 Willow Street
Southborough
(508) 480-9797

www.massdental.org

Massachusetts Interactive Media Council

43 Charles Street
Boston
(617) 227- 2822

www.mimc.org

Interactive-media companies and professionals.

Massachusetts Medical Society

860 Winter Street
Waltham Woods
Corporate Center
Waltham
(781) 893-4610

www.mms.org

Massachusetts Society of CPAs

105 Chauncy Street
Boston
(800) 392-6145

www.mscpaonline.org

National Human Resource Association, Boston Affiliate

19 Harrison Street
Framingham
(508) 879-4883

www.humanresources.org/
boston.html

Northeast Human Resources Association

1 Washington Street
Wellesley
(781) 235-2900

www.nehra.com

Public Relations Society of America—Boston

45 Broad Street
Boston
(617) 292-0470

www.prsaboston.org

Society for Marketing Professional Services

93 Concord Avenue
Belmont
(617) 489-4733

www.smpsboston.org

Society for Technical Communication, Boston Chapter

PMB #197
738 Main Street
Waltham, MA 02451

www.stc-boston.org

Society of Women Engineers, Boston Section

(781) 594-4SWE

world.std.com/~swebos

UNIVERSITY CAREER RESOURCES

If you're graduating from a Boston-area college and thinking about staying here, you could be in luck. Most colleges and universities have career offices that can put you in touch with alumni in specific fields. Because so many people who go to college in Boston never leave, chances are good you'll be able to find somebody local to talk to you about career possibilities.

INDEX

About

monstermoving.com

Because moving affects almost *every aspect* of a person's life, Monstermoving.com is committed to improving the way people move. Focusing on an individual's needs, timing, and dreams, the site provides everything for the entire lifestyle transition and every stage of the move. Free service provider content, interactive products, and resources give consumers more control, saving them time and money and reducing stress. Site features include cost-of-living comparisons, home and apartment searches, mortgage calculators and services, an interactive move-planning application, an address change service, relocation tax advice, and virtual city tours. Monstermoving.com is committed to remaining the most effective, comprehensive, and lifestyle-centric point of service for everyone involved in moving.

Monstermoving.com is part of the Interactive Division of TMP Worldwide (NASDAQ: "TMPW;" ASX: "TMP"). For information, visit *www.monstermoving.com* or call (800) 567-7952.